MW01105414

No Reason for Goodbyes

Messages from Beyond Life

Chassie West

BALBOA.
PRESS

A DIVISION OF HAY HOUSE

Balboa Press books may be ordered through booksellers or by contacting:

Balboa Press
A Division of Hay House
1663 Liberty Drive
Bloomington, IN 47403
www.balboapress.com
1-(877) 407-4847

Because of the dynamic nature of the Internet, any Web addresses or links contained in this book may have changed since publication and may no longer be valid. The views expressed in this work are solely those of the author and do not necessarily reflect the views of the publisher, and the publisher hereby disclaims any responsibility for them.

The author of this book does not dispense medical advice or prescribe the use of any technique as a form of treatment for physical, emotional, or medical problems without the advice of a physician, either directly or indirectly. The intent of the author is only to offer information of a general nature to help you in your quest for emotional and spiritual well-being. In the event you use any of the information in this book for yourself, which is your constitutional right, the author and the publisher assume no responsibility for your actions.

Cover photo: Paula M. Williams

ISBN: 978-1-4525-0125-3 (sc)
ISBN: 978-1-4525-0127-7 (dj)
ISBN: 978-1-4525-0126-0 (e)

Library of Congress Control Number: 2010917194

Printed in the United States of America
Balboa Press rev. date: 1/24/2011

CONTENTS

Acknowledgements

This book would not have been possible without the support of Pam Blizzard and the members who frequented the Web site Pam constructed, and moderated:

www.FriendsCommunities.org

Their encouragement and support kept me going through innumerable computer and word processing glitches. Their courage is evident in their willingness to contribute their experiences, the number submitted amounting to the majority appearing herein.

Sincere appreciation is also extended to those who heard about this project as word began to spread and who sent their narratives to attest to what they, too, had experienced. I am extremely grateful and humbled at the trust all of you had in me as your editor.

To those who have helped me navigate this spiritual journey (whether you knew it or not) - John Edward, John Holland, Robert Brown, Gena Wilson, Mary Jo and Bhrett McCabe, Patti Sinclair, Abraham-Hicks, Jennifer Farmer, Nancy Canning, Cheryl McGill, Joan Farmer, Jean Favors, Joan Fowler - my gratitude. I would still be groping around in the dark and doubting my sanity without you all.

And finally, to all the friends and family members on the Other Side who made their presences known to us and who appear on the pages to follow, including Elaine Flinn, who I suspect is now peeking over my shoulder and nudging me to work faster, and especially to Bob West, who started it all.....

Foreword

As a full-time professional psychic medium, I have spent hours and hours channeling the voices of those who have passed from the physical body. The information that I have received from them over the years is invaluable. I would like to share some of their divine insight with you. It is my intention, as it is the authors', to leave you feeling more confident that the spirit world is just a breath away. I want you to believe that your loved ones really do come to you in dreams. They really do sit on the bedside with you at night. They really do change the TV channel and turn lights on and off! As we attempt to strip away the doubting voice of the ego and loosen the grasp of the snake, we will come to find out that healing awaits us from the audible voice of Heaven.

To those who live in Spirit (Heaven), the physical body appears to be illusionary. They look down upon themselves while in transition and notice how light they feel without the body. They enjoy the freedom of a telepathic spirit-body. They are gloriously relieved of the struggles that they once dealt with in their daily existence. From the vantage point of an ascended spirit, the physical plane leaves much to be desired. When a human being has traveled beyond the earth, they live a life without the grasping coil, with the fear or doubt that absorbed them in the past. They live the life that God intended. They live a life full of joy, ineffable love, acceptance, magic and grace. The deceased live like the enviable winter vacationer. I often imagine them sipping something cool in front of a glassy blue-green ocean, the sun warm on their skin, the sky above a crystal blue and the silky sand wrapped around their toes. Their minds are empty but for thoughts of pure peace and understanding. Their cares of the physical world have slipped away like an autumn leaf down a rushing stream. They are finally at home. They have at last returned to the loving source of their creation. They are in reunion with loved ones whom they have longed for in life. Heaven, my friends, IS an enviable place to be.

In reading this book, you will encounter the stories of many people that you have never met. You will become engaged by each testimony offered by their loved ones. You will be in awe over the tenacity of their spirits from across the veil. You will become removed from your once skeptical mind and feel the sincerity of their journey. As you read, I pray that you too will become a believer in all things unseen. It is only when our soul can reconnect with our spirit mind that we truly can find peace in this turbulent physical and material world. It is through a guided, conscious effort that we can return to that place from which we came. We can have Heaven on earth by choosing love over hate, joy over sorrow and peace over war.

If you have ever wished to cast aside doubt, then I encourage you to do so as you read this book. Allow the messages of these real life encounters to open and expand your own heart center. Allow the ego its well-deserved vacation from the chains of skepticism. I pray that you read this book over and over, each time allowing the images of love and inspiration to bring you off the dusty, lower road and onto the path of an ever flowing stream of love and abundance. This is your birthright. May each day bring you the joy of Heaven, the love of God and the blessings of a thousand angels.

Be reminded that your loved ones are always within reach.

Patti Sinclair

Preface

The power of knowing that life continues on after death helps many through the grieving process. We do not grieve for the individual that passed on; instead we grieve for our own loss and uncertainty that our loved one can continue to live on. Religions through the world have based teachings, sermons, and doctrine on the assumption that healthy, balanced living on earth will lead to eternal life. It is reassuring to believe that your loved ones are truly living, loving, and growing in the world beyond our reality. What if you could KNOW that they are living?

The McCabe family is not your traditional family. Since the early 1980's, our family has seen the world, and the world beyond the world we all know, through a different lens. With a devout Catholic upbringing as a basis for our faith, eternal life was not a question. It was a faith and belief that was confirmed through the work of the family psychic/intuitive on a daily basis with grieving families, those searching for direction in life, and those simply wanting to understand that life continues beyond our physical world. When you have a mother who is a psychic/intuitive with an uncanny ability to connect to the world beyond now, the faith becomes a knowing, bringing reality to the hopes and desires of so many, that life surely does continue on.

The true impact that we learned was not necessarily the message that was delivered from the crossed-over to the living. While this information can have a healing power to the grieving process, the absolute healing is the confirmation of the faith that there is eternal life after death. This can be liberating to a hurting, grieving soul.

While uncertainty deepens the wounds in the emotional health, knowing allows the injury to heal. This knowing came through the communication that so many desire to have with their own loved ones, only in our case it came through the work of a psychic/intuitive.

Communication does not need to occur solely through the work of a psychic/intuitive. When we began working together as mother and son, psychic and psychologist, our goal was to help individuals find the understanding to appreciate the miracles of life. As a soul interpreter and a psychologist, we appreciate the pain that grief brings with it and the experience of living with grief. After-death communication, as detailed so eloquently throughout this book, offers many that confirmation of faith, the knowing, that strengthens the love we have for our crossed over family members.

Whatever your faith, it does not deny the desire many have to communicate with those that have moved on beyond the physical world. This communication takes away the finality, the endings, and instead, fosters a belief system of "until we meet again." Through smells, visions, or simple feelings, these after death communications provide the reassurance that the soul continues to live on. The confirmation of life after death is manifested all around each of us, some more formal than others, some big, some small, but always a miracle of living.

Whether you are searching for answers from the other side or answers in your daily living, your grieving process is a BIG part of living and is following the spiritual plan designed long before entering your current life path. Our work has grown over the years, evolving to help people connect and communicate with friends, family, and loved ones who live in another reality. Life continues, just in a different perception, but through your heart, memories, and prayers each and every day.

Life after death is real. The personal stories and experiences shared in this book will open your eyes to a larger world than you might live in today. You cannot read the words without feeling happy for those who know they have experienced one of the true miracles of life - the one that is available to each and every one of us – confirmation of life after death. Hear the joy, the warmth in the stories written. If you question the existence of life after death, read the stories, listen to the words, and open your heart. Your miracle awaits.

The Psychic and The Doc
Mary Jo McCabe and Dr. Bhrett McCabe

Introduction

Death has always been a topic never far from our minds. It is the ultimate mystery, everyone's personal boogey man, a fate we know we will never escape. It is only in the past few decades that our dread of the inevitable has begun to change for some, spurred by the publication of *Hello from Heaven* by Bill and Judy Guggenheim, and the work of Elizabeth Kubler Ross. The proof of current interest of both science and the lay population in spirituality, man's evolution into the next level of consciousness, the nature of the universe and all things metaphysical is now evident in the number of books, films, Web sites, live and on-line seminars and television features touching on the subjects, few of which existed when this project was begun in 2005. Ever so gradually, the prospect that we survive after physical death has begun to edge its way into mainstream thought. This book offers proof that not only do we survive physical death, we can let you know that we do.

The voices between the covers of this book are those of ordinary people – young, old, of diverse religious backgrounds and ethnicities, and from all over America, Canada, the United Kingdom and as far away as Australia. Among us are office workers, educators, writers, professional psychics, retirees, social workers, computer geeks and geekettes, homemakers, antique dealers, you name it. The one thing we all share is having been witness to something extraordinary, glorious and miraculous, the kind of thing with the potential to alter one's belief systems, view of life and everything we thought we knew, certainly in my case. Some of us experienced it one way, others in an entirely different manner. The bottom line is the same: we were on the receiving end of an afterlife communication, in other words communication from the departed. It's the kind of thing to shout to the heavens, to celebrate, to share. And the majority of us, before now, never said a word, never dared to.

In the majority of cases, our initial reaction to the phenomenon was to rationalize, run the experience through the wringer of logic, decide that we'd imagined it. The next stage was one of questioning our sanity. My reaction, after it had happened a second time, was to hie myself to my doctor's office for a physical. Pronounced hale and hearty, I then talked to a counselor who couched her response carefully, but suggested that what I'd experienced was more common than I thought. I didn't believe her. Why should I? Surely I'd have heard about it, read about it, *something*.

There are any number of terms for it: after death communication; discarnate communication; spirit communication. Prior to 2000 I was blithely ignorant about the whole concept. As a writer, primarily of mysteries, I spent most of my days in front of the computer putting one word after another, one chapter after another. There was nothing new about that; my first book at been published eighteen years before. I had retired from my day job to write full time. With groceries in the larder, money enough to pay the bills and buy cat food, and friends to chat with, I was (literally) fat and happy. Then one night my husband called me.

Let me be clear about this. When you've known someone for thirty-eight years and have been married to him for thirty-one of them, you know his voice when you hear it. And under other circumstances there might have been nothing unusual about his calling me. Since Bob West's ashes are fertilizing a holly tree outside my window, however, there was everything in the world unusual about hearing his voice. In spades.

The first time it happened I was awakened from a sound sleep by his voice. As Bob had been bedridden the last year of his life and in failing health for the previous three, I reacted to his voice exactly as I had during those anxiety-ridden years: I was out of bed and on my feet to find out what he needed. I was, in fact, halfway across the bedroom before I realized I had gotten up for nothing. Bob West had been carried from our residence by ambulance the day after Christmas in 1997 and had never returned. He died in April of the following year in a rehab facility. Obviously I'd been dreaming.

Surprised at how easily I'd dropped into that time warp, and marveling at how real the dream had seemed, I returned to bed. For the life of me I couldn't remember what I'd been dreaming or how he'd been involved. As far as I could tell, I'd been dead to the world, no pun intended. Regardless, not only had Bob been loud and clear in the dream – the way I rationalized at the time – he had sounded as if he'd been in another room, perhaps the kitchen. On top of that, he'd called me by the nickname only he used.

The second and third occasions changed the whole dynamics of the situation because I was wide awake. Just as before, his voice was loud, clear, and again seemed to come from the front of our condo. And lest you think my apartment is haunted and his activity confined to our three-bedroom unit, the fourth time he called out to me I was on Long Island in a hotel. The only difference on that occasion was that I heard him in my head instead of, well, my ears. Again, he'd used that accursed nickname. There was no way I could use dreaming as an explanation.

It made no sense. I was long past the grief that is part and parcel of accepting that someone you held as dear as life itself has left yours. In that, I'd been blessed because Bob and I had been graced with three months of borrowed time. After two weeks in a coma and an EEG that indicated that he was at baseline, with his brain keeping his autonomic functions going and doing nothing else, I had been told that everything that had made him who he'd been no longer existed. Knowing what he'd want, I arrived at the hospital on that January 1998 morning with his Advance Directive. It was time to pull the plug.

A doctor at the nurse's station stopped me as I nudged the document toward him. He wanted to warn me, saying only that things had changed. Expecting the worst, I entered his room to find him wide awake, alert and in command of all his faculties. The medical staff had no explanation. But from that point on, we said everything that needed saying.

His death in April came as a surprise, even to the staff of the rehabilitation center to which he was transferred after a month in the hospital. Once the shock of his death wore off, I was relieved for him. Had he lived, he would have remained an invalid, which he hated. I missed him, yes, in ways I would never have imagined. But I had settled into widowhood with relative ease by the time he decided to make his continued existence known by calling my name.

I was certain I'd imagined it. I tucked it into the back of my mind with all the other flotsam cluttering my thoughts. Then on a slow Monday morning while channel surfing, I saw a promo for *Crossing Over with John Edward,* a syndicated show featuring a medium. Astonished that a local station would carry something of this nature, five days a week at that, I watched out of pure curiosity and with the jaded eyes of a skeptic. The whole thing had to be fixed. Perhaps they used hidden microphones or the people being "read" by John Edward were plants.

That was my attitude on that morning, progressively less so on Tuesday, Wednesday and part of Thursday. A lot of the intimate information and seemingly insignificant details given to audience participants could not have been researched. Let's face it, you weren't likely to find out on the Internet that fifty years ago your Uncle Bucky once swallowed a live goldfish to make his sister sick. These days, yes, thanks to Facebook and blogs galore, but not back in 2001. I became convinced that the reactions of those gallery members read were genuine. And on that fourth day, John Edward informed a woman in the audience that, yes, her late husband wanted to assure her that she had indeed heard his voice, that he had called her name when she'd been this place or that – I forget. I will never, however, forget her astonishment. Or mine. The communication I had experienced was real? And it had happened to others, too? In an interview conducted afterwards, the woman said she had never told anyone about hearing that voice, that she was certain she'd imagined it.

I still wasn't ready to become a believer. It went against my whole concept of death. Watching *Crossing Over,* however, made me curious. And furious. Something was going on I didn't understand.

A right-brained person all my life, I metamorphosed into a left-brained fiend, determined to research and get to the bottom of the whole business. I was in for a shock. Whereas I began with the sole intention of finding out what might be available on the subject of after death communication, the more I read, the wider the arena became. It was humbling faced with how much I didn't know, the only consolation being that it appeared that the general public was no better informed than I'd been. Why? Because people were hesitant to talk about it.

I discovered to my astonishment:

That according to a 1981 Gallup poll, 42% of Americans polled confessed that they thought they'd had contact with a departed loved one, with the percentage as high as 70 to 80 percent for widows. In a more recent poll sponsored by a cable TV station, 25,000 responded. 99% believed in life after death. 70% reported having experienced an after death communication (ADC).

That universities and private institutions here and abroad have in the past or are still researching in one guise or another, survival of consciousness after physical death, among them: Duke, Boston University, Oxford University, University of Arizona, Nevada University, Stanford Research Institute, the Institute of Noetic Sciences, and too many more to list here.

That reports and scientific research on those who have had a near-death experience support survival of consciousness. Research into this phenomenon is ongoing.

I wound up with a library of books on a wide variety of subjects metaphysical. On after death communication, now in common enough usage that it warrants being referred to by initials – ADC – I learned the variety of ways that the departed can and do communicate. And was, again, flabbergasted at realizing that prior to resorting to calling me, Bob West had employed a number of methods to let me know that – *Guess what, honey. I'm still around!* On two separate occasions he went so far as to touch me, the first time across my instep, the second time just above my elbow as I sat at the computer. Scared me spitless. But the man had taught communications at a local college, so why was I so surprised? I simply didn't realize what was going on.

In spite of the number of scholarly and complex treatises on the subject, few have been vehicles in which ordinary people could voice their extraordinary experiences. For me, not feeling free to talk about what was happening was like a cancer gnawing at my soul. Many of those whose narratives you'll read expressed the same frustration and it was this that became the impetus for this book. The descriptions of ADC occurrences that follow are not fantasies, fabrications or flights of fancy. They are literally what we experienced. Those who have contributed have done so with the understanding that the purpose was publication. All were asked to sign their names as testament to their experience. Patti Sinclair, a professional psychic medium has contributed the Foreword. Dr Bhrett McCabe, a licensed clinical psychologist, who along with his mother, Mary Jo McCabe, a psychic intuitive for almost thirty years, contributed the Preface, suggested that respondents include information on what was going on in their lives when the communication occurred, whether they felt free to share their ADC with others, and reveal what impact it has had on their lives.

You hold the results in your hands. Again, this is what we experienced. Whether you believe it or not, dear reader, is up to you. *No Reason for Goodbyes* is our declaration of independence, so to speak, in our own words and various writing styles. If nothing else, we sincerely hope it makes you wonder whether the death of the physical body is all it's cracked up to be. And whether our dearly departed are no more than a thought away.

Chassie West

CHAPTER ONE – SIGHTINGS

Given the number of young men and women who have lost their lives in the service of their country, especially in more recent years, I thought it appropriate that we begin our testimonials with the moving contribution by Colleen.

The memorial service for my father was over. All that was left was to move the bouquets to the car and then get through the hours of the reception. Some time before the end of that longest of March days, my mother informed my sisters and me that another service was planned for him at Arlington National Cemetery during the Christmas holidays.

I couldn't believe it. Death had never been considered an ending in our family, just another door like countless others that lead to different experiences through a lifetime. His ashes were already interred at Arlington and I didn't understand why Mom wanted to prolong the mourning for the father and husband we'd all lost. I told her so.

"Your dad wanted to have a service in Arlington," she said quietly. "And I'm going to do it for him."

Dad was a Marine during the Second World War. He was a radioman and family legend puts him onboard ship where he witnessed the raising of the flag at Iwo Jima. We all remembered countless ball games and parades where the Marine Corps Hymn was played – Dad standing practically alone until the last bars faded. He had a look on his face I still can't describe. But even as a child, I knew there was something of deep importance for him in that tune and I always stood quietly while it played.

The seasons moved by and suddenly it was time for Christmas in Virginia. Family flew in from all over the country. Discussion at the dinner table centered on the ceremony to be held right after the holiday. Time hadn't changed a thing for me. I still felt the exercise was pointless and maudlin, but out of respect I kept my thoughts to myself.

It was cloudy, chilly and threatening rain as the ceremony began. Across the rolling hills in the gray light, the graves of Arlington marched away like stone soldiers. The reds and golds and blues of the Marines' uniforms seemed to be the only color. Military precision and the air of command captured my attention, but nothing changed the way I continued to feel – sad, uneasy, and vaguely angry. All I could seem to do was stare at the shoes of the honor guard. Patent leather polished to a high sheen moving like clockwork against the cold ground.

I really don't believe in death. I've had countless proofs that life continues. And as I sat there listening to the eulogy, I knew Dad was still moving forward through his experience, continuing to learn and grow. But the sadness wouldn't lift. I missed him. Alzheimer's disease is what sent him on and the most recent memories we'd shared were conflicted and frustrating and profoundly sad. I was lost in those memories as the service neared its end.

But then an odd thing happened.

Suddenly, something caught my complete attention, as if someone had called my name. I was instantly aware and looked up in confusion. And as I did, a sweet, deep sense of peace flooded my thoughts. Time stood still. I felt embraced and comforted and filled with joy. Although there were no words, a voice seemed to say, "God is Life and Life is forever. Life goes on forever and ever. Everywhere and everywhen."

I looked at the faces of my family sitting quietly and at the Marines as they crisply folded the flag. Everyone was glowing. Color poured back into the scene and the misty day now seemed to be sunlit and glistening. I was suddenly aware of the deep affection the Marines held for my father, even though they'd never met him. How much they held for us as his family. The care they'd all taken to prepare the service – the 21-gun salute, the immaculate uniforms, the powerful eulogy. I finally understood Dad's love of the Marine Corps. Had it been appropriate, I would have leaped from my chair and hugged them all.

And then I saw Dad standing there watching the service, too. Just standing there quietly, smiling, completely absorbed in the ceremony. He was happy and proud, relaxed and energized, as if he'd just strolled by during a morning walk. Even as the thought about how weird it all was came to mind, I was swept by the understanding that what I was experiencing was natural and normal. The way things are supposed to be. He wasn't an apparition. No séance had brought him there. He was just Dad.

I had no desire to go to him. It was enough just to see him whole and strong. To see my dad again with the clear light of intelligence and humor in his eyes. And I somehow knew I couldn't speak with him, even if I'd tried. But I knew that we would some day.

I know that we will.

Colleen Lester

Bottom line: Colleen's experience is a reminder of all the fathers, sons and daughters who have served, dedicated or have given their lives in military service to our country. And of course, once a Marine, always a Marine, whether on this side of the veil or the other.

****

Giving credit where it's due, the sighting experienced by Joyce Braga was the primary impetus for this book. A fellow member of a writers' critique group to which I belong, I'd known her for years. One day while we were discussing my work-in-progress, a mystery that involved a sighting, she dropped this tidbit, which didn't register at the time. Once I realized what she had said, I called her later and asked for an explanation, which she gave

me. Except for her husband and her sister, she'd never talked to anyone else about it. Since I'd kept mum about my own contacts from Bob, I was consumed by several emotions: pure joy that she'd been given such a gift; sympathy at knowing why she had never spoken of it; and outrage that we'd felt so constrained. I wondered how many others might be suffering in silence. I found out. So my sincere thanks to Joyce. And her dad.

My sister called me with the news that our mother had died at 6 a.m. from a massive heart attack. Because my parents lived in Florida, and she and my brother and I were in Maryland, we had to move quickly because my dad was now alone. He was suffering with Alzheimer's disease, and our mother had been his sole caretaker for everything, including food, clothing and bathing.

I will probably never know how Daddy was able to process Mother's death. By the time we arrived twenty-four hours later, he was slumped on the sofa, surrounded by a pile of papers. He'd been trying to read the death certificate and the paramedics' report.

He looked up at me, his thin gray hair still wrinkled as if he'd been sleeping. His grey eyes seemed to be looking straight through me. He had on a wrinkled white, mis-buttoned shirt. His pants, which were way too large, were cinched by a large leather belt he'd tied instead of buckled, and he wore no shoes. The only thing he said, "Dorothy." He either didn't know or remember my name, Joy, and it had been years since he'd used my nickname, "Mouse." I remembered Daddy's meticulousness in minute detail because I, like many small children, had spent hours watching my father shave and fuss in the bathroom, a habit I'd carried on until my teen years, when he allowed me to go on about my angst as he groomed for the day.

Arranging Mother's cremation was the easy part. I'd expected making arrangements to be difficult, since three siblings had to agree. Surprisingly, we all favored cremation.

The hardest part was the final goodbyes. My mother and I had been estranged for years and I had no idea what emotions I would feel. As I kissed her on the forehead, I felt a twinge of sadness and nothing more. The true difficulty was waiting in caring for my father in the limited time we had and the need to move him closer to us. He knew what going into a nursing home meant and so did I. I struggled with this decision, but knew it was the best option we had. We could only stay in Florida for a limited amount of time with family tugging in our home state of Maryland.

I was nominated to make the arrangements and drive him to the nursing home. Once we arrived, he said, in one of the few lucid moments he would have, "If you put me in here, I'll never come out. I'm waiting for mother's ashes." That was the worst day of my life. Not only did I have to leave him there, I'd also learned that my mother's ashes had been lost in transit. Thankfully the ashes arrived the next day, a Saturday.

We took the battered box of ashes to him on Sunday, and over that day and the next, he saw all of his children and our families. It never occurred to us that it would be the last time we'd see him alive. He died Monday night. It was not, however, the last time I'd see him

It was Thursday, the morning after his cremation. The day was sunny, May at her finest, and my husband, Mark, had hurried off to work. The house was quiet, settling. I was in the kitchen about 8 a.m. The initial shock of my parents' death was over. Now I was a mixture of frustrated, upset, almost angry. After all I'd done, the mad scramble to bring Dad north, the agonizing search and all the frantic wheeling and dealing to get him into a nursing home, he'd died anyway.

Then I thought I heard a noise in the master bedroom. Curious, but for some reason, not alarmed, I stood in the doorway of the bedroom and noticed that Mark had left the light on in the master bathroom.

The bedroom was very bright, with sun beaming through the windows, since the curtains were open. The master bath was on the left side of the room, next to a double-door closet. I went about midway into the room, perhaps a couple of feet. I could see the edge of someone's arm in the master bath.

This master bath was very small. If you used the sink to shave or brush your teeth, your arm would be visible in the bedroom. I stopped. Oddly enough, I didn't feel frightened, I was curious. I moved towards the bed so I could see who it was, then sat down on the edge of the bed and stared. It couldn't be....

The arm moved and someone turned. My father had stepped away from the sink and was facing me. He didn't move past the door sill. In fact, he didn't move at all.

The bathroom light was still on. He looked perfectly natural and normal. He had on the same clothes he had the day I dropped him off at the nursing home, except they were freshly pressed and clean. His hair had been washed and towel dried because it was a mass of white curls. He was clean shaven. His light gray shirt was tucked into his gray pants, his belt buckle properly buckled instead of tied, as he'd worn it in Florida. For years he'd had trouble with that and Mother always had to fix it for him. He wore light colored socks and the white open mesh shoes he always wore in the summer.

I don't know if I said or thought, "Daddy?" but he answered. He smiled, showing a perfect set of white teeth. His gray eyes were clear. He said very softly, "Don't be afraid, Joy, it's just me. I wanted to tell my little Mouse everything is okay. I'm fine. You did the right thing. Don't worry." Here was my father, who had suffered from Alzheimer's for ten years, sounding like a rational, clear-headed man. He was once again the immaculately groomed dad of my younger years. It was like time had been suspended.

I saw him move and turn sideways towards the mirror. The arm was leaning against the sink as if he was checking his face in the mirror. Then the arm disappeared.

I sat a few moments, hoping he'd come back. I got up and looked in the bathroom, but there was no evidence he'd been in there. I felt a great calmness, an elation, a serenity. I left the light on in the bathroom that day. He never came back. But I could live with that. My dad was alright. He'd come back to let me know.

I feel the timing of his visit was critical, considering how angry I'd been. But I think my father knew I needed to see him one last time. It made the grieving process easier. I still went through all normal stages of grief, but every time I had a memory that triggered a sad image of my father, it was immediately replaced with the image I'd seen in my bathroom.

Joyce Braga

Followup: Joyce relates that growing up, her father was the one she could confide in, and with whom she could share stories about psychic experiences she'd had, spirits she'd seen, unusual visions she'd had. He was very open, told her that he, too, had seen things and that her grandmother and great-grandmother had had "the power of sight." It was a secret she and her dad shared and he cautioned to keep such conversations between them to herself. His appearance after his death convinced Joyce he'd been telling her the truth.

She shared the news of his visit with her sister. To her surprise, it gave her sister the courage to tell her about experiences she had had and had never shared. The only other person Joyce told was her husband, who was supportive. And when his father died and his mother had a stroke, he told Joyce he was beginning to understand what she'd experienced. He is convinced his father was guiding him in solving his mother's medical problems. So Joyce feels that sharing was eventually beneficial, thanks to her dad.

****

Before beginning this project, I'm not sure what my reaction would be upon sighting someone I knew had made their transition to the Other Side. Depending on the circumstances, I might have convinced myself it was a look-alike, or my imagination, perhaps wishful thinking. I'd have probably wrestled the memory to the ground and killed it, secure in the knowledge that I'd retained or at minimum, had regained my sanity. Now, at least I'd take the time to wonder about it. Fortunately for Lorena, whose sighting follows, she had backup. What luck!

My Aunt Frances's partner, Ann, passed away in 1988. We were very, very close. Seven years later in April of 1995, my dad passed away at home from cancer. Most of my family gathered there, including Aunt Frances, my mother's sister. My husband and I had come out of my mom's house and were going off of the deck down three fairly narrow steps into the yard. The steps were just wide enough for two people to walk side-by-side.

Suddenly, just as we were to start down, my husband and I both at the same time, stepped aside at the top of the stairs and stood there facing each other to let someone else come up the steps. As soon as she passed between us, heading into my mom's house, my husband and I looked at each other with our eyes wide and our jaws almost to the floor. We had just stepped aside for Aunt Ann to come up! It had seemed so natural in the instant that it happened that it took a second for us to realize what had actually just taken place.

She did not look like a "ghost," she simply looked like Aunt Ann. It was so real that we had moved out of the way without thinking about it. As a matter of fact, she looked so real and alive and normal that I would probably have tried to convince myself it had never happened if my husband had not seen the same thing at the same exact time! I've always wondered if she knew it was a rough day and maybe she was there to be with Aunt Fran.

Lenora Shope

Bottom line: Perhaps a clue to this sighting is in Lenora's statement that she and her aunt's partner were very, very close. Given that, it is no surprise that Lenora would be able to see Ann. That her husband could share in this miracle was a bonus. The bottom line was love, Lenora's love for Ann and Ann's love for Fran and her family. Or course she would be there to lend her support!

****

Then there's this unusual sighting of Lenora's:

On October 23, 2001, I woke from a sound sleep at about 2 a.m. and for no obvious reason, looked past the foot of my bed and slightly to the right to the bathroom doorway. Standing there was my dad, my nephew, who had committed suicide several years prior, and his mom, my sister. It's hard to explain how they looked, not like an actual person and not like a "ghost" in the movies, but more like vapor or fog-like figures. Perhaps if you could see energy, that's what it would look like. Although I don't recall actually seeing facial features, I had absolutely NO doubt at the time who they were. I had a strange sense of calm, as though they were simply there to let me know that everything was okay, but I felt a little freaked out about it at the same time because my sister was not dead and I was confused as to why I would see her there with them. I blinked, they were no longer there, and I went back to sleep.

About 7 a.m. I came out of my room and into the living room. My daughter, Jacklen, nineteen at the time, was sitting on the couch. I looked at her and said, "Okay, I think we're watching ENTIRELY too much John Edward," to which she replied, "Mom, there's no such thing as too much John!" and laughed. I told her with a nervous giggle, "I am not kidding. I saw your Aunt Joanne in my room in the middle of the night, and Aunt Joanne isn't dead. I'm telling you, too much John!" We had a laugh and went on about our day.

About 4:30 that afternoon, my sister, Elizabeth, called and said, "Sit down. I have terrible news. Joanne is dead. She was murdered at work last night." She worked as a security guard at an apartment complex for AIDS-infected women and children. She was last seen about midnight and was found murdered about 5 a.m.

Lenora Shope, Blanco, TX

Bottom line: In this case Lenora was given both a heads up of things to come, along with an assurance that in spite of the circumstances, everything would be fine. Lenora could rest assured that her sister, Joanne, was still with family.

****

It is not uncommon for sightings to occur during times of great stress. For Erica, it came during a labor of love.

I have had a few experiences, but the most empowering was while birthing my firstborn son, Dalton. I had a very long and hard labor. I'd been at it for about sixteen hours and was exhausted. I remember lying there thinking, Oh, my God, what have I done here? And in that moment there she was, my dad's mom. She had passed away of lung cancer shortly after I told her of my pregnancy. Years before, even before I was married, a psychic told me she saw an elderly woman who loved to read holding my three children that were waiting to be born. It wasn't until this very moment that I realized who the psychic was referring to.

My grandmother was the most giving and amazing woman. She was strong, yet gentle in every way. I loved her with all my heart and never really felt as though I showed her just how much I looked up to her. Anyway, she was standing right next to me. I saw her clear as day. She was wearing the dress she'd worn at my wedding and was smiling at me with her eyes sparkling. She reached out and touched my shoulder. It was in that moment that I knew everything would be fine and an amazing peace came over my body. We would be just fine.

Dalton was born about an hour later and scored a 9 on his Apgar scale. I was healed and all set in two weeks. What a miracle and a blessing! I think of it often. It helps me to remember life is good!

Erica Cook

Bottom line: It appears that those in spirit are more accessible to us when our defenses are down and when, regardless of the circumstances – or perhaps because of them -- we are far more open than we are normally. Of course Erica's grandmother would be with her for the birth of her grandchild. And Erica, with all the usually barriers no longer in place, was able to see her grandmother, know she was not alone and gain the strength she needed to give birth to her son. Love will do it for you every time.

****

An open mind about life after death seems more common in the United Kingdom. Modern Spiritualism there dates from the mid-nineteenth century and there are currently well over 300 Spiritualist churches in Britain, where contact with the departed

is part of their services. **In the narrative that follows, however, contact was made elsewhere.**

I lost my fiancée in June 2005. From that point on, I needed to prove to myself that she lived on, that there really is a spirit world. I had had no spiritual experiences before her passing and had no real interest in the subject. Since her passing I have had what I would regard as three totally different but amazing and real experiences. It is the interactive one which I have chosen to relate, as I feel it demonstrates how, as John Edward, among others, says how spirit people are involved with our lives and listen in on our conversations.

It was the middle of November, approximately 7:30 p.m. My fiancée's mother and I still share the same house. We were in the living room, she doing her knitting and I was watching TV and having a conversation about a relative of hers who had passed over twenty years ago called Bert. I knew nothing about him, as we had never discussed him before. We talked about him for around half an hour – what sort of person he was, how he became her mother's second husband, etc.

At 8 pm I turned the volume back up on the telly for a programme I wanted to watch while she concentrated on her knitting. At 8:15p a chap appeared no more than four feet in front of me and, although transparent – I could see right through him to the TV - he was clear to the finest detail. He wore a smart suit, a tie, his buttons fastened. I could even see the different shades of the buttons, how much darker they were than the fabric of his suit, how much darker his tie was as well. Strangely, he had his right arm held up. He then spoke to me in thought and told me he had lost part of a finger on his right hand. He then disappeared.

I calmly turned around and said to my fiancée's mother, "You know Bert who we were talking about, did he lose part of a finger on his right hand?"

"Yes, he did," she replied.

"Right," I said, "because he just appeared in front of me and told me."

I remember this as clearly now as I did then. As regards to the finger, my fiancée's mother never thought to bring it up in conversation, adding to the shock in her face when I told her.

Darren Farrington, Lancashire, England

Bottom line: Occasionally there appears to be no rhyme or reason for a sighting, especially of someone we don't know. But after the death of his fiancée, Darren wanted proof of the continuance of life. Bert supplied that. Not only did he make an appearance after having been a subject of conversation, an indication that he had heard it, he communicated telepathically with Darren, giving him information he had not known, information which confirmed Bart's identity. Darren had wanted proof of life after death. He got it.

****

A very special Christmas gift:
In the winter of 2005, I experienced my first after death communication. I am the only girl of four children in my family. Christine, a cousin the same age as I and in the same class with me through graduation, was like a sister to me. We shared many childhood memories and the same talent for drawing and painting. She went on to college, then started a family and we grew apart, as friends often do when they take different paths.

It was heart-breaking when she was diagnosed with amyotrophic lateral sclerosis (A.L.S., also called Lou Gehrig's disease) during the summer of 2004. She had so much more life to live with her children. Within a few months she could not stand up straight, talk, or hold her head up. I did not want to see her that way, as I knew that would be my last memory of her. However, I came home from work one evening to find her sitting on the front porch with my parents and her caregiver.

She stood up, walked over and greeted me, her body sagging, her head dropping forward from the lack of muscle strength to hold it up. But she had a smile on her face. That was the last time I saw her. She died a couple of weeks later in the middle of the night.

I was raised believing either you went to heaven or you went to hell, so I was concerned that she was in hell because she told me once that she did not believe in God. This thought would come and go over the months after her death, leaving me wondering what had become of her. Otherwise, I didn't really dwell on it.

It was December 2005, her birthday, and Christmas was fourteen days away when I started having visions of her standing in front of me. I did not want to remember her as I'd seen her last, her body sagging, so I would say, "No," look away and the visions would disappear.

But she started showing up more often. Finally out of frustration I stopped and said, "Okay, I'll look at you." She stood there smiling at me with so much love and joy on her face. I looked down at her body and it was well. I looked back up at her face and when our eyes met, the vision disappeared. I was overjoyed and filled with a sense of peace. My lack of fear of death had been confirmed. She came to show me that everything was okay and for me not to worry about her. She was home and well again. And I smile.

Catherine Hahn

Followup: Catherine's Christmas presents that year were joy and peace of mind, thanks to Christine. Another was her loss of fear of Hell. She relates that she began her spiritual journey in January 2006, seeking the truth of who she is and why she is here. "It is up to us to see the light and know that we are not alone on this earth or in our journey here. Ego tells us we are alone and God tells us we are never alone." She continues her search for truth and light. And she smiles.

****

Vikki North is an artist in California who worked in television and film for twenty years. She is also more than familiar with

after death communication, as this and the visit from her mom's cat, recounted elsewhere in this collection, attest.

An unexpected visitor:

I'm an educated career woman. Educated people don't admit to believing in ghosts, at least not in mixed company. As illogical as that might be, there have been stories about the afterlife in every culture since history was recorded. At every station in life, from Presidents to paupers, people see ghosts. Most of us have had a firsthand experience with one. We just don't admit it, even to ourselves.

I'm sure you've heard many people say, "I'd have to see a ghost with my own eyes." I'm in complete agreement with that statement and that's exactly what happened to me.

I saw a full body apparition when I was about 16 or 17 years old. I was in my bedroom doing my homework and heard my door creak open. Thinking it was just my mother, I didn't look up from my studies. When I finally did, a young woman was standing in front of me. Her body was translucent. She looked to be about my age. She wore period clothing and some sort of bonnet or cap. It's an odd thing to remember, but I noticed her cap didn't have tassels. It was just plopped on her head and her hair was stuffed underneath it.

She didn't seem to be aware of me at first. She just stood looking around my room. I sat absolutely paralyzed. Then she turned and looked directly at me, with one of those, "Oh, there you are," expressions.

She started to walk towards me and simply put her hand out as if to say, "Hi there! My name is Betty the Ghost."

At my tender years, I had no idea what was standing in front of me. All that I knew was she wasn't part of our world. I think she realized that I was terrified. It wasn't the type of fear you feel when you suspect a burglar in your house or you think your life is at risk. It was more like a fear that you're going insane.

She started to reach towards me and touch my arm, as if to say, "Don't be afraid."

The moment her thin arm and hand reached out, I hit the floor and ran past her with the speed of lightning directly to my mother's arms. My mother left me in her room and reluctantly walked back to mine to see if the ghost was still there. She was gone, of course. My mother and I rationalized it; I must have fallen off to sleep in a prone position at my desk. That's it! I just dreamed up Bonnet Betty. It worked for my mother and me, but we both knew that wasn't true.

I think I was in my 40's before I ever admitted to my 'other world' experience. I'm 57 years old and the memory of my little ghost has never left me. Bonnet Betty, as I affectionately named her, never appeared again. I've often wondered what she would have told me if I had just had the courage to sit and listen. She obviously saw me as someone her age and maybe just wanted a friend.

Betty did leave me with an amazing gift. You see, it's not a matter of 'believing' in ghosts. I had one stand right in front of me and say, "hello."

So you may ask, "Would you admit it in mixed company?"

Not on your life. After all, I'm an educated woman.

Vikki North

Followup: Vikki says that having seen Bonnet Betty validated for her that there is definitely an afterlife. For her it's not a case of believing. She <u>knows</u>, has seen it firsthand.

As a child, she did share her experience and was told it wasn't real. She accepts that her family was simply reacting from their own fears of the paranormal and, because of that, weren't able to give her the support she needed at the time. Now as an adult, she feels no hesitation about talking to her deceased parents. It brings her comfort.

Vikki's art work and her encounter with a ghost in the Whaley House in Old Town San Diego are related on her Web site: *www.theredchairgallery.com*. Stop by.

****

Dawn's sightings launched her in a direction she hadn't anticipated:

My paternal grandfather, Harold, passed away in January 2002. I wrote a touching poem for his funeral that made us all smile, and then I tucked the memories of my grandfather somewhere into my subconscious mind.

Approximately two years later in January 2004, I started receiving impressions of my grandfather through thought forms and dreams. Sometimes I swear I even saw him around me! As time went on, a few of my intuitive friends also began seeing and hearing my grandfather. I didn't have any fear from his visitation because it was nice to see him again. Since my grieving process was over, it was like having an old friend come back into my life. Whenever he visited, he always gave the same message: "You have the gift of intuition and you need to start using it to help people."

Being the practical person that I am, I didn't believe him. How could I possibly be like those psychics that I saw on television and read about in books? Although I appreciated the visits from my grandfather, I didn't heed his messages and I continued on with my life. The only person that I could truly share this information with was my husband. I was afraid that my family would treat me differently and shake their fingers at me. I didn't want to be the person to ruffle everyone's feathers.

A few months later, a friend was holding a psychic fair for her charitable organization, so I went to support her and the cause. After arriving, I looked around the room and saw only one psychic available, so I went and sat down at her table. Her name was Nonie which, coincidentally, was what we called my maternal Italian great-grandmother. Nonie is a spirit artist - a medium who is able to draw a picture of the person that she is talking to in spirit while she is giving the reading.

She began my reading by telling me that my grandfather was present. He told her to ask me, "What are you waiting for?" She then asked if I knew what it meant. I did, of course, but I still didn't know what to do about it, so I decided to ignore it. At the end of the reading, Nonie turned her sketch pad toward me to show that she had drawn a picture of my grandfather, which still hangs in a frame above my desk.

Time passed and I began seeing my grandfather more often. I enjoyed his visits but I was still uncertain of his messages and I wasn't willing to trust my own intuition about becoming a professional psychic, let alone a spirit medium!

In October of 2004, I received a frantic phone call from a friend who is a psychic medium. She had been hired to conduct psychic readings at a prominent college during parents' weekend and needed another psychic to help. Each psychic was to conduct five minute readings for four hours straight. She had called all of the professional intuitives she knew, but they were all going to Connecticut on that particular weekend for a psychic event. When she asked her spirit guides who could work with her, they showed her my face. As she asked for my help, I heard myself saying, "Sure, no problem." After hanging up the telephone, I realized what I had just agreed to and proceeded to freak out! Two days later, I had managed to calm myself down for the psychic event.

Upon arriving at the college, we were bombarded with hundreds and hundreds of people! As they sat in my chair, one by one, I started seeing images and hearing information. I relayed the information and everyone seemed happy with the results. Halfway through, my psychic medium friend came over to check up on me. When she looked around the corner in my direction, she saw my grandfather standing behind me with his hands on my shoulders. It was at that point that she knew I would be fine. On the way home, I was so excited because the entire evening made me feel incredible! My grandfather appeared and gave me a wink and a smile.

The next week I received a call from my psychic medium friend. It turned out that all of the professional psychics going to Connecticut were told the *wrong* date and could have easily helped out at the college event instead of me, but apparently my grandfather had other plans.

Since then my intuitive abilities have grown and I communicate with the spirit world on a regular basis. I have clients all over the world and the quality of my life has greatly improved. I am truly amazed every day at how my life has unfolded, and I am so thankful that my grandfather didn't give up on me.

Dawn Carr
http:www.angelsofdawn.net

Bottom line: Clearly Dawn's grandfather recognized that she had a gift she hadn't acknowledged. It is just as clear that he was determined to see that she did. He never gave up. Now that's love!!

****

Valerie and her mother, Gail, can say that after death communication has become commonplace for them. This, however, Val says was a first.

Feb 15, 2002

My paternal grandmother was diagnosed with cancer when I was about two. They estimated she had six months or less to live, but she beat the odds to live five more years, dying not long after I turned seven. I have very few memories of her, and even when I try hard I can't remember her feeling healthy and enjoying life. I think it used to make my dad very sad that my memories of his mom were all of her being sick in bed and suffering.

The experience I'm about to describe happened on February 15th. The date is important because my dad's father's birthday would have been February 14th and the 16th was the anniversary of my dad's brother's death. The significance of these dates didn't occur to me until several days after this experience.

As I was driving home from work on the Beltway and was talking aloud to my dad – I do this a lot, as my 30-45 minute car ride is generally the only quiet time I get these days. I was telling him how much I still miss him. I told him I remembered how he told me he never stopped missing his mom after she died, and that I knew now what he meant by that.

A while later a very clear image of my grandmother's face appeared in my upper vision, sort of centered. She looked very solid, but she didn't block my view of the road, as she was above it. She looked young and vibrant, and she was just smiling the most beautiful smile at me. I turned the radio down, I have no idea why, and said, "Hi, Grandmom. Did you come to see me because I was just talking about you, or do you have something to tell me?" She just smiled.

A few minutes passed and all she did was smile beautifully at me, so I shrugged my shoulders and reached down to turn the radio back up. At that moment, a very clear thought came to me: "The frogs aren't just from your dad. We think they're hilarious and we've all been sending them." At the same time, the image of her face tipped back and started laughing. I think I laughed, too. Another thought came through very clearly and insistently: "Tell them." The image of my grandmother didn't disappear until I finally said, "Okay, okay, I'll tell them. I'll tell them, or at least I'll tell my mom."

When I arrived home, I called and left a message for my mom to call me. When she did, I relayed the message to her and the experience itself. We associate frogs with my dad because of a long-standing joke about him hanging a silly frog decoration on the Christmas tree each year. Since his death the previous June, we'd been getting increasing number of frog validations and thought they might be from my dad. This confirmed that they are from him and also from other relatives on the other side.

The next time I saw my mom, she pulled out pictures of my grandmother and had me identify which picture looked most like the image I saw. I identified one (from 1969 when I would have been at most a year and a half old) and told her it looked closest to what I saw, except "Her skin was a lot more tan." My mom's surprised response was, "She loved to be tan!"

I have told only a handful of people about this because it sounds unbelievable, even to me and I'm the one it happened to! The only thing that makes me believe it more is because it was my grandmother coming through. I think had it been my dad, I would have written it off as wishful thinking. I don't recall ever having anything like this happen to me before.

Valerie Ingson

****

Suicide leaves havoc in its wake, affecting even those outside the immediate family. When it's a young person, a spear of sadness pierces our hearts whether it's someone we knew or read about it in the local newspaper. So many dreams, so much potential lost. We feel helpless and peer at the youngsters we love with unwelcome concern. It is fortunate that our next contributor was given the gift of closure and was able to pass it along to someone who needed it most.

Four years ago my stepdaughter, Becca, had a friend she was close, to even though they weren't hanging together any longer. He was a super-sensitive guy and ultimately committed suicide when he was about seventeen. We were all pretty upset at this, since we all loved and liked this kid. Unfortunately he'd been going down a troubled road.

A day or two had passed since we'd heard the news and I was on my way home from work. Cameron had been on my mind since I'd heard he had passed, but at this moment, I was exhausted and wasn't thinking about anything except getting home and taking care of the tasks that awaited me.

I was driving along a state highway on which I have to get into a left turn lane. As I was driving and getting close, all of a sudden I'm looking at Cameron's face about a foot in front of me and up by my window visor, him looking down and grinning at me with a Cheshire cat grin that was pure Cameron. I just smiled back at him, 'cuz, man! He was RIGHT THERE with me and it just felt like it was supposed to whenever I'd see him in the past. He'd always been able to just swoop right in and capture my heart with that smile.

I jerked myself back to the present, realizing I was on the road and I saw that I was about to miss the turn lane to my street. I jerked the wheel to the left and jumped into the turn lane, slamming on my brakes to stop, because that light at the left turn was ALWAYS red! ALWAYS! In the six or seven years I'd lived there, it had NEVER ONCE been green when I pulled up to it and it was a daily M-F work route for me.

I was shock and amazed that: one, Cameron had been with me; two the light was green; and three, there wasn't another car

ANYWHERE in sight! ANYWHERE.. This is just weird because at 4 p.m. every day that route usually has plenty traffic.

I was blown away by the experience, overjoyed at seeing his face and that beautiful smile, but thankful for it, too. It took much of the intensity of my sadness away. I was also left with a knowing that we do live on.

I'd just recently read Walking in the Garden of Souls by George Anderson. It is a beautiful book and very touching, and my first real experience in how mediums work. I got a feeling that I should give Cameron's mom a copy of this book when the time was right, but I didn't know her and had never met her, though I had talked to her on the phone a few times when she was trying to locate her son when he was hanging out with our kids.

I believe it was the next night, still before the funeral, and I was in that state between waking and sleep, that twilight space, and all of a sudden I heard Cameron say from near the bedroom closet, "Tell my mom I love her." I bolted RIGHT UP, I don't mind saying.

I really deliberated about it for a while. Then about three weeks or a month later, I wrote a 12-page letter to his mom, telling her about this and had my stepdaughter, Becca, take the letter and book to her one day when she was going over to see her.

She called me several weeks later and we talked about it for a while. She told me that I had no idea how much of a gift my story was for her, that Cameron had never once in his life told her that he loved her, and this was just awesome for her. She also told me something I hadn't known: Cameron's father had also committed suicide, so she'd been dealt a double suicide whammy in her immediate family.

She moved from the area soon after and I never spoke to her again, although I hope that my experience with Cameron and the letter gave her some hope and strength to carry on.

Kim Hardie

Followup: Not too long after Kim sent this, her stepdaughter, Becca, ran into Cameron's mom. She told Becca that she could have no idea how much the letter Kim had written her had helped to save her sanity and her faith in life itself. She had read

the letter hundreds of times. It had given her more peace over her son's death than anything else in the world. She wanted Becca to convey just how much it still meant to her, that she reads that letter often.

For Kim the experience with Cameron left her remembering him with a smile on his face and love in his heart for his mother, instead of what could have been her thoughts of him as a young, tortured spirit in enough pain to end his own life – a beautiful gift in its own right.

Bottom line: Ghost stories to the contrary, of the many different ways in which the departed can manifest and validate their continued presence, making an appearance seems to be rare. Perhaps this is because it means that it requires that they lower the very high frequency at which they vibrate in the non-physical world to a frequency within the range that the human eye can see.

On the other hand, they may well have our health and well-being in mind, or for that matter, the date of our own inevitable departure from this physical plane. Most of us, confronted by the image of someone we have no earthly reason to anticipate seeing again might jolly well drop dead on the spot. But then, I'm only speaking for myself.

C. W.

CHAPTER TWO - WHEN THE MEDIUM BRINGS THE MESSAGE - PART I

Merriam-Webster defines a medium as: "an individual held to be a channel of communication between the earthly world and a world of spirits." Some are born aware of the ability, some recognizing it only after a traumatic event or, on occasion, the death of a loved one. For those for whom it is a profession, they do not take their ability lightly. Most take part in development circles or are trained with others having similar talents, where they hone their craft for a number of years. (Information concerning open development circles is available from Spiritualist churches, among other resources - see Appendix B.) In other words, they are constantly working at it, learning, refining their gifts.

Mediums raise their levels of vibration in order to meet those in the spirit world halfway, since the latter must lower their super-fast vibrations to facilitate the process. Understand, anyone can elevate his or her vibration; it happens most commonly during physical exercise, especially if it is aerobically challenging. Mediums, however, are able to raise theirs far above the norm. And the manner in which they receive messages varies. Some are more clairaudient than others, their strength the ability to hear the message from the departed. Some are more clairvoyant, able to "see" an image of the spirit. A combination of the foregoing is not unusual.

Some are presented with symbols requiring interpretation as to what is to be relayed, e.g., an American flag might be a clue for the medium that the contact was in the military and had a military funeral. For another medium, it might simply mean that the departed was very patriotic, again a matter of interpretation. Each medium has his or her own dictionary of symbols particular to his or her life experiences which the spirit world uses to convey what they wish to relate. It is important for the sitter to take into account that mediums are individuals and one should not expect that they all receive and relay messages from the Other Side in the same manner.

A reading with a medium is a unique experience in many ways. Perhaps because of the circumstances, one tends to approach it with a combination of skepticism, anticipation, and raging hope. You can be so determined not to be fooled, not to inadvertently reveal anything that will make it easier for the medium that you short-circuit the process. There's a tendency to have tunnel-hearing, on a par with tunnel vision, where you take what you hear literally and exclude any other interpretation. Told that a medium is being shown a badge, you might immediately think "police," and reject it, as no one in your family has walked a beat. The memory that your brother was a Boy Scout for whom earning his badge had been one of the most proud accomplishments of his young life, and which he was bringing up as validation of his identity, doesn't occur to you until later.

Another tendency is to develop a sort of amnesia. You may come to the reading with list in hand, your family tree back seven generations, yet still manage to forget your own last name, the names or nicknames of your children, the month you were born.

If you've done your homework, however, and have researched the medium in whom you're placing your trust, with the help of those with whom you have connected, you come away with a heart filled with joy.

Six readings with mediums, in both narrative form and transcripts from tape recordings have been included in this book, separated into chapters due to the length of several of them. They offer a glimpse at how different mediums connect with the Other Side. Hopefully, at the very least, it will make you wonder.

****

JOHN HOLLAND

John Holland has been working as a psychic medium for over twenty-five years, has been featured on television in Unsolved Mysteries, and the A&E documentary, *Mediums: We See Dead People.* With courses at the Arthur Findlay College in Britain as part of his training, and the author of several best-selling books (see Appendix A), he is originally from Roxbury, Massachusetts and has appeared nationwide with Sylvia Browne, John Edward, Robert Brown, Brian Weiss, Suzane Northrop, Lisa Williamson, Colette Baron-Reid and a host of others. A dynamic teacher as well, he conducts workshops across the country: Learn to Awaken your Psychic Strengths, and Learn to Connect to the Spirit World.

****

Pam Blizzard is the moderator of FriendsCommunities Web site (www.FriendsCommunities.org) an on-line group interested in the metaphysical. It is a place where one can be open, and learn. Pam shared this with the members as it happened. It's an experience we'll not forget.

In the six years that I had run the FriendsCommunities Web site, I had never had a mediumship reading. I never needed one. Others needed it more than me. I honestly, honestly felt that way.

My parents had a bitter breakup when I was thirteen and, of course, my whole life changed at that point. My new family and support became a circle of friends, a group of about thirty people who ranged in age from 14 to 19 or so. Our common bond was that we were outsiders. We didn't fit in with the athletes and cheerleaders. Our circle was our community, our family, our tribe. We were tight. We were loyal to each other. We spent almost every evening and weekends together as a group. When one was in trouble, we all came to each other's aid.

When I was fourteen I was totally unprepared to face death. No one in my rather small family had died; all my grandparents were either living, separated from the family anyway, or had passed before I was two. So I was totally devastated when a friend, Frank, who was seventeen, died in a car accident. It was devastating to the entire group. We were so young and had nothing to fall back on but each other. We were certainly not religious people. There was no one who could counsel us about death.

A week after Frank died, our friend, eighteen-year-old Larry, was hit by a car while on his motorcycle and had to have his leg amputated. Again we were devastated, wondering what kind of life this was, what kind of "God" could do this to young people, and why it could affect a whole group this way.

When I was sixteen, our friend, Dean, fifteen, was murdered in a home invasion. Then when I was seventeen, my friend, Rich, and my best friend's brother, Noel, drowned in a canoeing accident on a nearby river. They went over what appeared to be a small waterfall, but they had no idea about the undertow. Their bodies were not found for some time, leaving us to wonder (hope?) if they had simply run off, or if they were really gone. Noel's body was found about two weeks later, and then Rick's, his hand still clutching the paddle.

I was surrounded by death. I lived in a constant state of "who is next?" and wondered if it would be me. I honestly felt that I would not live to see my eighteenth birthday. Not only did my own sense of loss and fear devastate me, but watching my surviving friends crumble with grief and being unable to help them or comfort them left me feeling helpless and without power. These people were my family now and I was powerless to explain it to myself, much less to them.

When I was nineteen, our friend, Gary, committed suicide, leaving behind my good friend, Debbie and their five-year-old son,

Josh. My then-husband, Dave, and our best friend, Larry (who lost his leg) had to go into Debbie's and Gary's bedroom and literally clean what was left of Gary's remains from the room. It was a horror. Again, it hit the whole group of us very hard, leaving us to wonder about our own sanity, questioning if we were capable of the same thing. We all talked about how we could have prevented it, how we felt so guilty that we didn't know what he was going through, and at the same time, how he left us feeling angry that he could do such a thing to himself, to Debbie, to little Josh.

A year later, Gary's younger brother was murdered while in a jail cell, arrested for a petty crime. We rallied to support their mom as much as she would allow us to. Then when I was twenty, the news came that another good friend who had moved away, Bill, was killed in a car accident. Bill and I were very close when my parents separated.

When I was twenty-one, it was our dear friend, Rich, on his believed Harley. When I was twenty-two, it was my friend, Peggy, hit head-on by another car on the road I used to live on. She left behind children that had been a constant source of joy in my home.

Then when I was twenty-four, it was Phil, found dead in his car. They never performed an autopsy to find out if it was foul play or natural causes. They simply buried him. Thirteen years, ten friends. So young, no explanation possible. It was like Death was the thirty-first member of our "tribe."

In the last few weeks before attending John Holland's workshop in Chicago, I'd been frustrated. I'd lost my job without any warning, bills were due, the weather had turned. One day I was alone in my kitchen and it all just hit me. I thought of my upcoming weekend. How would I pay for gas to get there, or my meals? Thank God I had already paid my roommate for the room.

I gave in to the temptation to feel sorry for myself, something I usually resist. I thought of all my friends on the other side and I said, "Dammit, I need to hear from you. I really, really need to hear from you." I don't remember if I said it out loud. I said, "After all these years I just need to know that you ARE there, that the other side does exist. I've been doing this (expletive deleted) Web site for six years, and for God's sake, throw me a bone, okay?"

I was so upset with my feelings that I walked from room to room to try to get rid of them. I walked into my bedroom and said, "Okay, I got it out of my system," and "Whatever you can do, I'd really appreciate." I also said, "Mom, I'd really like to hear from you, please." She had died seven months before. I walked back to the kitchen thinking of Rick and Noel, for some reason. I thought to myself, now that would be efficient, if the two that passed together could come through together.

I looked out my kitchen window at another thing that bummed me out: I'd killed all the plants on the porch. It wasn't an accident, it wasn't a mistake. I had consciously let the suckers go by choosing not to water them. (Long story as to why I made that decision, but for now just know that I chose to let them go.) My husband had busted my chops for two weeks about killing the plants. I thought to myself, now THAT would be personal, unique and undeniably a "sign" if someone from the Other Side mentioned the fact that I killed the plants – not to mention embarrassing.

Real life set in, dishes, laundry, getting my resumé together, getting my son, Zach, off the bus, dinner – you know the routine. I didn't think about it any more.

On my way up to Chicago, I was so excited to have two and a half hours in the car alone. Time to listen to an inspirational author on tape. I settled on Ron Roth's "Healing Path of Prayer." He talked about how his prayer and meditation life developed, and how the "Our Father" has been mistranslated from an affirmation in a speech that begs "God" not to trick us and to give us just the very basics of what we need from day to day. He points out that when you trace the words back to Jesus's original Aramaic, the words come to life as an affirmation of what God already gives us. He said that God gives us everything we need – it's here for us; we just need to claim it.

When he said that, I said, "Okay, fine. I claim a reading this weekend from John Holland." I kissed it up to God and let it go.

Pam Blizzard

****

Following is the transcript of Pam's reading with psychic medium John Holland, edited only when messages came through for others in the FriendsCommunities who were there with her that day. This took place in Chicago in October 2006 with hundreds in attendance. Parenthetical comments are Pam's explanations.

JH: Bang! I'm coming over here.

PB: (I had to look at him two or three times to make sure he was walking toward US. He had a message from Lori Messer's grandmother, who had passed two weeks before.)

JH: (to Lori) Who'd you come with? (We all raised our hands and the whole place laughed.) Wait a minute. Alright, this is the way it's going to happen. This is compliments of the Barnaby lady. I've got a couple of kids who want to come through. They visited me before. I don't know where to put this. Is there a drowning connection for this group? Fluid to the lungs, a drowning connection?

PB: (I was stunned, because this is what I had asked for. No one else was claiming it, so I spoke up.) I have these two close friends that passed that way, actually drowning in a river.

JH: Is one female?

PB: No...

JH: That's okay. Is one more artistic, more sensitive? They could be gay. I'm not saying he was, sometimes that's how I get this.

PB: Yes. (Actually, Noel was very sensitive, very artistic, not the real "macho man" like the rest of the guys in our group. He didn't feel he had to go along with the crowd. He was definitely artistic.)

JH: Your mom has passed?

PB: Yes.

JH: She's coming in loud, loud, loud.

PB: (That would be my mom. She's boisterous and loves attention. As a kid, if I got separated from her in a store, I'd just listen for her voice because she'd be laughing with total strangers.)

JH: Are you the number one daughter?

PB: (I hesitated to say yes, because I'm not the first born, but—)

JH: She's putting the number one above you, Pam, because you either took care of her, or you're the oldest, or the responsible one.

PB: (Yes, I took care of her, nursed her through surgeries, the one who had to take care of all the details of my mother's health care, insurance, finances, etc., and I was always her "baby." She made no bones about me being her favorite and always said that my sister was closer to my dad, which is true.)

JH: I don't want to play favorites in case your sister is in the room, but there's a big 'thank you,' a big 'thank you,' a big 'thank you.'

PB: (I really needed to hear this, because I wanted to do so much more for my mom, but it was like she didn't let me, or she didn't want "more" for herself. I have wondered since her passing if she thought I should have done more, visited more and I wondered if she appreciated what I and my husband did for her.)

JH: Is there a connection to cancer in the lungs or emphysema?

PB: My father has emphysema, on this side.

JH: Your mom makes me aware that as hard as she tried to stay here, she knew you were ready for this. Do you understand this?

PB: Yes. (This is huge for me. My mother was on life support two years ago and they told us there was no hope. I was devastated because my sister could not come to be with me. We had to try and deal with it over the phone. On the way to visiting her the night before I was supposed to "pull the plug," I prayed and said, "I'm not ready for this. I don't care what I believe about the afterlife, I am just not ready for this. I need more time." When I got to her side that night, I verbally told my mom that it was okay to go, but in my heart I didn't mean it.

The neurologist called me the next morning as I was getting ready to go to the hospital to be there when they disconnected life support, and told me that she was starting to improve, which she did and lived on for two more years. But she had a painful, horrible quality of life and I wondered why God didn't take her the first time. This time when she became so close to death, I was ready to let her go, and my sister was able to come join me, which is a whole miracle story in itself. So this was very meaningful for me, almost like she stayed until I was ready to let her go.)

JH: How many sisters do you have?

PB: Just one.

JH: She's saying, "Hi to my girls, hi to my girls." I won't embarrass you but the other side will. What's this, you went in the garden, you killed her plants?

PB: I was saying to her, "Hey, I'm going to this John Holland thing. I'll be so embarrassed if she comes through and mentions the plants." (This is the sign I asked for, to mention the dead plants. They weren't hers, but she absolutely loved coming to my porch where I had hanging baskets and tons of terra cotta planters with herbs in them. She would go on and on about how much she just loved the plants and they were beautiful. She'd almost annoy me because she'd just repeat herself over and over about the plants. So she'd be busting my chops about letting them die, I just know it.)

JH: She's not upset, she's just saying, "Ask her about the plants," and I can joke with her, by the way.

PB: Yes. (Absolutely. My mother was the life of the party, always trying to make her doctors laugh and telling bawdy off-color jokes.)

JH: And, of course, she did, because you asked her to, and she heard you. She's coming through with the greatest of love and greatest of respect. Were you with her when she passed?

PB: No, we just missed her. We think she did it on purpose.

JH: Sometimes they do that. You can be with them for twenty-four hours a day and you can go to the bathroom and they go, because they don't want to put you through that.

PB: (There's a whole story to the timing that she passed. We're fairly sure she waited until we were in the parking lot pulling into the hospital, because the nurse had just checked her and rolled her over, and then checked her again, and she was gone, five minutes before we walked in the door.)

JH: She's saying, "Thank you for letting me go." She tried to wait as long as she could. She tried to wait until you were ready.

PB: (This goes back to me not being ready two years ago, and being ready this time.)

JH: She was very dizzy, always nauseous. She's saying, "Look at the crackers in her bed."

PB: Yes. (She was always complaining of being nauseous, always dizzy when she stood up. We knew it was a side effect of the medications that she was taking.)

JH: September is significant.

PB: It's my wedding anniversary. (I totally forgot until the next morning. It is my sister's wedding anniversary month, too. From here the reading switched to someone else. Later, JH returned to me.)

JH: There's an adoption connection here.

PB: My son is adopted. (I totally forgot at the moment that my husband and his two siblings are adopted. One of those siblings, his sister, gave up a child for adoption and then later adopted a child.

My sister, Patty's first two children are adopted. It's a very huge validation.)

JH: Pam, I hope this helped you, too.

PB: (I misunderstood and thought he was talking about the Dad thing with Lori.)

JH: No, the drowning thing. There's no real message there, just to come to you.

PB: (This makes sense, because I said, "I just need to hear from you," and I'm not connected to their families or anything. I just consider them to be representatives of that "group of young people" that I know on the Other Side.)

This reading was SO meaningful for me and has given me a renewed sense of knowing that the Other Side really does exist, that we do not die, and that my loved ones are still connected to me and can see what is going on in my life. I believed it before now, I KNOW it. The Other Side is awesome. John Holland is an awesome medium, teacher, and a warm, funny loving spirit. I cannot emphasize enough how lucky this world is to have him in it.

High Five, Rich and Noel!

Pam Blizzard

Then there's this October 2006 postscript from Pam:
When my mom passed on March 6, 2006, my sister took care of all the details, including clearing out my mom's room at the nursing home. She gave my mom's clothes to Good Will and brought the family pictures, mom's glasses, and our children's drawings in a box to me. I put them in a corner in my bedroom and hadn't touched the box since Mom passed. I just wasn't dealing with it.

Tonight I was in my bedroom re-reading John Holland's book, "Born Knowing." I got to the "Quickening Chapter," where he describes his very first mediumship experience. Near the end of the chapter, I put the book down and decided to finally look in the box of my mom's things. Maybe I'd find the Ritz crackers, I thought to myself. What I found was even more amazing.

What I had thought was a silk flower arrangement in the box was a REAL LIVE PLANT! I looked at the dried up flowers laying on the crusty, dry dirt, and the obvious white dust laying on the glass planter from the last seven months.

I did it! I really did kill HER plant! John Holland was more accurate than I thought he was!! When my sister gave me the box, I had no idea it was a live plant. I honestly thought it was fake! My jaw dropped.

But that was NOTHING. Upon further investigation, my heart stopped. There is new growth, a new sprout coming out of a dead plant that hasn't been watered in seven months, that has not seen sunlight in the corner of my bedroom!! The new sprout can only be a few days old! How can this be??? DOUBLE WHAMMY!! I am in total shock right now.

Pam Blizzard

CHAPTER THREE - LUCID DREAMS

There are dreams and then there are Dreams. Lower case dreams are those we experience each and every night. Some we remember upon waking, perhaps full-blown, perhaps in wisps and they may or may not make any sense. Some may not pop into our consciousness until much later in the day. Innumerable theories exist to explain the purpose and meanings of our dreams; it's not my area of expertise and as someone who rarely recalls them anyway, I feel my best approach on the subject is to sit down and shut up.

Uppercase Dreams, however, are another matter entirely. Most commonly called lucid dreams, the primary difference in them is that they seem so intensely real as they're happening. And oddly enough, even as they're happening, you are firmly aware that you are indeed dreaming. Once you wake up, you remember them vividly in full, glorious color and details for days, years and decades afterwards. I've had only two, the first fifty plus years ago as a freshman college student, involving what I realized later was an angel. To this day I have no idea what it meant, but some five decades later I can recall it and everything about it, even how I felt as it played out.

My second experience with a lucid dream is much more recent, in fact, less than a year after Bob West left this mortal coil. I was in the midst of a lower case dream, about what I don't remember. Suddenly there was a shift, a difference in the quality of the moment. The dream stopped as if someone had hit a switch and cut the current. A new type of awareness suffused me, one in which I knew without a doubt that I was asleep and lying on my right side. Just as suddenly I knew I was not alone, that Bob was there.

It was summer, the only cover required, a sheet. I felt it lifted from my body. I felt the mattress depress. I felt him get in and snuggle up behind me, just as we'd slept, spoon-fashion, for so many years. I settled into the familiarity of it with no alarm, only complete and utter contentment. He didn't speak; there was no need. I'd missed this. It was pure bliss.

I can't say how long he stayed, but my feeling is that it wasn't long. Finally I felt the sheet lift again, then the give in the mattress lessen as it released his weight. The sheet settled over me again. And he was gone.

Still on my side, I woke immediately and sat up, knowing I'd been dreaming and astonished at how real it had seemed. Then I realized that, inexplicably, my back was still warm with the feel of him! That lasted less than a minute, the warmth gradually fading. I got up, checked windows and doors and sleeping cats in the other room, knowing full well I hadn't given an intruder a few minutes of respite. I knew in the depths of my soul that Bob West had been there. And only learned much later that I had experienced a lucid dream, one that serves as a common mechanism for the departed to make an appearance.

That's not to say that each and every dream of our loved ones qualifies as a lucid dream. It's a whole different animal, and if you've ever experienced one, you know it. It makes sense. In our sleep, our usual defenses and logical thought are dormant. We're open, the channels for communication free of static. So they come.

****

A mother-in-law keeps a promise:
My sister-in-law, Beth, and her husband were coming to see my father-in-law, and we were all to meet for lunch. Beth and I were

the main caregivers for Mother her last six weeks of life. We kept her at home and nursed her with assistance from Hospice and other family members. Because Beth lives overseas, I had not seen her since Mother passed.

My dream: my dear mother-in-law, who passed in 1997, was talking to me on the phone. Mother was telling me that she would be at lunch with us. I told her that would be so nice, that I missed her and wanted to see her. I had said a few weeks before to my husband, Phil, that I could not remember her voice or laugh any longer, and I missed it. What a gift that laughter was. And suddenly, there she was, sitting crocheting an afghan, with that wonderful soft smile and lilting voice! I was so thrilled to see her!

She was younger and was working with ease. Her hands were beautiful and not at all arthritic as I had always known them to be. She said I would see a blue butterfly and that is how I would know that she was with us. I remember at one point she laughed, but wouldn't say why. At that point my alarm clock went off and I tried very hard to keep contact, but she faded off with the 'blue butterfly' reminder as her parting remark.

The first thing I did was write the 'visit dream' down. I told Phil about it and proceeded to get ready for church. He went off to work, saying he hoped that indeed I would see the blue butterfly.

I kept wondering how I might see a blue butterfly – someone's pin, perhaps, a child's sticker, a book cover, etc. As I was getting ready for church, I noticed that the scarf my little dog, Ginny, was wearing had fallen off. I picked up the scarf and called Ginny over to put it back on. She did, with no fuss and wagging her tail exuberantly! That was a surprise because she normally isn't that compliant when getting her scarf on.

Off to church I went, then straight to lunch with Father, Beth and John. We had a great time, but I saw no blue butterflies. I knew Mother was there anyway, because she said she would be. I got home, made dinner, and had to put Ginny's scarf back on again. I thought it was odd that it had fallen off a second time, because they don't normally untie that easily.

After a bit, I finally sat down to enjoy some 'down' time after a busy day. Our older dog was next to me and Ginny was curled up on Phil's lap. I looked over and here was a beautiful big blue butterfly, in fact, over half dozen of them. Ginny's scarf was covered with them! I hadn't noticed them in the morning or just before dinner when I'd had to put the scarf back on the dog. I was thinking so hard about finding one that I missed it when the scarf lay out in the middle of the floor - twice. It turns out Mother had said hello early this morning and late in the afternoon, but I didn't get the messages until that night. I could almost hear her laughing.

It became another step in the healing process, a reminder that she was only a thought away, an experience I readily shared with Beth and my father-in-law and others. It was a great comfort to them. Like me, they were pleased that she was no longer hurting and was still aware of what her family was up to.

Thank you for the blue butterflies, Mother - it's so appropriate for you. Close enough to be your symbol, different enough to be unique. Thank you for the laughter, the smile, the love and the visit!

Sue Purdy, Lancaster, PA

Bottom line: Butterflies are a symbol of transformation and renewal. As Sue said, how appropriate!!!

****

Gen's experience, from Australia, qualifies as our first two-fer, a lucid dream with the bonus of a message to be passed along.
My nephew, Jamie, passed away at about 2:30a.m. on a Thursday morning, 14 October 1999. He was only 17 years old, the victim of a car accident as a passenger in his own vehicle. He was later cremated and my sister has his ashes at home.

From the moment he passed, I feel he tried to contact us any way he could. The most amazing of them was a dream I had about twenty-four hours after learning of his death. I never saw him in the dream, but boy, did I <u>hear</u> him! When I woke up, etched in my mind was: "Please explain, Property of, Earring, and Nigel." I admit that I was skeptical, uncertain if it was really a message from Jamie or just a dream.

As our family has a history of strange dreams, I told his mum. She told me that she had just received the property bag with Jamie's clothes and personal effects and that it contained only one of the pair of the gold earrings she had given him for Christmas the year before. She didn't hold out much hope for finding the mate, however, thinking it may well have ended up in the gutter at the crash site. And the opportunity to go through the wrecked car itself might never arrive.

I found the dream difficult to dismiss. Jamie had been short on patience in this life and didn't believe in wasting time. To get this message to me so soon after his death meant to me that he wanted answers and action A.S.A.P.

The following January I had to travel to Adelaide. For the life of me, I can't even remember why, and I couldn't afford to. Still I just knew I <u>had</u> to go. I managed to get down there with my husband and all of my children. Turns out my twelve-year-old niece from Queensland was going to be there. I hadn't seen her in eight years.

I wanted to see the wrecked car; my husband and my younger and older sisters didn't because it reminded them of how Janie had died. I didn't look at it this way; I just wanted to see it and take photos of it, so I could show my own children as they got older. Since my children all wanted to see the car as well, my husband had no choice but to join us. He needed a change of shirts, so my sister lent him one of Jamie's polo shirts.

My sister then changed her mind. She wanted to see the car. She bundled Jamie's ashes in her knapsack/bag and came with us to her ex-husband's house. And there was the car.

Suddenly, my sister said, "I must find that earring."

The car was a total write-off, a mangled mess, but I agreed that earring had to have been in the car somewhere. After the accident, all the stuff that had been splattered on the road – glass, etc., bits of metal – were all put in the boot of what was left of the car. My sister put Jamie's ashes on a bench in the shed and we all went about looking.

After an hour of searching, the earring was finally found on the back seat of the car UNDER a McDonald's wrapper. Jamie's mum had gone inside briefly to make us all cuppas when it was found. I took it in to her. We were absolutely rapt that we had it. My sister had given the other earring to Nigel, so she decided to let Nigel have the one we found.

All the while we were searching, I took photos, and we took them to my younger sister's house to show them to her and Nigel and the niece from Queensland. I took more photos of their reaction when they were handed the small gold earring.

It was like we ALL had to be there in the flesh to see what was left of Jamie's pride and joy, his car, and to find the earring. It wasn't until later that I noticed that in one of the photos I took of the back seat through the window, there is what looks like the earring under the McDonald's wrapper.

Geniene Gordon, Whyalla, South Australia

Followup: Not surprisingly, Geniene says the experience had a positive effect on her grieving process. It was proof that consciousness continues after death. It also enlightened her; it showed her how receptive she was to messages from the departed and taught her to trust her instincts more.

There was, she says, never an issue about talking with her sisters about the experience, as they often discuss their dreams. Finding the earring served as validation for her, and especially to Jamie's mother, that consciousness survives.

****

Another two-fer, this one from Lori. She did not, however, consider her assignment a bonus:

There was one occasion in 2006 when I had to be the messenger for the departed. I learned one important thing: never deliver the message to someone who is driving!

I'd had a dream about my husband's parents, who had both crossed. It was incredibly real and vivid! I could hear them, see them, touch them, feel them! Mike's mom gave me a hug and said that she had been wrong about me, that she should have known I would take care of her son. We didn't get along well in life; she thought I was after the family's money and did not care for him. In the final weeks of her life, my husband, her son, had a stroke. I have taken care of him ever since, over eight years now. That was a BIG validation for me, as she was not lucid enough to understand his condition at the time. They were even in the same hospital at the same time at one point.

His father died shortly after we were married in 1996, so I did not get to know him well. In the dream he told me to tell Mike that he understood now, and that there was a mistake made about the roll top desk. He said he was sorry that the misunderstanding had caused a split between Mike and his brother, but he knew now and wanted him to know he understood. He asked if I would tell him. I said yes in my dream and woke up.

A few days later, this dream still nagged at me; I hadn't said anything to Mike yet. We were in our car on our way somewhere. It was time to bite the bullet. So without warning, I asked him if there had been issue with a roll top desk. Mike's face turned white and he had to pull the car over.

He asked me point blank why the hell would I ask that? I told him about my dream and he began to weep. Apparently there was a HUGE fight shortly before his father had died. My husband had gone to get a stamp out of the roll top desk and one of his brothers accused him of trying to take a watch of his father's before he died so the other brothers could not have it. It upset his father because he was disappointed that Mike would do that. His brothers refused to believe him. It was at that point that he was all but cut out of one of his brother's lives. He wouldn't listen to reason, and his dad had died thinking that Mike had done something wrong. It had bothered Mike all these years.

I was lucky enough to be the messenger for him. Word of advice, though: wait until they park before you give the message!

Lori Messer

Bottom line: Even under the best of circumstances, it may not be easy to pass along to someone a message from a friend or loved one in spirit. But as Lori advises, pick the time wisely!

****

Occasionally, our lucid dreams contain a warning. We're always free to ignore them or take them to heart. Fortunately, Lori did the latter.

I had a dream that I was driving a van (we didn't own one at the time) that I assumed was my mother-in-law's. In my dream I had my kids and my mother in the car with me. My husband's father, who had just recently passed away, was also in the car with us. He was not sitting down, but rather leaning over my shoulder telling me to be careful, that this truck was going to hit us. I looked up to see a white semi with the name of a nationally known moving company in blue letters coming onto an on ramp on the highway. He did not see us. He sideswiped us and our van flipped and we were badly hurt.

I was extremely shaken up by the dream, but didn't think about it again until about a month later. We were on the same stretch of highway driving my new van. I got a sudden blast of cold air on my neck and a déjB vu feeling. I heard the word "Remember," and suddenly the dream came back. I looked over just in time to see a white semi truck with the same blue letters barreling down the on ramp. I moved over quickly into the next lane and watched as he almost sideswiped the car in back of me. If I hadn't moved, we would have been badly hurt. My husband's dad warned us that day!

Lori Messer

Bottom line: Once again Lori's father-in-law came through out of love for his family. So we'd be well advised to pay attention to our dreams. There's almost always something to be learned from them.

****

There are occasions when a lucid dream brings with it a message impossible to relay by any other means. Amanda's dream, though not strictly an ADC, was the vehicle used to alert her to her mother's wishes.

My mom was in a coma. She was sixty years old, had contracted bacterial meningitis and went into a coma on November 8, 2000. She was on and off life support, and in and out of the Intensive Care Unit several times. She had seemed to be improving, at least enough so that she was taken off of life support and put into a regular private room, even though she was still in a coma.

On Christmas Eve night, after coming home from being with her, I dreamed that I parked on the top floor of the hospital's parking garage and got out of my car to find her standing by the passenger side. She looked healthy and whole and well once more, even better than she had looked for the past four or five years. I was so happy to see her like this! I started to hug her and I remember saying, "Oh, Mama!"

She gave me a stern look, one I remember seeing a lot growing up. She looked me straight in the eyes – even now years later I still see her eyes clearly as they looked then as she looked into mine – and said, "I need you to leave me alone." I remember opening my mouth to speak. I'm not sure what I was going to say, but she shook her head at me and gave me an even sterner look, like "don't argue with me." And she said again, "I need you to leave me alone. I'm not giving up, but I NEED you to leave me alone." That is where I woke up, and the phone was ringing. It was the hospital calling to tell us that they had returned my mother to the ICU and that she was once again on life support.

For days after that dream I was upset and puzzled and hurt. I felt that she didn't want me to visit her any more, didn't want me there. I was so insistent that she not give up! I feel, though, that she was sort of sitting on the fence between this side and the other. I think I was probably too hard on her, and maybe too hard on myself, too. I finally came to the conclusion that maybe I was keeping her from making her own decision about leaving this world. Maybe my constant attempts to make her fight and to wake her up was hindering her. Maybe I was flat out annoying her. I don't know, but I tried so hard. My sister and I both did. And as silly as it sounds, I was actually mad at her for a little while for telling me to leave her alone.

I still remember that dream like it yesterday. It feels like a gift now. She just needed for me to back off a little to see that. And in the end, it all played out like it had been written that way. She was on and off life support and in and out of the Intensive Care Unit several times before she took an even worse turn and we chose to have her life support removed on January 4, 2001.

The whole family spent that last day and night with her. She passed peacefully in her hospital room on the morning of January 5, 2001, with my sister and I on either side of her, holding her hands, and my father and brother close by the bed, telling her that it was okay to go and that we would be okay. She took her last breath while we spoke to her and kissed her cheeks. There was no struggle, no pain, only peace. Her face was relaxed, she seemed finally at ease. And finally we were at peace with the decision we had made.

I think we fool ourselves that we made that decision. Mama made the decision. She was waiting for us to catch on and let go on our own before she left. That was just like her. She always thought of us, never herself. She had to help us and give us time to let go a little, so that she could.

Amanda Miller

Bottom line: Apparently lucid dreams can be used as a connection between one conscious mind and another. In Amanda's case, her mother made her wishes clear while still in the physical world. And as difficult as it was, Amanda listened and let her mom go in peace. Out of love.

****

The pain of losing a child has no parallel. Therefore it is a special blessing when a parent experiences a visit, as related, again, by Amanda.

In February of 1994 I was pregnant with my first child, Jessica. One night I dreamed of a little girl with long, dark brown hair and brown eyes. She appeared to be about three years old. Somehow I knew it was Jessica. She simply stood on some steps and looked at me. I stared back. Then she waved at me and I woke up.

The next afternoon after the dream I felt pain and began to lose blood. I went to the hospital and learned that I had lost her. I've always felt that the dream was a gift, that Jessica was saying goodbye to me and allowing me to see what she would have looked like in life.

After I came home from the hospital I was in bed and crying, begging God to bring her back. Inexplicably, the light above my bed turned off and then on again. I thought I felt her presence, a warm, loving feeling that came over me. And even though I only carried her for four months, Jessie's still with me. I can call up the memory of her visit any time and still see her beautiful little face any time I want to. It makes me long to hold her as I do my other two children, but it brings me peace as well.

I had my son almost a year to the day that I lost her, and he looks like a male version of the child I saw in that dream. Same color hair, eyes, it amazes me! And I still feel as if I have three children. I once found myself unconsciously looking for the "third" while I was grocery shopping with my other two children and trying to keep an eye on them.

Yet another visit via lucid dream was courtesy of my grandmother, my dad's mom, whom we called Granny. She had passed away in October of 1992. While I was pregnant with my son, she came to me in a dream. She rubbed my belly and said, "He's going to be okay." I was very anxious during that pregnancy since I had lost Jessie less than a year before. This visit from my grandmother calmed my fears a great deal. Also, it let me know that he was indeed a boy and not the Rebecca Lynn I had decided to name him. Rebecca arrived almost three years later.

Amanda Miller

Bottom line: Even though Jessica was not destined to remain in the physical world, she left her mother with a gift she could hold in her heart for all eternity, her "picture." And Amanda's grandmother in spirit was there to assure her that the next child to come, this time a son, would be fine. And that love never dies. Never.

****

Another daughter comes to bring comfort:

I have had many recent encounters with my daughter, who took her life on May 25, 2005. She suffered with depression over her son's illness. He has diabetes and had been in and out of hospitals, with no end in sight. As his illness got worse, her depression did as well. She also suffered with disintegration of her spine and at times was in severe pain.

Then six months before her death, her soul mate died from a massive heart attack while shoveling snow for his elderly parents. They found him the next day lying in the snow. She fell into a deep hole of depression, and counseling as well as my support did nothing to help her. In May, her son was once again hospitalized in severe pain from diabetic complications and went into a coma.

The night she died, I was visited by the dark angel in the late hours of the night. I knew it was my daughter telling me she was in trouble, and I felt great fear for her. The next morning I called her house, but was unable to contact her. I found out she was missing that night. She was not found until two days later.

About this same time I needed colon surgery and was admitted to the hospital. The day after my surgery, I heard a knock. My back was to the door. I turned to see who had come into the room and my daughter was standing near my head. I was astounded and said, "Bev, you're here." She said, "Of course I'm here, Ma. I love you and will never leave you." She knew how devastated I was by her death and how much I needed to know she was in heaven, in spite of her suicide.

The next night she came to me in a vision. She knocked on my room door and said, "Ma, take my hand. I am going to take you to the mountains."

I said, "Where are we going, in the mountains in New York?"

She said, "No, Ma, it's the biggest mountain ever." My daughter took me by my hand to a mountain that was made like the Incas or Mayas.

I clearly saw everything in great detail. We walked up the granite-like stairway with steps on both side of the mountain to the very top. Once we got on top, it was flat and you could see valleys and awesome landscapes.

She told me the field of flowers never dies, even when you step on them. I was frightened to be up so high. She stated there was no need to be afraid, that nobody got hurt here. There was no pain or tears in this place, only peace and happiness. We could lie down on the thick, soft grass. While we were lying there, I could see people walking up and down the stairs smiling, holding hands and full of peace. I also saw my husband walking up the stairs, and asked her what he was doing there, as he seemed to be struggling to climb the stairs. She told me that he, too, would soon be going there. In doing so, she was preparing me for his death.

My daughter then took me to a place where there were many people playing all kinds of musical instruments I had never seen before. The music was playing all over, the sounds so peaceful, and yet the music did not clash with the other players. She told me there is music playing all the time and for me to just sit and listen to it. She knew I would love hearing it. Then she left, and I woke up.

She has shown me that she is around me in many ways, by the frequent smell of her perfume. Many times I can smell cigarette smoke and nobody is smoking. I have seen her standing in my kitchen. She smiled at me, then was gone in a second.

Her visits have had a huge impact on my life, giving me hope that we will never truly be disconnected. It was so comforting to know that she lives on to help guide me through my life. I hope that this will help others who search for answers regarding the passing of their loved ones.

Beverly Morningstar

Followup: Sadly, Beverly's visit from her daughter was prophetic. Her daughter was indeed preparing her for the pain of finding her husband of thirty-six years having made his transition during the night, less than three years after his daughter. It helped her to realize that our loved ones truly never leave us and can act as guides to welcome other loved ones when they transition to the Other Side.

She shares her visits with many family members and friends who have had similar experiences, and who also believe our loved ones are always close to us after they leave us. Beverly says: "Allow your mind to be still, and their presence will be known to you."

****

To be blunt, guilt is a butt-kicker. Guilt following the death of someone dear is even worse, because we can never undo whatever we've done. It's a kind of poison that eats into one's soul. Fortunately, the departed are a forgiving lot, if we're lucky enough to discover that.

Elaine and I had been best friends for ten years and had spent many long hours debating the existence of life after death. Elaine had lost both her parents by the time I met her, and she had never really gotten over her grief. I would often try to explain to her my personal view of the life that goes on after our physical death, but she just never believed it. I would laugh sometimes, because she had been raised and was still a member in good standing of a local church, and I have a wide and varied view of the spiritual world that did not include organized religion.

The plant where Elaine and I had been co-workers for ten years suddenly closed. I went on to school and got another job. Elaine, however, never recovered from the shock of losing her job. She became increasingly depressed and began drinking heavily. Eventually I stopped all contact with her, and her daughter avoided her as well.

Her death was sudden and unexpected. I was torn with both grief at her passing, but also guilt that I had not spent more time with her. I spent many nights asking "what if....?" If I had been a better friend, perhaps I could have helped her stop drinking. Perhaps I'd have recognized that she was becoming ill.

Several months after her funeral I had the most amazing dream which I knew, even as I had it, that it was her message to me. In the dream I was upstairs in Elaine's home with her daughter. We were cleaning out her mom's storage stuff.

I pulled a box from under the bed I was sitting on and opened it to find that it was full of books. As I pulled out one after the other and laid them on the bed, I saw that they all had to do with reincarnation and life after death. I looked up at her daughter and said, "I didn't know that your mom was into this stuff."

Just then I looked across the bed and there stood Elaine with the most amazing smile on her face. I wish there were words to describe how joyful and peaceful she looked. Imagine the look of a mother when she gazes into her newborn baby's face for the first time – all the love and joy and wonder at the miracle of life, that is the closest I can come to explaining it. And even though she never spoke I KNEW that she had two messages for me. One, that life after death was real and so much more than what we had talked about and, two, she wanted me to tell the daughter she was closest with about her "visit" and let her know that her mom was still with her and was incredibly, amazingly happy.

Even as I tell it to you I can still see Elaine's face in my mind's eye in that "visit." I cannot begin to describe the joy I felt when I woke up, but I was nervous about sharing the dream with her daughter, who had a more conventional religious belief system. There was every chance to expect that she would dismiss me as a kook, but I knew I had to tell her. To my surprise and relief, she accepted the news with no doubt, almost as if Elaine was there with us, confirming that it was all true.

I think this experience opened my eyes and my heart to see the miracles that have occurred in my life so many times. I have an even more personal relationship with God than ever before. My ADC seems to have blown open a door inside me that before had only been opened a crack.

I have no doubt that our souls live on after our physical body dies. Before Elaine died, I knew on an intellectual level what I believed, but now I FEEL that belief every day. I share this story with people all the time in hopes that perhaps I will have the opportunity to open that door in someone else's heart.

Cathy Dague

Followup: Every bit as important to Cathy, she came away from this experience with a sense of total forgiveness from Elaine, who didn't blame her friend for her actions. She wanted Cathy to share that with her daughter, and for them both to know that she was finally truly at peace and happy. Their guilt is now a thing of the past.

****

Parents. They never leave us. And moms remain moms:
My mother, Isabel Wilson Allen, crossed over on May 3, 1982 from breast cancer. My mother was an English/Home Economics major in college at Louisiana Tech and taught elementary school for many years before her death. English language was always very important to her, and if my brother or I used a word incorrectly, she immediately pointed it out to us and was forever correcting our grammar. She was also very involved in tennis as a teenager and young adult and taught tennis on several occasions. Foolishly, as a college junior and the #2 player in my college tennis class, I challenged her to a tennis match. I was nineteen and she was forty-three and had not picked up a tennis racquet in many years. She reluctantly accepted, and after running me all around the court with her perfectly placed shots for four games, all of which she won handily, she declared she was quitting because she was not getting enough exercise and just standing in one place. I happily agreed to ending the match, as I was sweating profusely and was sore for three days afterwards.

About six months after she crossed over, I was awakened one morning and in my drowsy state saw that I was on some type of tram with a lot of other people I did not know. My mother, however, was at the front of the tram showing some of these people a new tennis stroke she had learned. She seemed to know everyone and they seemed to know her; they were all talking and laughing like old friends. She had on a short tennis skirt and looked to be in her twenties or early thirties, the picture of health and happiness.

I ran up to her and hugged her, telling her how much I loved her and missed her each day. She told me she loved me and missed me also. I said, "But Mom - you are dead!" She quickly explained that "Death is like ending one sentence and beginning another sentence in the same paragraph." This is not something that I could have ever come up with, since I was neither an English major or ever even very fond of English classes, much less sentences and paragraphs. We talked some more about how my job was going, and I began to walk back to my seat. She stayed at the front of the tram with her friends, still talking and laughing with them.

The tram stopped at the bottom of a hill in front of a very large white marble building with immaculate landscaping and a path leading up to it with marble benches placed along the walkway. You could see the lovely path winding up the hill, all beautifully landscaped. Everyone got up from their seats and began to exit the tram, still talking and laughing and seeming to know where they were. I got up as well and started to follow them out, but then remembered that I had brought my mother a present and had stored it under my seat on the tram. I ran back to my seat, retrieved the present and was about to exit when the tram doors closed and the tram took off with me on it.

I knew when I finally awoke that I had indeed seen my mother, and I can still see the details of this "dream" or "visit" as vividly as if it had just happened. My mother's reply that, "Death is like ending one sentence and beginning another sentence in the same paragraph," is definitely something that only she would have said. I could not possibly have made that analogy because I do not put anything in the context of English grammar, do not know enough of it to do so and was never very interested in it.

I also had a "visit" from my grandfather after he crossed. He sat on the edge of my bed and talked to me for a long time about my father, mother, brother and how college was going, even giving me some tips on getting better grades. I had also said to him, "But, Papa, you are dead," and he replied, "People say I am dead, but I am really not dead." At the end of our visit, he said to call him sometimes, and said he loved me. I assured him that I would call him and as soon as I woke up that morning, I tried to dial his telephone number, but, of course, the number no longer worked.

I have had several other "visits" from friends and family members after their crossing, but I think the one from my mother is the most memorable and remarkable. I do hope that more and more people can see that this life is just a stepping stone in a much longer journey of the soul.

B. J. Allen, Matlacha, Florida

Bottom line: The lesson here is that no matter where they are, on this side of the veil or the other, mothers are forever mothers, passing along wisdom they hope we will take to heart. And the visit from B.J.'s grandfather reminds us that those in the spirit world are just as involved and interested in our lives now as they were when they were here with us. Some things change. Love makes certain that important things don't.

****

With sisters as close as Debra and Gail are, it should come as no surprise that a message might be passed along to one for the other:

It was early in the morning and I was having my usual dreams which make no sense and fade quickly from my memory shortly after I wake up. All of a sudden, my dreams switched scenes and became very vivid and colorful. I found myself on a cruise with my sister, Gail, where I had gone to a part of the ship to sit on a couch.

Gail's husband, Phil, who had died months before, sat next to me, and it was the most vivid and colorful dream I can ever remembering having in my life. He had jet black hair and was probably in his early forties. It was so real, it was like it had actually happened and is a memory to me even to this day, as clear as any real events in my life.

I asked Phil if he was just visiting, or was he going to stay awhile, and if he wanted me to go to the cabin and get Gail. He said it was just a visit and wanted to let Gail know that she needs to let go and move on with her life. I was so excited in my dream that I ran back to my cabin to get my camera, because I didn't think anyone would believe that Phil came to visit me and I wanted to take a picture. At that moment, I woke up. Normally I am a very slow riser in the morning, and it takes me several minutes just to open my eyes and get out of bed. Not so after this dream. I immediately sat up on the side of the bed and had a very strong feeling of love and warmth that was unbelievable. I said to myself as I woke up that this was so great. I actually saw Phil.

Debra John

Followup: The adventures of Gail, her husband Phil, their daughter, Valerie and Gail's sister, Debra, continue throughout this book. The connection between them all remains as constant now as before Phil made his transition into the world of spirit. Little has changed. The love between them all is still strong. No surprise there.

****

As I collected these narratives, I was struck by how many involved contact from grandparents. Apparently the relationship between grandparents and their grandchildren is very special. A friend commented after the birth of her first grandchild that as much as she loved her children, she had no idea how intensely she could come to love this new little soul. So it's no surprise that the following series warm the heart.

My third child was born in September of 1992. I was so happy! I sent pictures to my grandmother in Mexico City. I was named after her and she had raised me and five siblings since our birth here in California. To me, she was my mom.

In 1980 she went back to Mexico to live with my uncle, and in January of 1994, passed away. I was devastated and mourned for her. I would cry myself to sleep, so hurt that I hadn't been there to say goodbye to her and that she would never meet my son, Diamon.

One night my grief seemed even more intense. I remember sobbing uncontrollably until I fell asleep, yearning to see my grandma again. That night I had two dreams that changed everything. In the first, my grandmother stood in front of me with her arms wide open. I went to her and hugged her. I felt her body just as I had remembered it many years before and I could smell her scent. I held her tightly until I felt okay to let her go. It was so real. I cannot describe my joy at being in her arms again.

The second dream took place in our car. I was in the front passenger's seat and Diamon's dad was driving. I glanced back to see if Diamon was in his car seat and he wasn't there! Behind me was my grandma with Diamon on her lap. He was snuggled in her arms, being held close to her chest. I was surprised, then immediately very calm. I smiled with joy.

When I woke up I felt rested and healed of my deep pain. It could not have come at a better time. I had so yearned for her to meet Diamon. I was so unbelievably happy to have been able to hug my grandmother in my dream and say goodbye to her. I also felt the image of her holding my baby meant that she DID know Diamon and that she was with him and taking care of him. I felt cleansed and reassured by the dream of that night.

When my fourth child was born in 2002, I knew and still know that she watches over him, too. I still mourn her and miss her very much, but all I have to do is remember those dreams and I feel enlightened and peaceful. I feel that my grandma came to help and heal me that night as she had many, many times before when she was physically with me. I told my siblings, and one day when they're old enough to understand, I'll tell my children about their great-grandmother's visits. I'm proud to be Guadalupe, after her.

Lupe Ramirez Peterkin

****

And again....

My grandmother, Mary, was a wonderful part of my life. She and my grandfather (my father's parents) lived with us from the time I was six until she passed away in 1975. Because of this, we never came home to an empty house. There was always the smell of something cooking or baking when we got home. Those alone are the most wonderful memories I have – aromas. You simply can't beat them.

About a year after Grammy passed away, I had this wonderful dream of her. She was in the church basement sitting beside a piano with her favorite red and blue print satin dress on. She had a Mona Lisa smile, not too broad at all, but sweet. However, when she laughed it was a delightful trill. She was so special. She never said anything to me in the dream. I was way up in the right hand corner of the dream, looking down and across from her. She smiled so sweetly at me, I think to let me know that she was okay and for me not to worry about her. I smiled all day after that dream. It was the best gift in the world to me.

My dad's father passed in 1954 when I was twelve years old. It was my first funeral. Granddaddy was a quiet man. But, not unlike my dad, when he spoke, you wanted to listen to every single word. He was a well-read man who would tell wonderful stories. I loved every single one of them.

My after death communication of him is still a mystery to me. He showed up in my dream dressed the way he knew I would know him in a minute – black pants, white shirt with no collar, and his slippers. Granddaddy's shirts would wear at the collar and my grandmother would turn the collar and hand sew it back on. During the summer it would be too hot for a collar, so she would take them off and stitch the cowling closed so it appeared to be a short stand-up collar. He had on one of those shirts in the dream. He had this wonderful full mouth smile on his face with sparkling blue eyes, pointing at the radio – again, no words, just smiling and pointing at the radio. I have tried to decide what the radio was about other than to recognize the importance of communication.

But the wide wonderful smile my grandfather had on his face melted my heart. I miss his wonderful stories, his pipe tobacco aroma, and those beautiful blue eyes. It was so good to see him again.

Ellen Siddons

Bottom line: What struck me about Ellen's telling of her lucid dream was the detailed description of how her grandparents looked, what they wore. They made certain that their appearance would align with her memory of them and reassure her that they had not changed. They were still the beloved grandparents they had been and would always be and that she was still loved in return.

****

Once again, a grandparent brings comfort:

In my dream my grandmother came to me sitting in the park. She was not the elderly woman I remembered, but looked like she did in her forties. She sat next to me on the bench and stroked my cheek. She said to tell Sandy thank you for taking care of her, and not to worry, that we had done the right thing. She stood up and twirled and said, "Look at me!"

She kissed my forehead and stroked my cheek again and then wrinkled her nose at me. She brushed my hair out of my eyes and said, "Oh, that hair! I can't see your eyes! I could just take a pair of scissors and...." She laughed, hugged me and walked away.

I woke up crying, but happy. I had to laugh about the hair thing. She was always threatening to cut my hair when it was in my face!

I'm very fortunate in that I believe that the deaths of my mother and my grandmothers unfolded and played out exactly the way they were supposed to. That is not to say that I did not grieve their loss or was not affected by losing them. Quite the contrary. Losing them was the hardest thing I have ever been through. I was able to say my goodbyes to them and be as much a part of their deaths as they were a part of my birth. I held them as they slipped from my world like they'd cradled me when I came into theirs. The three of us have a very special relationship and looking back, I realize that we have always been a trilogy of strong women, each of us giving strength to one another, learning from one another and always loving one another, even after death. I still have and feel that bond with them. They are always with me watching over me and protecting me now as they did in life.

Lori Messer

Bottom line: Lori's ties to her family remain as strong as they've ever been. Their visits and reminders of their love for her are proof that the death of the physical body changes nothing. Parents and grandparents are with us for eternity. So is love.

****

And yet again:

I was extremely close to my grandfather. He was retired by the time I was born and was at our house every day. He rocked me, visited, and took me for walks in the stroller. I went to his home for lunch all through elementary school, had dinner there with him and my grandmother, who was still working, more than I did at home. And I spent a great deal of my weekends there. I was twenty-five when he died after a long illness of about four or five years.

After his death I talked to him every night when I got into bed, and couldn't help crying as I did. It was the first death of anyone really close and grief was new to me. I felt badly about it and kept saying, "I'm okay, Pa. Don't pay attention to all this crying. It's just something I have to do." I would always say to him, "I just wish I could KNOW that we're still connected, that you still love me. I still love you and miss you so much."

I dreamt of him virtually every night for about three months after his death. He died in the hospital where I worked, and I kept dreaming that I would be up on the wards and find him alive. Since everyone had thought he had died, no one had been to see him. They were very disturbing dreams.

Then one night I dreamed that I was sitting on the couch in my grandparents' living room and he was sitting next to me. It was the shortest, most meaningful dream to me. He hugged me, pressed his cheek against mine and said, "I love you, you know."

That was it. I woke right up and I could still feel the tingle on my cheek from his whiskers, as though I'd just been with my grandfather. I didn't fully realize what had just happened, but I knew it was special, more than a dream. It gave me such a feeling of peace and hope to know that we were still connected. To this day I can't tell that story without crying. That was in 1980 and it's as vivid now as it was then. All of the emotion of that moment just wells up again. It wasn't until I read John Edward's book that I realized that what I had experienced was called a visit. It validated what I already believed, that I would be with him again.

The only one I told at the time was my mother, who was totally supportive. She confessed that she, too, had had odd dreams about her father. We were able to talk about it openly, which helped us both through the grieving process and created an even stronger bond between us.

Mary Ellen Gray

Bottom line: How fortunate it is that Mary Ellen was able to share her lucid dream visit with her mother and her mother could confess to similar experiences. Love at work again, strengthening ties between this plane and the next.

****

Tory went to bat for her dad and received a thank you she considers out of this world.

My dad had cancer for two years before he passed on December 14, 2006. The last few months were rough. My mom had also died from cancer and suffered terribly before she passed in her home in 1994. Seeing my mom suffer compelled me to move heaven and earth to ensure that my dad did not suffer as she had.

He was going to need 24/7 care. His girlfriend lived next door, but was not in good enough health to take on the task. I live an hour and a half away and have a very demanding job. The hospital discharged him to a nursing home. I was SO distraught. My father had cared for his father-in-law in the 1970's so he could die at home. And in 1994 my father cared for both his wife and his mother at the same time so both of them could die at home. There was NO WAY I was going to let my dad pass in a nursing home. I had him out of there within three days.

Even though I did not have the money, I hired 24/7 private duty nurses to care for his personal needs – cooking, washing, diaper changes, etc., and we had Hospice for his medical needs. Hospice was covered under Medicare; it was the private duty nursing that was not.

Pain management was priority #1 for me. I worked during the day, then made the trip back home at night to be with him. On his second day home I found that his girlfriend and the private duty nurses were trying their best to keep his pain under control using the meds they had been given, when it was clear that he needed a pain patch or some other form of medicine that could be administered other than via pill. However, no one had made a loud enough fuss to get what was needed. I called Hospice, demanded his primary care be contacted to call in a prescription for a pain patch to his pharmacy. They did that.

After waiting an hour with no call back, I found that his doctor STILL had not called in the prescription. It was at this point that I became a person I never thought I could be. I contacted the doctor's office directly, and the receptionist was as helpful as she could be. After getting no satisfaction, I told them that if I did not receive notice from the pharmacy that his prescription was ready within fifteen minutes, I would drive to her office and create such a scene that only the police would be able to remove me. The pharmacy called in five minutes, my dad had his patch within fifteen minutes, and he passed that night peacefully, pain-free and AT HOME.

I left my daddy's house at roughly one in the morning. It was the night that a meteor shower had been predicted, but it was also very foggy. As I was traveling through the fog, however, one area became clear enough that I could actually see just a split second of the meteor shower. Dad passed at roughly 2:30a.m. I now believe that was a clearing for him to ascend and/or a message that it would be okay.

My dad and my fiancé were close. My fiancé passed in August 2004. In January 2007 I had a dream and Rob came to me with my dad standing in the background. Rob said a lot, talked up a storm. Unfortunately, I don't remember a THING he said!

My dad stood by quietly. After Rob was done, my dad stepped forward. He said nothing. But I knew he was thanking me for what I had done to help him die the way he deserved to die. In my forty years, my dad never told me he loved me. My mom told me she loved me every day, ten times a day. I never needed my dad to say it because I knew by his actions that not only did he love me, I was his "everything." That's why his standing there saying nothing meant what it did to me.

Tori Thomas

Bottom line: If we're fortunate, when the time comes for final goodbyes we will have little or nothing left to regret. Knowing that we'd done everything we could do, said everything to be said, especially "I love you," can make all the difference in the world to those of us left behind.

****

What follows is not only a recount of messages from beyond, it is also an introduction to a little-known congenital disorder as well as heart-warming evidence that our loved ones celebrate our successes along with us.

My father will always be around watching over me no matter how old I get on this earth! These after death communication experiences with him surrounding my smile surgeries give me great comfort and joy.

In 1997 I found out I was misdiagnosed with cerebral palsy, when what I really have is a rare congenital disorder called Moebius Syndrome. The main characteristic of people with Moebius Syndrome is facial paralysis. We are born with little or no ability to make facial expressions, due to our sixth and seventh cranial nerves either being underdeveloped or missing. This includes the inability to physically smile or frown. My family and I discovered this through the national news when a little girl named Chelsey Thomas made the headlines with her "smile" surgeries. People with Moebius have characteristic looks about them. Just seeing Chelsey on television, we "knew."

My father really wanted me to look into the surgeries, but I was not ready at the time. I was working on my second college degree in Art (first one was in psychology) and didn't want to take the time off required for surgeries. Plus I just didn't really want to go through such a major operation. I remember my father saying to me, "Oh, it's not MAJOR surgery." And I'd argue back, "Sure, it's not YOUR face they will be cutting on!"

Through all of 1997 I continued working on my Art degree. My father was sick but for the longest time kept it from me and my older sister, because he wasn't sure what was wrong. It was around Christmas time when we found out Dad was going to the doctor for a battery of tests. In January of 1998, one day after New Year's, he was diagnosed with lung cancer and only had one chemo treatment along with radiation. He crossed over shortly thereafter on February 5, 1998.

I ended up getting my second college degree in May of 1998 and went to work right away. A few years passed as I tried to adjust to the loss of my father and a new life on my own at the same time. Someone at work was testing a new digital camera one day and took a picture of me. I couldn't stand the result. My face made me look mean and I didn't feel it reflected who I was as a person. Did my father arrange for this to happen so I could see clearly what I needed to do? I'm not sure. At any rate, I think it took this for me to finally start surfing the Internet and really looking into the Moebius Syndrome.

I found the Moebius Syndrome Web site, which had lots of before and after pictures of people who had gone through the "smile" surgeries. I was very impressed with how natural all the smiles looked. And what an improvement!

In June of 2002 I attended the Moebius Syndrome Conference in Chicago. There I met with plastic surgeon, Dr. Ronald Zuker, who works mainly with children but also is a partner to Dr. Ralph Manktelow, who oversees adults. Dr. Manktelow was not at the conference that year so I was very grateful that Dr. Zuker agreed to see me. Just one look is all it took. He knew that I had Moebius as well. I was told I was an excellent candidate for the surgeries. He took a few pictures of me to take back to Dr. Manktelow.

Immediately after returning home from the conference, I made an appointment with a neurologist who gave me the "official" diagnoses I needed for insurance purposes. The next thing I knew, my mother and I were on our way to Toronto, Ontario, Canada, the only country in the world that specializes in the "smile" surgeries.

Making the decision to go through this was huge. I don't where the courage suddenly came from. Perhaps my father was giving it to me? The whole ordeal involved traveling to Canada twice for two surgeries lasting eight hours each. The first surgery took place in November 2002 – on America's Thanksgiving Day. This involved my right side, where they took my right Gracilus muscle (inner thigh) and transplanted it to the right side of my face. The second surgery took place in March of 2003 and involved the left side of both areas. It took two months after the first surgery for my right side to start moving. The nerves had to re-innervate to the new muscle and I literally had to teach my brain how to smile. And likewise it took two months after the second surgeries for the left side to move.

I must relate what happened at Toronto General Hospital when I had the second surgery. My father was a major dog lover in life, not only for his own dogs but for others' as well. He was always bringing home lost dogs and keeping them safe until their owners were found.

And my dad knew that I loved stuffed animals. They have always given me comfort, even in adulthood.

I recovered faster after the second surgeries and was able to be admitted to my hospital room much sooner. In Canada they have an area you go to after surgery called the step-down. Then after you recover enough in there, you are admitted to your hospital room. I ended up taking someone else's bed because she was not ready to be taken from the step-down area. When I was brought into the hospital room that was not originally for me to be in, there were two other people sharing it with me.

One lady was unable to find her bag of clothes a relative had dropped off for her while she was in recovery. My mother helped her find them by looking in all the closets in our big room. Mom eventually found the clothes, but before she did, she found an adorable stuffed Basset Hound! For the rest of the stay, the stuffed Basset Hound kept us all company. I wanted to take him home if nobody else in the room wanted him, but my mother thought we should leave him there. Ironically a woman suffering from cancer talked us both into taking him home. (Okay, I admit I didn't need much convincing.) I now refer to my Basset House as my "Angel" dog. I really feel like my father was giving me a present for my hospital stay – the gift of letting me know he was there.

My father knew that I had always been a vivid dreamer. I remember him saying, "I wish I could remember dreams like you do." So it's no wonder that this is his favorite way to visit me since he has crossed. A few months after both surgeries were done and I had the ability to smile my full smile, I had a visit. We often meet at the "old house," the house I grew up in. In this dream/visit, we were in the kitchen. In life this is where I would talk to Dad the most.

In the dream Dad said to me, "I would like to see your smile." I walked over to him and he put his hands on either side of my mouth. I could FEEL their warmth. I could FEEL his presence. I've never experienced anything so vivid. When I woke up it took a few seconds to realize that I literally had a smile on my face. And the warm sensation I had on my face in the dream was felt in reality and lasted about a minute or two after I had woken. I'm sure my father had seen my new smile before, but he literally wanted to FEEL it and he knew the dream state was an ideal way to communicate with me.

I really think most of us who have relatives who have crossed over are still being looked after and guided by them whether we are aware or not. My father is still guiding me today and I feel especially blessed that my awareness of his existence, along with all my other guides, keeps expanding.

Tina Tipton
http://www.moebiussyndrome.com Http://www.smile-surgery.com

Followup: Even after years since her father made his transition, Tina confesses that she feels that grief never really ends. For her there will always be a sense of loss. She awakens from dreams of her father and other family members and feels as if a part of her has been literally ripped from her body.

"I truly believe that when close ones have passed," Tina writes, "they do take a part of you with them. I guess it's similar to when you have a relative move to another state or country. They are not physically with you, but you know they are here. The only difference is that communication is a bit more challenging with those who have crossed over."

In a sense, the journey through grief is not unlike a move to a foreign country, one unlike any place we've ever know. It takes longer for some to accept and adjust to than others. It's one of life's harder lessons. We can take comfort in the knowledge that our loved ones are trying their best to tutor us through it.

****

Gena Wilson is a social worker, professional psychic, medium, animal communicator and Reiki Master who lost her fiancé in a work-related accident. What brought her through, along with the support of family and friends, was love, for which the divide between this world and the next means nothing.

My fiancé, Tom, was a tree trimmer and take-down expert. He was in a tree in a yard in Arlington, VA. It had rained a lot that summer and he was reaching around the tree to help guide the limb that had just been cut. The limb kicked and a small leaf hit the main power line. It arced through him and, unfortunately, he had on metal climbing boots.

On the way to the hospital after the initial call from his job that an accident had happened and that I needed to get to the hospital immediately, he came to me, dancing and doing flips and saying that he had made it and was so happy!!

I said, "Tom, go back to your body. Please don't leave me. Go back to your body!" I was crying. I knew he was over but just thought he was having a near-death experience and would be alive when I got to the hospital. But, of course, he was gone.

The night he died I finally fell asleep and found myself in a tree. I was electrocuted, just as he had been. I could feel and hear the buzz, and then I was out of my body. It was so easy to leave and did not hurt at all. I felt he was showing me that dying is easy and not painful at all.

A lot of activity occurred during the first week. I would smell the massage oil that we both loved and that he'd used on me, massaging me and I him. One night he came to me and woke me up making love to me. I could feel him touching me and I was writhing up to meet his body, just as in love making. I could feel him kissing me, wanted the moment to never end. He said that he loved me and wanted to make love to me forever. I cried and cried.

By the time of his funeral three days later at the church before all arrived, and with my two psychic friends side by side with me, we all heard him crying hysterically. He was saying that he made a mistake and wanted to come back to me, that he realized that he would just have to come back to the earth plane and do life all over again to learn the lessons he was supposed to learn, and that he was not sure he would get to come back and be with me. It was so awful for me. I felt so helpless.

I had told the priest that I could not speak – I was sobbing most of the time at that point. He said okay, but then asked me to come up. I was shocked, but he just wanted me to come and place a flower on his coffin. I distinctly heard Tom say, "Don't you dare pick the pink flower!" It was a funny moment in the middle of such a tragedy, but soooo Tom.

In the beginning when he came to me, I was elated, moved to tears. But it was never enough. I wanted more time with him, always more. People would say how lucky I was to be able to connect with him. To me it was a blessing and a curse – a blessing that I could link with him and that helped, especially over that first year. But it was also a curse because after each contact it was like losing him over and over again.

I did share with family and friends. It helped people who had lost a loved one and it helped me as a professional social worker and intuitive reader/spiritual counselor to be even more understanding with clients.

It was, however, the hardest thing I've ever gone through. I was already very spiritual and doing God's work. I admit I had a hard time understanding the why, what losing Tom meant in my soul's journey, that is, until I received the message from spirit that he and I had been together through many lifetimes. Now we both had to advance separately. I miss him, but know he'll be waiting to welcome me Home some day.

Gena Wilson

Followup: There came a point where Gena was faced with a choice. She'd been diagnosed with several blood clots in her lungs, and as she lay near death, Tom came to her. She had to decide whether to live or die. It was not an easy decision, but she chose life. There is a special place in her heart for Tom, and gratitude for the love they shared.

****

Let's go shopping!:

My father was a shopper, a shopper extraordinaire. Until he became ill, my mother never shopped for food, a TV set, or even for a meat grinder.

One of the things he loved most was to help his "girls," my mother, my sister and I. It could be hunting shoes, clothing, or even jewelry. Saleswomen in clothing departments used to get glassy-eyed when he walked in with us – and ask for him when he wasn't with us. Daddy would just pick dresses, etc., off the rack and send them into the dressing rooms for us to try on. And would be disappointed if we didn't succeed.

My father suffered a massive stroke in December of 1976 and died on October 20, 1980, the date of my parents' wedding anniversary. I hadn't heard him speak in all of those four years.

One night some time after my mother died and I was sleeping in my grandmother's room, because I couldn't bring myself to sleep in the master bedroom that had been my mother and father's, I dreamed of my father standing in the doorway, beckoning to me, saying, "Come on. Let's go shopping!"

He was dressed casually, as usual – slacks, a pullover, maybe a drizzler jacket. (Only a wedding or fancy dress dinner could get my father into a suit. He was a wholesale produce merchant who went to work at midnight and returned at mid-morning.)

Now that was a gift! I hadn't seen my father stand in many years, hadn't heard him speak since 1976. To hear his voice again was wonderful. And, of course, to go shopping with him would have been the most natural think in the world.

Binnie Syril

Bottom line: What a delight to discover that once a shopper, always a shopper, whether on this side of the veil or the other. And what a delightful switch to have a father happily embrace the label and return to his daughter to reassure her that he still wore the label proudly.

****

B.J.'s lucid dream is in a category of its own:
It was one of those warm summer afternoons on the lake where we lived. People were boating, skiing, sailing, wind surfing, and

having picnics on their pontoon boats. My husband, Tom, and I loved to sit on the deck and watch all the activity. When the wind began to gust, we went inside for a nap.

A couple of hours later, we were awakened by the sound of sirens. They were close. We scrambled into our clothes and hurried outside just in time to see a policeman stringing yellow crime scene tape around the property directly across the small cove that separated our houses.

We discovered that a man had jumped off a pontoon boat to help a young woman whose wind surfer had tipped over. He had drowned. They thought that perhaps the board of the wind surfer might have hit his head. Divers were brought in. People in different uniforms milled around the edge of the water. I heard a hysterical woman crying out because she was not allowed to cross the yellow tape line. I knew it was the man's mother. I went over to the distraught woman, hoping I might be able to help in some small way. I knew what it was like to lose a child, even if the child is grown.

I settled her on my deck where she could see what was going on, got her a cup of hot tea, and a throw blanket for her shoulders, and encouraged her to talk to me. She told me about her son they were looking for, and another son who had been murdered a few years earlier. She told me about their lives, the struggles they'd gone through. Never taking her eyes off the search area, she talked and cried, and talked some more.

The sun went down. The search was called off. The poor woman was forced to return home without knowing what had happened to her child. My heart was breaking for her. I wanted to help, but had no idea what else I could do. I prayed about it and hoped God would show me a way.

By daybreak the following morning she was back and shortly after, the search was on again. The day ended the same as the day before. They couldn't find the body. On the third morning, as my husband and I walked out on the deck, he looked at me and said, "Do you know where he is?" Sometimes I felt things or knew things that didn't make sense. I pointed to the opposite cove from where they'd been searching. To this day I don't know why I did that.

Cadaver dogs and a psychic were brought into the search. With the man's mother, I watched as they boated the dog, his nose hanging out over the edge of the boat, up and down the search area. I became more and more convinced they were looking in the wrong place. I tried to talk to a couple of those in uniforms, but was summarily dismissed.

When I retired on the third night, the man and his mother on my mind and in my prayers, I didn't think I would ever get to sleep. But sleep finally came and so did a dream I will never forget. I was under the water. I fought against a current and through the cloudy water that hampered my vision. Suddenly I saw him. He was tangled in tree roots. His eyes opened. He looked at me and said, "Help me!"

I could feel my air running out but I swam closer, pulled, tugged, tried my best to unloose him from the black craggy roots. My lungs were about to burst. I swam upwards and emerged through the surface of the water screaming for someone to help me. My screams awakened my husband. Still shaking, I told him about the dream. We threw on our robes and hurried out on the deck. Just as the sun peeked over the horizon, the man's body popped up in the exact place I'd pointed to the day before, the end of the opposite cove that had a big tree right at the end of it.

Later I learned there was a river that used to run through where they'd built the lake. Apparently when the man went under he was caught in the current and carried away. Although I've forgotten many things in my life, that dream is as clear in my mind today as it was the day it happened.

B. J. Rogers, Arizona

These are a small sample of the broad spectrum that lucid dreams can assume. And they don't always feature the appearance of someone who is now among the non-physical. One thing is certain, however; once you've experienced one, you'll never forget it.

C.W.

CHAPTER FOUR – WHEN THE MEDIUM BRINGS THE MESSAGE - PART II

JOHN EDWARD

Psychic medium John Edward is internationally known, having been introduced to the viewing public with his syndicated TV series of the early 2000's - *Crossing Over with John Edward*. I would hazard a guess that for the vast majority of those tuning in, it was probably the first time we had seen a medium up close and personal. For quite a number of viewers, it opened many doors, launched many a spiritual journey, mine included. John tours to sold out houses across the country, and the world. His most recent television show, *Cross Country with John Edward* appears on WE, Women's Entertainment network.

****

Gail, Valerie, Paul, and Mary Beth's reading at a John Edward seminar, Atlantic City, December 7, 2001 at the Taj Mahal showroom:

I, my daughter, Valerie, my son, Paul, and my daughter-in-law, Mary Beth, went to our first John Edward seminar. It was not televised and there were many more people than at the *Crossing Over* TV show. The seminar was six months after my husband crossed over. He'd had the chance to watch the show for a few months before he died and came to believe, as I did, that John was real. I told him during one of our talks, "Now you know what you can do later." Valerie said she asked her father to try coming through with something no one could know about.

A seminar lasts two and a half hours, and no one wants to leave the room during it. John came out from behind the curtains to a very warm welcome from the audience. He was wearing a black sweater and blue jeans. He was also wearing his glasses. To us he looked basically the same as he does on the TV show. He told us he can't stand still because of his energy and that he would do a lot of pacing on the stage. That's also why he often runs up the steps on the *Crossing Over* TV show.

Right at the beginning John stated this would be a little different from most other seminars because he was going to skip the lecture part and go right into readings, with a few questions and answers mixed in. A big cheer rose from the audience, because that is what everyone was really there for.

A few of the very first readings were a bit difficult, with people who either couldn't or wouldn't validate some of the things John was saying. The rest of the readings were great! Many of them made us and John laugh. He stayed on the stage for them, only walking off occasionally for someone way in the back. We guessed he is not supposed to leave the stage for his own safety. He was asked about how he knows whom to read. John said there is an arrow of light and a pull over people he is meant to go to. About two-thirds of the way through the seminar, our incredible experience started. He looked at our general area and—

John mentioned a dog puppet that looks like a particular dog and was used to "play talk" to a dog. John was talking fast and making puppet moves with his hand. He was pointing in our direction from the stage and he stated this was coming through for someone right at the end of the aisle. We were twelve rows from the stage. No one on the other side of the aisle looked remotely like they were going to own up to this. Mary Beth, who was sitting in the aisle seat, spoke up. We all knew about her dog puppet, but were reluctant to speak at first for fear that we would be reaching out, trying to make something fit where it didn't. John came down from the stage and stood right in front of us, next to Mary Beth. She has a dog puppet that looks like her basset hound, and it's a big part of their lives right now, because her then 15-month old son adored it. Her father, who died three weeks before my husband died, often played with the dog hand puppet with Andrew, my grandson. Her father would make the mouth move and the dog "talk" to him. Andrew loved it and it made him laugh.

John then started his rapid fire talking. He stated there was a mother coming through and he mentioned the date, November 23, that had just passed. November 23rd was the anniversary of Mary Beth's best friend's mom's passing. She had a very strong personality and Mary Beth had been asking her to help others come through. John then said there is a new baby. Mary Beth's baby, my new granddaughter, was one month old the day before the seminar.

The name Katherine came through. Donna, another member of the John Edward Web site we belong to, was sitting next to us with a friend of hers. The friend's grandmother's name was Katherine and was the person she wanted most to hear from. She thought it was a quick "hello" from her. At the beginning of the seminar, John had asked us to look around at the people near us, because often the Other Side considers us to be together and will come to them also.

John started mentioning and emphasizing a back brace, back surgery pain, or severe back problems, like two lower discs being crushed. He kept repeating and repeating the two discs, making a crushing motion with his fingers. He wouldn't accept me trying to make it fit by saying Phil's cancer had spread to his spine. He looked dubious about what I thought it was and finally gave up on it.

Shortly after the seminar, we remembered that eight years ago, Valerie had lower back pain that made it almost impossible to stand up. An X-ray showed her two loser discs were compressed. They talked about surgery to fix them but Valerie said no. She had to wear a back brace for over a month and do some exercises. It finally stopped hurting without surgery. We were very concerned about her. It was exactly as John had described it.

John mentioned dittos, a ditto machine. A ditto machine is what the old copier machines were called and the ink on the copies had a strong smell. Valerie looked at John and made a quick hand motion of taking a ditto sheet, lifting it up and smelling it. John looked excited and nearly jumped at her. She said you can REALLY feel the energy when it's directed at you and she later asked if a spotlight was on her! John said, "YES! Exactly! Why did you do that?" He sees pictures and images in his mind and must have seen a ditto paper being smelled. He amazes himself when someone gets the meaning of what he sees. She felt like a real idiot. She was so glad this wasn't taped, because she couldn't think of anything specific and just said, "I used to love to smell them in high school." John laughed and asked if she was well known for her ditto sniffing in school. That got a big laugh from the whole audience.

We also discovered by seeing John at other seminars that he does have a very bright light surrounding his body, and that is what Valerie saw. I have seen him surrounded with a white light, yellow light, and blue light. He is bright enough that it is distracting to watch him. Valerie also has some of the psychic abilities that other people on my husband's side have.

At the end of the seminar as we were getting ready to leave and standing by our seats, Mary Beth reminded Valerie of a ditto incident. It happened when her father was in the hospital and a few days before he died. Valerie, Paul and she were alone in the room with him. He was in a morphine-induced coma at that point and would never come out of it. A nurse came in with a sheet of paper she was using for marking down his vital signs. Valerie held it up and sniffed it. All three of them smelled it and it reminded them of how a ditto sheet smelled. It's a very strong and intoxicating aroma. They launched into a whole discussion about how they thought ditto machines were obsolete, and how they all used to love getting dittos back in school because they smelled so great. I was not present at the hospital for that conversation. Several times while Phil was in the coma, they had talked about whether he was aware of everything that was being said and going on around him. This was his way of confirming that he was. Many times on his show John has brought through people who confirmed they were aware of everything going on around them, even while they were in a deep coma.

At the seminar, John said there was a father coming through that had a non-acceptance of an interracial relationship. He was staring right at me when he said this. It took a few minutes for me to remember that when I first started dating Phil, who was half Filipino and half Lithuanian, my father made a big issue of the difference in race. That made me angry with him. This was especially significant for Valerie and Paul because I had never told them about it. They looked at me in surprise. Long before Phil and I were married, my father got to know him and learned to love and respect him. I had a microphone in my hand and was telling this to 1,400 people! I did talk to my parents before the seminar and had asked them to come through.

John said there was a big gambling problem on that side, too, and that this person would be downstairs right now on the slot machines. My mother had a huge gambling problem with playing the slot machines and losing the grocery money in them. The machines used to be in all Maryland grocery stores. She would have skipped the seminar to play the slots.

John mentioned there were a LOT of fathers all coming through together in our area. Mary Beth's dad had died in May, Paul and Valerie's dad died in June, and my father had died a long time ago. Between them all they made a lot of fathers and grandfathers for our group.

John started mentioning seeing a foot amputation. Mary Beth knew what it meant. Her dad, a diabetic with serious complications from it and cancer, had a bad infection in his toe. The doctor was talking about amputating it, but her dad died before it could be done.

The last thing John said was he saw someone in jail, a jail connection, and he was looking at me. I couldn't think of anything, but the people right in front of me were all shaking their heads, "yes." John laughed when I handed the microphone to one of the men. John thought I just didn't want to answer him. There was a BIG jail connection to them, a son who died in jail and another son now in jail. John had said earlier that people sitting near each other are considered to be together.

We were all amazed in a state of shock and disbelief at having received a reading. It was so awesome. Any small shreds of doubt we may have had about whether John Edward is for real were completely erased. The information he gave, one thing after another, fit us too well to be guesses. The ditto was the greatest one. Valerie remembered she had asked her father, if he did come through, to come through with an obscure validation that no one could have found out about and the ditto certainly matched that.

There were 1,400 people at the seminar and everyone there was hoping to get a reading. John says only the strongest energies can get through at a seminar and the people who are meant to get a reading, do. He only had time to do about twelve and we were all so happy we got ours. A lot of things fell right into place to give us the chance to go. For the first time since Phil died, the knot of grief in my chest was gone. I am still grieving but not with great pain.

Gail Ingson

CHAPTER FIVE - MESSAGES BY SPECIAL DELIVERY

There is nothing like receiving a message from someone from whom you never again expected to hear. In truth, this category can overlap with others, since messages from the departed may occur as symbols or reminders, in lucid dreams or in any number of ways. On occasion they'll use things on the wing – birds of all sorts, butterflies, moths. Sometimes a message might arrive via feather. They'll use what's handy, a path of least resistance.

The manipulation of electrical energy, for instance, is allegedly a breeze for them and is frequently a means used to alert us of their continued existence. There are innumerable accounts in other books on the subjects of their turning on and off lights, electrical appliances, televisions and radios.

In my case for several weeks after Bob's death, the phone would ring. Nothing showing on the Caller ID, and upon answering it, I'd hear nothing, no white sound to indicate a live connection, no heavy breathing, not even light breathing. The phone company had no explanation. And I admit it was not until I was typing these words that I remembered what a phone junkie Bob was. He loved talking on the phone, even before it and the computer became his lifelines to the world beyond his bed. Our long distance bills occasionally resembled the treasury of a Third World country. Years later I learned that this kind of mysterious call with no one on the other end is not an uncommon phenomenon, one of many ways the departed attempt to "reach out and touch."

Finally the calls stopped and then the doorbell began to ring. I'd answer the door. Nobody, and it's easy to hear traffic going up and down the steps to the other five units in my building. On one occasion I was at the door, about to open it for a friend who was leaving. Doorbell rang. I snatched it open immediately. No one there. I replaced the bell with a new one with a completely different sound. Oddly enough, to this day I continue to hear the old one. Don't ask. I still don't understand this one.

Then there was the hospital bed. A custom model ordered for Bob, it was the size of a double bed, weighed four hundred pounds and did everything but fry eggs. It took me a while after he died, but I finally decided to use it, since most movers had no desire to tote the thing out. It was comfortable, adjustable four different ways with the use of a wireless remote. I rarely bothered with the latter feature; I was used to a flat surface.

One night I awoke with the feeling that something fishy was afoot. The bed – mattress and foundation – was slowly rising, the motor purring softly. Shades of *The Exorcist*, right? I groped for the remote, found it hanging on the headboard where it had been gathering dust. I had been burrowed under the covers like a mole, my arms under my pillow. For once the cats were nowhere in sight, so I couldn't blame it on them.

I pushed buttons to stop it. No dice. It kept elevating to its maximum position, the motor continuing to purr even after it could go no higher. I had to get up, wiggle my way under the bed and unplug it. My electrician couldn't explain it, especially as he found that there was a problem with the motor which should have rendered it completely inoperable. I slept in the guest room until I found movers willing to haul the thing away.

There were other anomalies with the bedroom television cutting off inexplicably. I blamed it on the cable company, a convenient scapegoat any time. All the above occurred before The Call in the Night from him, and at the time they occurred meant little except something to grouse about. My point is that the voice of Bob West reverberating in the ether and only on one occasion from one side of my brain pan to the other and NOT my ears was, in effect, a message, to wit: *What do I have to do to get through to you, huh?*

So, in many instances that's the sole purpose of a message, to let you know the sender is still around, aware of what's happening to you, and supporting you every step of the way.

On occasion it may be a warning, a heads up. The following narratives are only a sample of messages sent and received.

****

Clearly this adopted and beloved aunt was keeping an eye on Lenora:

My Aunt Frances's partner, Ann, passed away in 1988. We were very, very close and I know I felt her presence at her funeral service.

A few nights later, I had just put my four-month-old son to bed and had gone to bed myself and was drifting to sleep when I heard her, plain as day, say, "Honey, don't you go to sleep and leave that on!" I sat up, rather startled.

I decided to go to the kitchen to get a drink before trying to get back to sleep. I went around the corner and there, on the ledge of the bar, sat a burning candle. I gasped, blew it out and said, "Thank you," to Aunt Ann.

Lenora Shope

Bottom line: How reassuring it is to know that our loved ones continue their roles as protectors. And will relay important messages any way they can!

****

A grandparent weighs in again:

My most beloved grandfather passed away unexpectedly when I was fifteen. He was so loved and the entire family was in deep, deep mourning. I cried and cried. I just couldn't get over the burden of his death.

One day a couple of weeks after he passed, I went out into one of his cattle pastures behind the house to be close to him, since this was something we shared, a love of the land and his love of cattle. He often took us grandkids with him on his daily cattle checks, so this place was filled with a lot of "together energy" and love for me.

I walked around, still bawling my eyes out, until I found a place in the tall pasture grass where I wanted to sink into, and as I was sitting there sobbing away, all of a sudden, I felt a large heavy hand on my left shoulder, and I heard my Papa sigh in a very deep, weary sounding way. Then I heard him say, "It's gonna be alright," still sounding slightly weary, but comforting me, too. The feel of his heavy workman's hand on my shoulder filled me with such peace. Hearing his voice was a miracle to my ears.

I turned to look but there was nothing there, no physical sign of my Papa, but he'd been there for an instant. All of a sudden I realized that the deep, overwhelming burden of loss had been instantly lifted. My heart was filled with happiness and joy, with laughter, grace, God's glory and a peace that words have no capacity to describe. It is definitely one of the most beautiful moments in my entire life, thanks to my Papa.

I knew then that he loved me and is still with us. He was the most awesome human being I ever knew and that hasn't changed. He was awesome in Life and he's awesome in Spirit.

I told my mother, who was comforted and awed by it as well. In fact, many of my family members had various communications from her grandfather after his passing, in lucid dreams. All received much comfort.

It truly is because of this experience that I KNEW without a shadow of a doubt that we do continue to live on after we pass. We may not understand it, but we do NOT die, we do not cease to exist. There is nothing anyone can say or do that would convince me otherwise. I KNOW what I experienced and I can't deny that. What a beautiful gift I was given that day. What an amazing legacy.

Kim Hardie

Bottom line: Kim's gift from her grandfather clearly left a lasting impression. To lose the fear of death and know that who we are doesn't change once we leave our physical body is indeed life changing.

****

Mothers will eternally be mothers, whether on this side or the other. Nan Crowley seems to blush her way through this account, concluding that she and her mom hadn't quite grown into our "both of us are adults now; let's be friends" mode. As a result, her first contact from her mother when she was 40-plus rocketed her back into a time warp.

My mother died in January 1981 when I was 28. She'd not been 100% for several months before she passed, and it was not an easy passing physically. It was very difficult; she and I were all that had been left of the family, as Dad and my brother had died some years before.

In the early period after mom's death, I had great difficulty shedding the memory of her last days in the hospital. I still talked to her, but with two small children and a household for which I was sole provider, I seldom looked for evidence that I was heard.

Fast forward about fifteen years or so. The kids were grown and I was headed back to school. I had sort of invented underachievement in high school, or at least had elevated it to an art form. Not something to be proud of, but it was what it was. So I was terrified. I didn't know if I could "do it right" this time, or if they'd even let me in for "real" credit, considering my past academic history. After the first semester, I received a letter from the school suggesting I sign up for Honors Program. Oh, my heavens!! So I did and didn't humiliate myself. GPA 3.85-ish. I was thrilled.

Late one night a year or so later I was sitting at the computer table when I saw my transcript next to the computer. I picked it up, looked it over thinking, "Ya know, I didn't do half bad. I actually did pretty darn well."

And before I could think another thought, the words, "Well, I <u>knew</u> you could <u>do</u> it, Bitsy," popped into my head – in my mother's best *I told you so* voice! (The name she used was a childhood nickname, not "Bitsy," but I just couldn't quite bring myself to use the actual nickname here.)

My immediate reaction was typical teen response, even though I was 40-something: "Oh, Maaa...."

Then it hit me. That was my mother's voice! I wasn't hearing the normal "voice" you think with, i.e., my own. I had heard <u>my mom's</u> voice, one I hadn't heard for twenty years.

And how very true to life the words were, too. "If I'd heard, "I'm proud of you," it wouldn't have had nearly the impact that the phrase, "I <u>knew</u> you could <u>do</u> it," had. It was <u>exactly</u> the sort of thing my mother would have said (and did, on occasion). It was a brief, but oh-so-normal conversation between me and Mom.

It was my mom. She was <u>there</u>, just being Mom. Her praise of my accomplishment was the first unmistakable evidence that not only was she still on the job, she could voice her support. And make herself heard.

Nan Crowley

Bottom line: The departed are no less interested and involved in our accomplishments after their transition into spirit than they were when they were here with us. They cheer us on and celebrate with us. Given half a chance, they'll also let us know. Stay open to it and never doubt it!

****

Moms and messages again – with me as the medium.

Halfway through my telephone consultation with a psychic intuitive, she complained that a woman kept poking at her, someone whose name sounded like Ellen or Eileen. Stunned, I asked if it was Elaine, a writer friend who had made her transition several months before. Evidently Elaine's affirmative reply made the psychic's ears ring, which was typical of my friend. I was told that Elaine wanted to get a message to her daughter, simply: Hello.

"That's all?" I asked.

"Yes, that's it. Just 'hello.'"

After our conversation ended, I chickened out. Rather than picking up the phone again and calling Kelly, I sent her an e-mail, explained what had just happened and gave her the message her mom had asked me to relay. And held my breath.

Not five minutes later, I received a joy-filled response and an explanation. While Elaine lay dying, she promised that once she arrived on the Other Side, she would let Kelly know by saying hello. In doing it, she put me square in the middle, but by God, she kept her promise!

Chassie West

Bottom line: Becoming a messenger can be daunting. There are the religious beliefs of the recipients to consider and whether the message will be well received or rejected out of hand. But since those in the spirit realm had trusted me with their gift for their loved ones I felt I had no choice. And in the end, things went well. Their gratitude was overwhelming. Once again, love made the difference.

****

How many times in this life did our mothers try to warn us about something and we paid little or no attention? Imagine our moms' frustration at trying to get a message through when separated by the veil!

My two sons, my goddaughter, and my friend, Denise, and I were sitting at the table about 9:30pm trying to decide if we wanted to go and get some ice cream at the new shop that just opened up down the road. I don't see very well at night and try to avoid driving after dark when at all possible, unless it is close. The store was a straight shot down the interstate from our home, so I volunteered to drive.

While we were discussing whose car would have enough room in it for all of us, an old accounting calculator that sat on the table "went off" and rotated the cartridge as if it was going to print. Then it stopped. I was not touching it in any way and the switch was in the Off position.

I started laughing and Mollie asked if it had belonged to Grandma Bobbi, my mother. I told her it was what Mom had used at work every day for twenty years. She got a bit misty-eyed and said, "Hey, maybe she is saying hello to us," and smiled. I said that she probably was – and it rotated again! I just smiled, because I often get small "hellos" from her like that.

We continued to plan our late night fat attack. I offered to drive again and the machine went off once more. Mollie was a bit unsettled and asked why it kept going off. I said it was probably Mother scolding me because she didn't want me driving at night.

Until now the machine had only made one keystroke at a time, but just as I said that, the tape also started to run and multiple key strokes went off. I laughed and said, "OKAY, MOTHER! I WON'T DRIVE!" and handed the car keys to Denise, at which point it stopped. We talked about some good memories of her for about fifteen minutes, then left the house hurriedly, realizing the store would close in about ten minutes.

On our way to the ice cream shop, we passed a very bad accident in the intersection. The paramedics were working with someone in the street, doing CPR as we drove around it. The entire car was quiet, and my son said, "Momma, if we hadn't been talking about Granny so long, that might have been us." I was stunned. He was right.

Thanks, Mom, for keeping us safe that night.

Lori Messer

Bottom line: Lori's mother was not to be ignored. How clever of her to use an old-fashioned calculator to get her message across! And how fortunate it was that Lori finally listened.

****

This time, with a different goal in mind, Lori's mom checked in on-line:

I was finishing the last paragraph for my post for a Health and Transformation chat on body image and literally, as soon as the last period was typed and I hit Submit, I got an e-mail alert.

Here is what I had written: "I think a big part of the reason I am finally successful at losing weight is that I have found what my soul had been craving and THAT has replaced the craving for food. Finding that inner happiness has replaced the need for outside comfort and allowed me to see myself for who I am and not for what I look like."

The e-mail alert was junk mail from some pharmacy. But the name of the person from whom it had come was "VIOLA ROSE."

That's my mum's name. Thanks, Mom!

Lori Messer

Bottom line: An e-mail from spirit. How's that for a very special message!!

****

Phil and Gail star in a remarkable love story. They had been married for thirty-six years when he died. A devoted couple, they often commented that their children's ethnic backgrounds amounted to alphabet soup, since his parents were from the Philippines and Lithuania, and Gail claimed ancestors from France, Germany and Canada, the latter a member of the Cree Indian nation. Phil was the computer guy, so it's logical he would use it to deliver a message:

My husband, Phil, was diagnosed with lung cancer in May 2001. About six weeks after hearing what the doctor had found, Phil began going through the dying experience. He began to withdraw from us. What he started doing is described in a powerful little blue book, "Gone from my Sight, The Dying Experience" by Barbara Karnes.

One morning Phil came out of his bedroom and looked dazed. I had moved to the guest bedroom because he was so ill. There was a monitor next to my bed so I could hear him if he called out. Phil described a vision he had just seen: he saw the "Light." He looked into it and saw people standing on both sides of it. They were all dressed in white and were smiling at him. He recognized his mother, father, and brother, who were already there. Phil said there were more people, but he didn't look at them. Phil began kneeling on the side of his bed at night and reciting the prayers he learned as a child. He was raised Catholic and was an altar boy for many years. His faith had gotten weak over the years, but it came back to him now.

Tumors which had to be surgically removed began to appear on his face and neck, but on several occasions the sites of the incisions bled profusely. Hurried visits to the emergency room became routine. The cancer was also eating into his spine. His legs were getting weaker, but he could still walk. His doctor said he might lose the use of his legs and have to use a wheelchair.

I was sleeping on the last night Phil would have at home. About 1 a.m., I heard him yelling for me. I ran into the bedroom, clicked on the light and saw blood all over his pillow and sheets. I grabbed a bunch of dry wash cloths and had him hold them tightly on the bleeding tumor while I called 911. We live only ten minutes from a major hospital, and the ambulance came quickly. I think I was in shock when they arrived, because I was too calm. My mouth felt numb.

In the ER, the doctor was trying his best to stop the bleeding. Nothing was working until they put on a very tight sticking, special bandage. It stopped the bleeding and was never removed. Phil was awake and talking. He was given at least three units of blood and needed more. I stepped out of his room and one of the orderlies showed me Phil's blood count figures. They were extremely low.

I had to go home after a few hours to let the family know where Phil was and get a few hours of sleep. When I arrived at the hospital the next morning, Phil was in the cancer ward. He was alert and looked pale, but in good spirits. He was hooked up to a morphine drip and had no pain. He could even smile and joke around. Inside, he already knew the end was close.

Over his last few days and before he went into a final coma, he got to talk individually to my daughter, son, his only living brother, and my son's wife, and during his last hours, only those who he loved the very most were in the room – me, my daughter, son, Phil's brother, my oldest brother, and my brother's fiancée. She was a nurse and standing alone by Phil's side.

She came over to us and said, "It's time." She knew the signs, what to look for. We all circled the bed, held hands and said the Lord's Prayer. I watched Phil's face closely and was blessed to see a quick, bright and tiny light leave his body. He was in a better place.

The day after my husband passed, I logged onto my computer, and it did some very strange things. In the middle of my paradise island screen saver there was a 3x6 inch rectangle showing white clouds and blue sky. This was new.

I decided to check the Word section of the computer, a place I seldom looked at, because I knew Phil had been documenting his illness there. I wanted to get rid of some junk things in it and being computer illiterate, didn't know how. Without going any further, I decided to turn off the computer. It would not turn off without my unplugging it. Later, I discovered my daughter's computer would also not shut down without a lot of help.

The next day my daughter and I were looking at my Word section and deleting unnecessary items in it. One item was labeled P1. I knew it was one of Phil's things. We opened it and this is what we found. We read it with streaming tears. It had been written six months before my husband died and I had never seen it. I asked that it be read at his funeral, as his last words to me.

Dearest Gail,

I've thought over and over what I want to say to you and find it very hard. I thought that it would be easy to put my thoughts on paper but each time I start, my eyes fill with tears at the thought of leaving you, our children and grandchildren. I know I can't write exactly what I'm feeling, but I'll try....

I know some would describe me as a "laid back" or an "average" sort of guy. I've been blest with meeting, marrying and loving you for over 30 years. How can anyone be so lucky!!! You've always been the light of my life. Through good times and bad, you've been there for me to share the good, and to help me get through the bad. I've never known anyone else with such a great disposition, with the ability to light up a room with her personality. You've blest me with two of the greatest children a father could have. There are many more things I could say here, but when I stop and think about it, just having a great wife and children is more than enough to make my cup runneth over and take me out of the "average" category.

My mind keeps wandering to various vacations and events in our lives, so many warm happy memories. I know that like most husbands, I didn't always say "I love you" enough times to you. For that I sincerely apologize. Somehow, just to say, "Gail, I love you," seems totally inadequate. My mind tells me to say that I love you for all eternity, which I do.

As you know, I do believe in God and rewards/punishment for our lives. Now that the good Lord has decided to call me to him, I hope and pray there is some way we can be together again in the future. It seems to me there must be something in Our Father's grand design for our lives.

I hope my message to you is not as rambling as it seems to me. More than anything else, what I wanted you to know is that I will always love you and will miss you.

All My Love, Eternally
Phil

Followup: Gail says that the love letter Phil left for her to find and finding it when she did, had a tremendous impact on her. "Words can't express what I felt while reading it. The closest I can come is that it was an incarnation of his love for me. I have always believed we go on after death. Even with already believing, it still feels so good to receive tangible evidence of it."

Gail says that all during Phil's illness, he managed to buy cards to give her on special days. He signed them all "Forever and Eternally, Love Phil." He knew that he would still see her after he crossed over. She simply hoped he would find a way to let her know. He did, in spades. The unorthodox route he took for future contacts appears in a later chapter.

****

If there is a hell, losing a child has to be one definition of it. No matter the age of the child, they remain with us in one guise or another. Leigh's experience was proof to her that her infant daughter could still send a hello.

Back in 1991 my husband and I were expecting our first child. Her name was to be Robyn Elizabeth Dicks. I had a wonderful and normal pregnancy. You do all the right things to insure a healthy baby and, well, things don't always go the way they are supposed to. Robyn was born on November 4th with a heart condition called Epstein's Anomaly. She was immediately transferred to the Children's Hospital of Eastern Ontario. The week that followed was a horror story for us because she was a very sick little girl. She had a misplaced right valve and had to have an operation to rebuild this valve. The operation was too much stress on her little body and Robyn passed away on November 11th.

I think the best thing I did after losing Robyn was joining a support group. And you do your best to try and bring some normalcy back into your lives. So I went back to work as a bartender in a little English pub.

It was not until seven years later that I would feel her presence so strongly, a crucial point for me because, for some reason it felt like the first year. I had begun to question a lot of my beliefs in what happens after we die, whether Robyn was really in heaven or just where she had been buried.

One day a lady came in and handed me a flyer and walked out again. The flyer was about a "baby memorial" being held at the church just down the street for anyone who had experienced the loss of a child. I thought about it and decided I would go and go alone, so I could cherish my memories of my baby and not have to share that time with anyone but her. On a whim, I also printed 150 copies of a poem that had been given to me by Robyn's ICU nurse, called "God's Lent Child." I thought it would be nice to share these comforting words with others. On my way into the church I asked if it would be okay to put them on the table with some other information they had available. The lady at the door read it over and said by all means.

I proceeded to find my seat and chose to sit on the third row from the front. I sat beside a single lady who smiled at me, but we didn't speak. After a few minutes, she got up and walked to the front and started to play a beautiful stand-up harp. She played ENYA. I was astonished because that is all I listened to when I was pregnant and after Robyn had passed as well.

But it was what happened next that literally blew me away. The speaker for that introduced herself as "Reverend Robin-Lee." I could not believe my ears. My name is Leigh, my daughter's was Robyn. I knew instantly that something very special had occurred. For some reason I was drawn here and I am not one who attends church regularly. I just knew my being drawn here and all these little connections were truly a sign from her.

I didn't really understand the impact of the experience until years later, and I'm so grateful to the lady who came into my workplace and handed me that flyer. I have always wondered who she was. Is it possible she was an angel sent to those in need?

Losing Robyn was the most difficult thing I will probably ever face in this lifetime. Truly knowing in my heart that this is not all there is and that when we die we do get to see our loved ones again has changed my outlook on life and death forever. Whenever I find myself wishing for another message from little Robyn, I recognize that I don't really need it to know that Robyn is truly still there.

I do believe many coincidences have far more meaning to them; you just have to open your mind and heart to see the true messages. The power of the universe will never cease to amaze me. I will forever hold this experience close to my heart.

Leigh Brown

****

The message for Leigh's son, however, is an example of how the departed can manipulate electrical appliances using their extremely high rate of vibration. Was your loved one a channel flipper? Don't be surprised if your television occasionally seems to surf with no help from the remote. It's a message, and not from your cable company!

We moved to Newfoundland in 1999, at which point my son had never visited Robyn's headstone. I felt he was too young, but he knew about his sister, had seen pictures, and we talked about her often. When Tyler was perhaps six years old, I found him in the basement where he had made a circle on the floor with pictures of little Robyn and a candle that had been lit at her funeral. When I asked what he was doing, he replied that he was wishing his sister a happy birthday. It was indeed Robyn's birthday. I hadn't forgotten, but was so touched that he hadn't either.

After being gone for five years, we moved back to Ottawa. It wasn't until November 2006 that my son showed an interest in going to see Robyn's headstone. So we both went on November 11th to put flowers and pick a wreath. When it was time to leave, he kissed her headstone. I was glad he had come.

About a week later, Tyler and I were watching a TV show called "Much Music." It is based out of Toronto and shows all music videos. This particular night they had set it up so that you voted for your favorite video. They would show three different videos back to back and you could call in your vote or go on-line. Half the screen aired the video and the other half had a section showing the percentage of votes and a place where you could text message for 75 cents and your message would appear on the screen. No name of the sender was shown unless it had been included in the text message.

We were watching these videos when we both saw the text message coming across the screen, the first one making me laugh, but the second blew me away. It said:

"Hey Tyler...love your shoes."

The next one said, "Robyn would like her family to know she loves and misses them very much."

My son, fourteen at the time, had a newspaper route and had bought his first pair of Phatfarm runners, costing him 160 big ones. He was absolutely obsessed with keeping them clean. He was proud to the point where I came home one day to find him in his room with newspaper down, Q-tips, bright light, and cleaner removing every little speck of dirt. It is our belief that the text message was a sign for Tyler, acknowledging that Robyn was there with him when he visited her stone.

With each after death communication I feel more and more blessed to see them for what they are, and especially how meaningful they have been for my son.

Leigh Brown

Bottom line: What a priceless gift from sister to brother! Leigh can rest assured that her family is still intact. Robyn will always be with them, bringing comfort to her mother and the occasional "I'm watching you, big brother!" for Tyler. Love wins every time!

****

Let us not forget dads. This one made the ultimate sacrifice:

I was seventeen when my father was admitted to the hospital on a Sunday night in 1980. It was a stormy time with lots of lingering rain. We called my brother and sister, who had a long drive to get home. They went straight to the hospital where the rest of us were on Monday afternoon, and they stayed while we went home.

It was early evening on March 17th, which is still winter in upper Michigan, when we got a call from my sister that Dad was really bad and we had to get back. It had cleared up outside, a clear, cold night in the country when we left. We had to drive no more than a mile when we turned onto the main road to the hospital twenty-five miles away. I looked up at the sky and saw a falling star. I KNEW at that moment my father had passed. I looked at the clock in the car, and when we got to the hospital we learned it was pretty much the time

Dad had passed. I can still see that star in my mind and feel the cold, crisp air. While I did not "hear" from Dad, I just knew.

In early May I was looking out of my bedroom window in the woods and feeling very frightened, since we had no money. My mother was babysitting a couple of children at the time for extra money when Dad passed, and I had no idea how things were going to work out. Our finances were dwindling, there was every possibility we would lose our home, and I was overdue for surgery on a severely infected appendix. I felt as if I was hanging onto the last little thread at the end of my rope.

I was also angry. My father had been there for my siblings' special occasions, especially my sister's graduation from college. He would not be there for mine. I wanted to know who would take care of me now? How was I going to make it through life without anyone to talk to for advice? Then I "heard" a voice. It was not my father's voice, but very strong, soothing and authoritative, saying, "I will always take care of you." We were a very religious family and I took that voice to be that of God reassuring me that He was still there for me, since my father wasn't. It left me with an inner knowing that no matter what, there was no need to worry. I would always have a roof over my head and whatever I might need to live. It strengthened a certain portion of my belief in God, that He would always take a personal interest in my life as a stand-in for my father. In hindsight, it contained my father's stern matter of fact type love; he had never been able to express affection or tell us kids that he loved us.

Only in recent times – the past five years – have I come to know that it really was my father, that he had already done what he could to take care of me. Had he survived, I would not have received his Social Security benefits, since by my graduation, I would be eighteen.

He has taken care of me ever since. No matter how bad things get, "something" always comes through in the end to take care of it. He has been gone since 1980 and I have never "heard" from him since that one time.

I told no one about that experience for many years. It was a special gift for me to help me with something I had lost. I was also worried that others would try to convince me it hadn't happened. A reading with a medium, however, confirmed that the voice I heard was my father's. His apology for leaving so early was an immense source of comfort, that and knowing he's around and still helps me. With the wisdom of age, I know now that his loss was an important step in learning the lessons I had to learn. My dad had done what he had come here to do. For the continued growth of my soul, he had to leave.

But that experience is still as vivid in my mind as if it were yesterday. In fact as I write this, in my mind I can still see out that window and "hear" what was said. I have not been in that house for twenty-five years, but it's still that fresh.

Paula Mae Williams

Bottom line: Sometimes, especially when we're still mired in grief, it is difficult to see the bigger picture. For Paula it came with age and the wisdom accompanying it. Her father's gifts to her will remain with her forever.

****

And fathers-in-law:

My father-in-law passed away. I really felt that I had helped out a lot with him – making meals, keeping his medicine straight, fixing his meals regularly. After his death, I told him that I didn't understand why he wasn't sending me any signs. Guess I was being selfish. It wasn't _my_ dad, but I'd done my part.

The mail came the next day and there was an AARP envelope addressed to my father-in-law. Since they used to live beside us, we still get his junk mail from time to time. Usually I just toss them. I actually had it over the trash when, inexplicably, I felt an urge to open it.

Inside was a note pad that said: *A note from Dean.* His name. I felt this was the sign I'd asked for. He'd sent me a note. We still have it up on the refrigerator.

Deb Tanner

Bottom line: How clever of Deb's father-in-law to use AARP and the US mail to get his message across! Those in spirit will use what's closest to hand, ours that is, to let us know they're still with us and always will be.

****

For Malcolm, a writer who lives in Australia, communication from the Other Side is not uncommon. In spite of this, on one occasion which he relates later in the narrative he sent, he too needed bolstering of his beliefs. What follows is the first accounting he sent.

Saturday, 21ˢᵗ December 2002. I had spent a good part of the morning in the garden, despite the tropical heat and humidity, and after returning indoors, having a shower and turning on the air conditioning, I slumped down on the lounge and went into one of those very relaxed states where one could easily fall into a deep sleep. There was also that very satisfied feeling that comes with the knowledge of having accomplished many of the jobs that needed doing. These thoughts wandered off into the past to a time when gardening was absolutely essential to bolster our war time rations. The allotment allocated to my dad was a good twenty minutes walk, and to be honest, I hated it. We had to push the old pram, now converted into some kind of barrow, loaded with seed potatoes, manure, shovels and forks. I couldn't help thinking that he would have been proud of what I had got through that morning so many years after he and my mother had crossed over.

Then I heard her soft voice saying, "We know. We were watching you." It was loud, but very clear.

Malcolm Hutton

****

Sadly a few months later, Malcolm had more to report.

I am in the depths of sadness, though the shock is receding. My dear wife, Ede, passed away on 30ᵗʰ May. Edith had a lung taken out when she was only fifteen and this was a major factor in her ill health late in life. Admittedly she had been very ill, but had always recovered in the past, and as recently as the end of April. I have taken it very badly, though subsequent events have helped immensely.

After the funeral I flew down to Melbourne to be with my daughter, Fiona, for a while and to see my son, John, and his family. After only two days with Fiona, something extraordinary happened. Around ten to one in the early hours of Monday, 11ᵗʰ June, I was woken by Ede's voice calling to me loud and clear: "Malcolm, can you hear me?" There was no mistaking her. The pitch, tone and accent could only have been Ede. For a moment I was a little frightened and then thought that Fiona had been calling me. But the room was dark and silent.

The next night it was Fiona's turn. Unlike myself, she had never experienced hearing voices or anything like it. She too thought somebody was calling out to her. The only difference was that to Fiona the voice was jumbled and she couldn't make out what was being said.

On Wednesday morning I took a train into Melbourne and went to the VSU to get a half hour reading from one of their mediums. In spite of having had contacts from my parents off and on, I still needed confirmation that it was indeed Ede that Fiona and I had heard. At first, the reading was all about my father and grandfathers. The medium said that his name was Edward, which isn't quite correct, for it was John Edward. However, I do know how difficult it is to get a name when most communication is by images, and so an initial is usually the first or only name connection.

About ten minutes into the reading no other names came up until the medium straightened himself in his chair and solemnly looked at me, and said, "Who is Edith?" I could hardly answer him. It was so much more than I expected. Having muttered that she was my wife, he went on. "And isn't it true that she sometimes like to be called Edie?" One more I was taken aback, for her son, Michael, named on of his horses "Eadie May." He put the 'A' in so that race callers wouldn't say, "Eddie." Eadie May won one of her first races in Brisbane, and Michael was presented with a framed photo recording the win. He gave it to his mother, and I placed it on the other side of the room so that she could look at it most of the time.

It was hard for me to concentrate on the rest of the reading, partly because my eyes were doing more than watering. Alan then told me that I had given her some jewelry which she highly treasured. This would have been the Ankh with small crystals set in it that I gave Ede before she went into the hospital at the beginning of April. After she came home, I saw her out of the corner of my eye, holding and running her fingers over that Cross of Life.

He said that she was also thanking me for explaining the afterlife, because until her death grew near, she had many doubts. I had assured her that her mother and sister would be waiting to help her over and recover from her suffering in this lifetime. Ede also delivered a very important message: she and I have been together in a previous life. We had our moments of disagreement, yet I find it hard now to remember those times and can only recall vividly all the good and happy times we enjoyed together.

I think with all spiritualists, there are moments when we question or still have some lingering doubt. Ede's communication kicked me back onto the path of solid knowledge that life continues into the next world and next life. It was also what my daughter, Fiona, needed to hear.

I've told many people of my contacts from the next world. The usual response is an admission that it has happened to them or someone they know. By passing it on, it has helped many who have just lost someone and need to know that their loved one is still around.

I know that even though I need no more proof of an afterlife, every little piece is like one more in a vast jigsaw. The more we hear and learn, the more the whole picture can be seen.

Malcolm Hutton, Cairns, Australia

Bottom line: I'm so honored to have had Malcolm share his journey with us, especially as his wife, Ede's transition to spirit occurred as this book was still being pieced together. It was a reminder that even those of us who have received messages from

the departed occasionally have doubts and begin to wonder. Fortunately Ede persisted and nudged him back on track. And in sharing his experiences, Malcolm discovered how many others have also been on the receiving end of communication from those beyond this physical plane.

****

Another granddad brings a family together:

Hours prior to the death of my grandfather, I was sitting at his bedside with my mother, two of my uncles and their wives. I kept hearing this music. I kept waiting for the air conditioner to stop, but when it did, the music kept going. I was never able to place the song, as there was absolutely no melody. Oddly enough, my mother, one of my uncles' wives and I were the only ones that heard that music, and they both described it as I did. It had absolutely no melody.

My family is pretty religious, but started questioning everything they've always believed immediately after he passed. They questioned the existence of heaven and if their father would really be with their mother, who had died a little over two years before.

I drove home later that morning and took my mother home. I was exhausted, so I stayed at my parents' house and had breakfast. I was lying on the couch when all of a sudden I heard as loud as day: "It's beautiful here." It was as if someone in the room had spoken to me. I asked my dad – it was definitely a male voice – what he had said. He said he hadn't said anything. I turned to my mother and told her she got her answer.

What makes this even more unusual is that the voice in my head that told me, "It's beautiful here," also woke me up prior to my grandfather's passing. I was physically and emotionally exhausted. I had closed my eyes while I was lying on his real bed. As I was falling asleep, there were all these voices going on in my head — something I had never experienced before or since – and I asked them to stop. I fell asleep and the voice woke me up ten minutes prior to his passing, telling me that I needed to get up. My aunts and uncles had all gone to bed. So it was only me, my mother and his dog in the room when he passed. We figured it was the way he wanted it. His three girls were with him when he passed and he was going to meet his #1 girl, my grandmother.

I don't know if there is any significance, but the voice both times came from the left side. I didn't recognize the voice as being his, but I recognized it as a male voice.

The impact of these contacts has been huge and life-changing. As a result of it, my memories of my grandfather are of the good times, instead of his final illness. Also prior to this experience, I had been afraid to die. Now, dying does not scare me. It has made me really realize that spirit cannot die and has made me start to think about past experiences and synchronicities.

I was concerned about how my co-workers might react, but I've shared it with them and friends and discovered I needn't have worried. Not one has questioned my experience. They say they've known me too long and too well to have any doubts. I have also met some terrific people and have made lifelong friends.

Erin Connors

Bottom line: The loss of a loved one can bring with it a tendency to question concepts about life and death. For Erin it came at a time when her family was questioning the existence of heaven, and wondering if her grandfather would really be with her grandmother. Since some of her family were there when this ADC occurred, it was a great comfort to them, and another demonstration of her grandfather's love for them all.

****

So think about it. Have you received a message that you ignored? Or passed off as coincidence? Or wishful thinking? Forget expecting words from the Other Side to be accompanied by the blare of trumpets. It might instead come in the blare of the volume of your television when you haven't touched the remote, which may remind you of how loudly your dearly departed once listened to it. Open your mind to all possibilities. There are a variety of ways they can be dropped outside your door. Next

time check the peephole if you must, then open the door. And prepare to be surprised.

    C.W.

CHAPTER SIX - WHEN THE MEDIUM BRINGS THE MESSAGE - PART III

WIND DANCER

This from Sharon, nicknamed Kaydy, was conducted in a chat room on-line. As a result we have no further information as to the identity of the medium involved.

I visit a Web site called Spirit Space where they have classes to help people tap into their gifts to hear from spirit. I had this reading four years ago. It is copied from a log of the reading, which was conducted in a chat room and is embellished with my own interpretation of what it meant to me.

I had been trying to get on the reading list for quite some time and never seemed to have any luck. I would forget about the time and miss my chance. So on this particular Friday I made the list, but the list taker sent me a private message that there were so many people ahead of me that I probably wouldn't get a reading. They said unless more readers showed up, my chances were pretty slim. I decided to just hang around and watch the other readings. All of a sudden I noticed a lot of people log on and they were all readers! I'm not very familiar with Spirit Space, pretty new to the site, but in my limited experience there, I had never seen that many logged on at one time. I was hoping maybe my luck was turning.

I had been watching three different readings and the people being read didn't seem to be able to validate anything at all. But I could relate to about half of what was being said. The names and events coming through were really right on for me and my family. I thought this might be the "me too" syndrome I've heard about. I just sat there and asked my people on the other side if this was their way of reaching out to me and letting me know they were there. After the third reading, I was private-messaged and told they were moving me to a private room because they had someone waiting there to read me. WOW! I was so nervous and it took me three times to type in the command to get in there.

My reader's name was WindDancer. I felt an immediate bond with her (or him, I guess I don't really know for sure). I can't say enough about the kind and loving people over there. Here is the reading, plus my inserts of what I felt spirit was saying to me.

WD: Kay, I will work with you here. I am new to this format, and appreciate your willingness to allow me this time to share with you. Smells good. Are you eating popcorn, or is it significant for the loved one you were hoping to connect with tonight?

KD: No to eating popcorn, but it is significant. (Here's the deal with popcorn and my family. WE LOVE IT!! It is our favorite food and we have been known to have it for supper with lots of butter and salt. Some of us like it with milk and sugar, like cereal. When I was a kid it was my job to pop the corn. My aunt lived on a farm and they always grew their own corn and, of course, shared it with my family. We would spend a whole day taking it off the cob, and then us kids would have to make sure none of the chaff was in it before packing it in bags. My grandmother used to live with us and she had a huge apartment-like room upstairs in our house. Whenever we made popcorn for a snack at night, I would take it to her upstairs, because she had arthritis in her knees and couldn't easily use the stairs. She used to say she really loved the smell of the popcorn popping.)

WD: Kay, for some reason I am now hearing Zipp-a-doo-da, zipp-a-day, my, oh, my what a wonderful day – the song – from Song of the South. Does this have any meaning for you? Ha ha ha – seems to be the emphasis on "Mr. Bluebird on my Shoulder." Am hearing that line over and over!

KD: Maybe yes. (A little background here concerning the "blue bird on my shoulder." Last year my mom's gentleman friend of twenty-five years was diagnosed with cancer of the colon, which had metastasized to his spine. About a year before, I'd started my spiritual journey and credit John Edward and his show *Crossing Over,* for setting me on this path. Roy was 83 years young at the time of the cancer diagnosis.

Let me say that I am smack dab in the middle of a bunch of skeptics here. There is absolutely no one, except my 18-year-old daughter and my 28-year-old niece who will even entertain the possibility that there is any way anyone could get signs or communicate with someone who has passed away. So as you might well imagine, any talk of such things brings some pretty strong reactions. So I don't talk about it in front of them any more.

About a month before Roy passed, my mom said that Roy was talking to her about his impending death. He told her he wasn't sure if there was a heaven, but when he died he would come to ME and let me know what it was like...if he made it! She asked why he would come to me and he replied, "Because I know she believes in that stuff." I told her I would love to hear from him and thought we should get together and discuss some sign he might give me so I would know it was him. I have things happen to me all the time and I never really know who is doing them. Anyway, Roy and I never had the conversation. He crossed over on January 3, 2002.

At a huge party for my nephew I brought the log of my reading with me to show my niece. I told her I could validate everything but the zippidy do da song. She looked at the log and said, "Don't you remember? Roy's sons had that bluebird poem in his casket with him and that fake bluebird sitting on his shoulder!" I had totally forgotten that! I was so floored that I got the shakes and felt something go through me that is hard to explain. It was the most powerful thing I have ever felt. There were a lot of things in Roy's casket; his family hardly left any room for him! But I don't remember what the poem said, can't even remember if I read it. But my niece says she doesn't think it had anything to do with the song. She doesn't even remember it. I'm guessing that Roy was trying to tell me the song to remind me of the bluebirds in his coffin.)

WD: (((((Kay)))) I am not "seeing" any ONE person – but in the distance – can hear children's laughter, see what looks like a forest or wooded area...

KD: ?

WD: Seems to be playing peek-a-boo from around trees, with a gentle male figure. Seems to be older – there – playing with children.

KD: Maybe.

WD: I don't understand what it means. But seems to be older male. With children...can hear laughter.

KD: I think I do.

WD: Feels like this gentleman was very playful, loving and kind.

KD: You got that right. (My Daddy. If there was a man who loved children, it was him. He was everyone's angel. Neighbor kids flocked to our house and he was always taking everyone for ice cream or for pizza. He would plan parties for no particular reason and have all the kids in the neighborhood over. When my dad passed, the light went out of our life! I'm thinking the kids on the other side are really enjoying my DAD!)

WD: Is there a Gerald – Jerry – that has any meaning for you? Either here, or one who has crossed over??? J or G. Soft G sound. Or J..not sure.

KD: Not sure.

WD: Will let it go...

KD: Can I ask a question?

WD: Sure, Kaydy.

KD: Could it be Jeremy?

WD: Yes, that would be a J...or soft G.

KD: Okay, yes.

WD: Gerald and Jerry...and Jeremy sound alike.

KD: Yes they do. (My nephew, Jeremy, graduated from the Omaha Police Academy the morning after this reading. Jeremy was born just one month after my Dad passed.)

Sharon Michalski

CHAPTER SEVEN – REMINDERS – THESE FOOLISH THINGS...

An acquaintance lost her fiancé some time ago. An avid collector of coins, he had a special affinity for dimes. Before he died he told her that he would be with her as long as she needed him, that he would make certain she knew he was around.

For several years afterwards, she would find dimes. She'd get out of her car in a parking lot and see a dime twinkling against the tarmac. She would clean her kitchen or vacuum her carpet, leave the room and come back to find a dime on the counter or in the middle of the freshly vacuumed rug. She came upon them in the most unlikely places. That continued until she met the man she eventually married.

The contributions that follow play out this theme. So often we miss signs from the Other Side because they seem so insignificant. Sure, there'd be no mistaking a bolt of lightning that leaves the name of our dearly departed scorched across the lawn. That's not the way it happens. It's the little things, the seemingly insignificant incidents that pop up that are so frequently shrugged off as coincidence. Can you imagine how frustrating that must be for the sender?

****

Contacts from mothers begin this section - no surprise since motherhood is one of those callings that become a lifelong commitment – and apparently after life as well. And one's first Christmas after the loss of a loved one is always the most difficult. So it's not surprising that this became the initial occasion of what would become many "hello's" from Lori's mother.

My mother died almost four and a half years ago suddenly from undiagnosed ovarian cancer. Going on without her has been a daily struggle for me at times. We had the kind of bond where we knew what each other was thinking. We would answer each other's questions when no questions were spoken aloud. She was my best friend in life and I miss her dearly.

It was around Christmas time and I had just bought a new computer program for photo editing. My husband was in and out of the house puttering and I would talk to him about all the neat things it could do. He came up behind me and sat down, looking over my shoulder at what I was doing. I could see his white shirt out of the corner of my eye. I went on chattering for about twenty minutes, and suddenly had the feeling you get when you are excited to share something with someone you love, a very familiar feeling, and at the same moment, several things happened.

The thought crossed my mind that my mother would have loved to see this program. As soon as that thought entered my mind, I felt Mike's hand on my shoulder, as if he were comforting me. I turned to look at him and smile. There was no one there. He came out of the garage wearing a BLUE shirt, not white, and asked me who I had been talking to. He had been in the garage for the last forty-five minutes! I am convinced it was my mother sharing that moment with me. It was like having a hug from her one last time. I could feel her spirit, the familiarity of her presence. She WAS there with me, touching me, loving me, and comforting me as she always did. It happened in just a moment or two, but if felt like I was experiencing all of those feelings we had shared together in my entire life in that instant. It was a rush of emotion that was nearly overwhelming and brought me to my knees afterwards. It gave me comfort knowing she was still there looking out for me, and it gave me the courage to move on and bring my grieving to an end. It was undoubtedly the most precious Christmas gift of my life.

Lori Messer

The relationship between Lori and her mother was an extremely close one, to such an extent that messages of support from her mom are common. It is not surprising that her mother would want to share in Lori's successes, be they large or small. And clearly this was one of those occasions. But wait. There's more from Lori's mom:

Mom was the most caring, giving and generous person I had ever known, and it is only as an adult that I can really appreciate the strength and courage she possessed and the sacrifices she made for us when she was alive. Even when she was facing a possible diagnosis of terminal cancer (only two days before her death), she exhibited such a presence of grace and dignity. Her last thoughts and words were for her family and friends. They were not words of fear or regret, but words of love, compassion and kindness. She was a truly incredible woman.

She told me that even if it were cancer she would leave this world with no regrets. She had a family who loved her, friends who cared about her, and had had a full and wonderful life with all of us. She told me that if this was her time to go, what more could she have asked of life than those things. I could only hug her and cry as she stroked my head and comforted <u>me</u> in her last hours.

I miss that comfort. I miss those times when I would sit at her bedside and just talk and work out my problems out loud. It was nice to have that feedback and to use her as a sounding board. I miss that so much

Just when I was at my lowest point recently, she made herself known in a BIG way, not only in my life, but in the lives of those around me. I had started to have doubts about my path again and prayed for guidance. I prayed for a sign that all of this was real and not imagined. I got several signs over the next few days, and they are things I can't explain but have to accept as more than coincidence. They came to not only me, but to me through friends as well.

The first "hello" came to me at work. I had been making some of my daily calls to out-of-state attorneys I work with for updates on various cases. I called a number I routinely call every day and the number had been disconnected. I thought that was strange. I'd talked to them yesterday. I brought up the call on my screen to check the number to be sure I had dialed it right.

I didn't recognize the number at first and then it hit me like a ton of bricks. I had unknowingly dialed my mom's old phone number. It had been more than two years since I had even thought about her number, much less dialed it! Talk about floodgates opening. As I reached for the tissues, a small, white feather dropped from the tissue I pulled out.

Later that afternoon I received a phone call from a friend who told me she had something strange to relate. She said she hoped I wouldn't be upset by it, but felt compelled to tell me. She said she had gone to lunch with some friends, and as she was sitting in her car with the doors shut, a feather floated down into her lap, and she had the strangest sensation that it was from my mom. I smiled and told her it probably was.

As I was getting ready to leave work, a different friend called with yet another message. She was coming home from work, driving down one of our major highways going about 60 mph when a butterfly landed on her window ledge. The funny thing was it landed there while she was driving, not stopped at a red light, but driving! She said it stayed there for a good fifteen minutes, just hanging on and looking at her. She tried to shoo it away, but it would not budge.

She said she suddenly thought of my mom. It made her smile, and she laughed at it and said to the butterfly, "All right, Bobbi! If you don't cut it out, I am going to tell Lori!" At that exact moment, the butterfly took flight and yes, a feather landed in her lap as well!

That evening my sister called me. She is actually my best friend of thirty years and to my children she is Aunt Kelly. My mom practically raised her with me, as she was a constant companion.

My mom even introduced her as her other daughter when talking with other people.

The first thing she said to me was, "I had lunch with your mom today!" I told her to not say anything else, and to let me guess. "Was a feather involved?"

She was astonished. "As a matter of fact, yes, and how the $#*! did you know?"

I just laughed and told her the events of the day. Apparently she was having lunch and feeling a bit overwhelmed herself. She said her thoughts drifted to my mother and at that exact moment she felt a warm presence, and a feather blew into her car.

It is my belief that even now, after her death, she continues to try to "show me the way." I know in my heart that it was she who orchestrated my meeting with John Edward, the medium, and that it is she who continues to push me to seek more meaning in my own life. Even in her death she still continues to mother me and help me grow and find my own way. She is always there when I need her most. When I am at my darkest moments filled with doubt and fear, she is there. Thanks, Mom. And I love you.

Lori Messer

Bottom line: There's not a whole lot to say since Lori has said it all. Her mother is still on the job, still watching over her daughter, loving her and being loved in return.

****

A mother's admission - "You were right!"

My mother's name was Ruth. She simply didn't believe in life after death. I tried and tried to talk her into watching *Crossing Over with John Edward,* and told her of my experiences in the gallery and at two of his seminars. She simply wasn't interested in "such nonsense" and remained a skeptic.

The last time I spoke to my mother she was in a coma. I read to her a lovely story about what to expect as she slept on, The Next Place by Warren Hanson. Before I left her, I put a tape recorder on her chest with the music she liked. I told her that I loved her, and couldn't resist saying, "And don't forget, when you get to the other side, let me know that I was right and you were wrong!" I left her in the early afternoon, and she passed during that night. She was 88 years old. Although we knew she was failing, we thought for certain that she would leave us in November. My family seemed to be coming and going in November. My father passed on November 18th and my sister on November 21st. My three grandchildren were born in November – the 4th, the 11th and the 18th. Mom fooled us; it was August 25th. Then I remembered. It made perfect sense. My dad's name was AUGUST!

Mom had been very determined to be as independent as possible. When she was living in her own apartment, she routinely rode a bus for senior citizens. The price was $1.10 and she would write checks for each fare, her spidery handwriting belying her age and infirmity. To make it easy for her I got small yellow envelopes and put a Dollar bill and a dime in each one, so she could just grab the envelope when she needed it. When she moved to an assisted living facility, she apparently put all the dimes she had left into a change purse, since she no longer needed them for the bus.

The afternoon after my mother's death, I had been on the computer and saw a little ditty on a message board from a father and former skeptic, whose daughter had crossed over. In it, the penny found was from one departed relative, the dime another, etc. I signed off the computer to meet with my sister. I was bringing a pair of my husband's shorts downstairs. As I folded them across my arm, a dime fell out of the pocket onto the stair, just kind of popped out. I laughed and said, "Okay, if this is you, Ma, I'll be seeing a lot more dimes and they'll be from you." I put it on a knick-knack shelf so I see it when I go up or downstairs, and I smile.

Perhaps two weeks later, my daughter and I packed up the last of Mom's things at her apartment, and I found an old pocketbook at the bottom of her closet. Sure enough, inside was a change purse with a large pile of dimes. Without even thinking about it, I told my daughter to give them to my wannabe banker 13-year-old grandson. About ten minutes later, it hit me! I remembered reading the experiences of an on-line friend for whom finding pennies had become a "hello" from her father, another friend who found pennies from her mom and, of course, there was that on-line friend I'd read about that very first day when I was sent my first dime. I had to tell my daughter that I was sorry, but I was taking the dimes back because they were going into my private "momma-dime" stash of "found" dimes only. I didn't count them at the time, but when I did, it was exactly 30 dimes!

Two months after Mom crossed over, as I was driving to the grocery store, I was "talking" to Mom and laughed at something I remembered. I was extremely tired as I put the groceries on the conveyor belt, when two boxes jumped off the belt, both snacks I enjoy. As I bent down to pick them up, there was another dime, waiting to let me know she was around! Granted, people drop coins at the cashiers all the time, but except for the occasional penny, it's rare that they don't pick up a dime. I couldn't resist saying, "I told ya so, Ma!" I love it!

It seems that what I didn't find, others did. I am not the only one finding dimes in my house and yard. My hubby actually asked me if I was planting them around! I cannot begin to list all the various places that dimes have been found, but I can say that at present I have well over a hundred dimes. Even the skeptics who patiently accepted my dime stories while rolling their eyes are finding them. The day of my mother's service, my sister said that apparently Mom had left something for me on a table in my sister's den: a dime! And frankly, I loved the look on her face when she said it.

My son found an antique dime in the roots of a tree while picking up dog poop. There have been dimes – not pennies or quarters – in various areas of the yard, even where no one usually walks.

Mom's always with me. I was going to Wethersfield for a deposition regarding a lawsuit. Obviously I was feeling some trepidation. I was getting ready to leave and grabbed a blazer I hadn't worn in a couple of years. I put my hand in my pocket to find a DIME!

As Christmas approached I was thinking about Mom and that it had been a while since I'd noticed any validations. I asked, "What's up?" I came downstairs and saw (of course) another dime on the rug in our hall. Had to say, "Thanks, Ma."

When I ask, I have come to realize that she will always find a way to bring me dimes. Recently, she brought me two at once. One was just inside the back door and the other was just outside the door. She finds very creative ways to send me "hello's."

Granted, sometimes I still do reality checks. It just seems too good to be true, and there have been two occasions when I specifically asked for a quarter so I wouldn't doubt myself regarding her listening to me. And sure enough, I stepped on a quarter partially under a guest bed. On the other occasion, a pocketful of dimes, a quarter and an angel coin fell out of a pair of my husband's pants after I asked her to keep him safe while he was out of state. I find dimes to this day. I truly do!

Adrienne Baumgardner

Bottom line: What a heart-warmer, to say nothing of being a piggy bank filler. And what a delight to know that Adrienne's mom is still living up to her end of the bargain.

****

Six cents from heaven?

My daughter-in-law, granddaughter and I went shopping for our son's birthday (on Mother's Day this year). As we were heading back to the car, granddaughter, Eva, was parroting everything we were saying. We were laughing about that and swapping stories of embarrassing things kids say during this time period of their lives.

I had just finished telling my daughter-in-law about a flowery phrase my son, her husband, said to my mom in the middle of the grocery store when he was two. I told her how Mom had admonished me to be careful what phrases and words I used in front of him. As I finished the story, I stepped off the curb to get into the car and look down. Lo and behold, there was a nickel and a penny.

That is a definite hello from Mom and probably a reminder to watch my mouth around Eva. Mom <u>always</u> used to say if you have a nickel and a penny, you're rich. So that is the sign she has given me a few times these past ten years since her passing. And think about it, that is an odd combination of change to see side by side on the ground. I know it wasn't there when we got out of the car because I am always scanning for 'pennies from heaven.'

Hi, Mom. Thanks for shopping with us.

Sue Purdy, Lancaster, PA

Bottom line: Aside from the validation the combination of coins provided for Sue, it also filled one of her most fervent wishes. Her mother had made her transition to the Other Side before Sue's daughter-in-law and granddaughter became a part of her life. As a result of finding the penny and the nickel during the shopping trip, Sue was assured that her mom was with them, aware of the additions to the family, and continuing to enjoy one of her favorite activities: shopping. How cool is that?

****

Message from an autumn rose:

My parents were visiting from out of state. They hadn't been back for several months and as a result, hadn't heard any of the tape from the reading I'd had with John Holland, only what I had typed out for them in an e-mail.

There was one small part I wanted my dad to hear, a very important message from his mom for him. So I asked him to come with me to pick up the kids from school, and I popped in the tape for him. He's a healthy skeptic, but gets a little spooked out with these things. I have to say he seemed very impressed with John Holland. He was glad to hear what my grandmother had to say.

My other grandmother, my mom's mom, had come through loud and clear in the reading. It is obvious that she watches over everyone in the family. As we pulled up to the school, we got to the part where John said he was letting lots and lots of roses popping up all over. He said that roses are a big "hello" from her and to watch out for them.

113

At that point we got out of the car and walked into the schoolyard, talking as we walked. "So what do you think?" I asked.

"It's something!" he said.

"It sounds like Grandma is around quite a bit."

"Great!" he said with a smile and a roll of his eyes. I laughed, too.

Now I love to look for synchronicities, but when it comes to "hello" from loved ones on the other side, I don't go out of my way to look for them. If they want to get my attention, they certainly will. And they do.

We got the kids and started back to the car. The sidewalk was ankle deep in fallen leaves. The kids went ahead of us, lugging their backpacks and kicking up the leaves. As I walked through them, something caught my eye, but I continued a few feet and stopped. I turned around and bent over to pick out of the dried up brown fallen leaves one perfect new healthy red rose petal. "Dad. Check this out! Wow! What do you think of that!"

"Well, if I didn't know any better, I'd have thought you put that there yourself!"

"Yeah." I rolled my eyes, and smiled. "Right."

Then my daughter piped up. "But Papa, I saw it first! I was in front of you."

As I loaded the backpacks into the car, my father went back to look around for a rose bush or something to explain why that single perfect rose petal was there. Nothing.

Laura Wooster

Bottom line: Laura was already open to communication from the Other Side, so there has to be a certain satisfaction in helping someone else begin to wonder.

****

As I read Jenny McDaniel's narrative, I was struck by how much her love for her mother permeated every word. Moms, in general,

tend to be special to us. For Jenny, her mother was Special, with a capital S. What a woman!

My mom was what my grandma describes as a pleaser. She loved to make people happy, especially her family. She was an outgoing Leo who always made our friends feel welcome, and even when our friendships grew distant, she still kept in touch with some of them and knew what was going on in their lives.

She had her faults, too. She had quite a temper and if she was displeased with something, you and everyone within hearing distance would know it. She was by no means a quiet person. But for the most part, whenever she "let loose," it was because she cared.

My mother's name was Jeanette and when she was diagnosed with breast cancer the first time in 1997, she wasn't exactly quiet about that either. She was very open about her illness and, as a result, she got tons of support. Church members, friends and family prayed for her and visited with gifts, flowers and cards. She especially loved when our pastor would visit with scriptural teachings and prayers.

About a year and seven chemo treatments later, my mom was weaker but getting better. We thought that the worst was behind us and that she would now be fine.

Then she started to complain about numbness in her hands and feet. She went to the doctor and learned that she had thyroid cancer and a suspicious mass on her left lung. For the first time my mother was quiet about something. She told no one, but started to make plans for a family vacation.

My family was clueless, but I knew something was up. We had our vacation and everyone had a good time, but for me there was a nagging worry about my mom's health.

When she finally told us, she did it separately and for me it was devastating.

What followed was just terribly sad. The chemo drained her of all her energy and she got weaker and weaker. Bit by bit the bright shining light that I knew as my mom faded, and in the end she was a shell of her former self.

I had been watching *Crossing Over with John Edward* for a few months before the day of her actual passing. I knew she was going to a better place, and that it didn't mean that it was the end of our relationship as mother and daughter. I was actually able to tell her it was okay to go. I knew she was ready to go HOME and I kind of envied her.

So on her last day she was surrounded by family and friends at home in her own bed. As she was leaving someone suggested that we put on some music. The CD was already in the player. It was my mom's favorite Christian gospel CD by Andy Griffith. When she drew her last breath, "I'll Fly Away" was playing. We were all astounded when she opened her eyes after being in a coma-like state for over twenty-four hours and this HUGE smile lit her face. It seemed like her entire soul was beaming through. She looked at us with so much love that it was almost painful to witness. I was the last person she looked at and it was as though she knew exactly where I was. I told her to GO in my mind and she did. She closed her eyes and took two shallow breaths and was gone.

Our pastor had informed us to call him at any hour when the time came. It was close to midnight, but he came and spent a few minutes with my mother's body and a few hours with us, talking about arrangements and other things.

The next day he came by again. We were talking about how she left and the song "I'll Fly Away" was mentioned. He took out his planner and informed us that when he had spent time praying over Mom's body the night before, that was the song that had been playing, since the entire CD had been set to repeat. He said he normally didn't write stuff like that down, but that it had felt right at the time.

So that was one of the songs we sang at her funeral. My stepfather had never even heard of after death communication, but it was enough for him to have the song title "I'll Fly Away" engraved on her headstone and enough to have friends and family frame the song, some with artwork and give it to us as gifts.

I have received this song from my mother on at least two occasions. One was when I was having a really rough time at work with a co-worker. On the radio I was really surprised to hear a very unusual version of the song with an electric guitar on a hard rock station. I knew Mom was aware of what was going on and telling me everything would be okay. The other time, another co-worker and I were having a discussion and he handed me a CD from the rack at our store and told me, "Here, you need to get this." It was a gospel CD with another version of the song on it. He had no idea of my connection to this song and what it meant to me.

My mom also likes to give me egrets as signs, long slender, graceful white birds that wade into shallow water, sometimes standing still for long stretches of time waiting for minnows and other small fish or whatever to come close enough to catch. This bird does not fret about looking for sustenance, but KNOWS that food will come to it if it stays still long enough.

I know there is a higher spiritual purpose for her sending me those. I will admit that I am a big worrier. I can stress about all kinds of stuff and make a mountain out of a molehill. I believe that the universe, God and my mom are telling me that I need to learn to have patience, trust and KNOW that what I need will always come to me, that my most valuable lesson in his life is to "let go and let God."

So, whenever I hear the song or get an egret, my heart fills with happiness because I know my mom is telling me to rise above and soar.

Jenny McDaniel

Followup: In response to a question about the timing of her early contact from her mother, Jenny's reply is worth quoting:

"I had gone to my mom's grave on her birthday and at first I was very bitter and thought to myself that this would be the first birthday that I wouldn't have to worry about finding the perfect gift for her. The need to give her something was overwhelming. Then I thought to myself, 'I can give her something and this will be the best present she ever got.'

"That whole day I thought about all the good times we shared. I thought about all the Christmases, birthdays and special occasions. I thought about how outgoing she was and how generous she could be, even though that sometimes got her into trouble. I thought of how the house would smell when she cooked, and how safe and secure I felt as a child with her as my mom.

"All day long and into the night, I did this and the next morning I woke up and felt better than I had in ages. It was really a good feeling, and I vowed to do it every birthday for her. I know she felt it and appreciated it, because for my birthday, which was two weeks away from hers, I got my first egret picture from her, and even though I didn't realize it until two months later, the egret signs just kept coming."

Bottom line: There are so many ways to honor those we have lost, from simply lighting a candle, placing flowers or flags at the grave site, and on and on. But Jenny's birthday present for her mother makes me reconsider how I've marked special days of my own. A gift of happy memories from this side of the veil to the other. Even the thought makes me smile.

****

Moms and flowers, a winning combination:

My husband and I went to a garden show in Harrisburg. While walking through the parking lot, I saw a penny and said to Phil, "Pick it up. It is a penny from heaven. I wonder who is saying hello today."

We went into the display area and saw all of these lovely gardens, trees, and flowers. The first thing I saw were pansies and daffodils – my mother-in-law's favorites. Then we saw a bank full of trees. They were almost the same density as those she planted on the bank in her yard. There was a rose of the coral color that she absolutely loved.

Phil and I both have a weakness for pussy willows and I kept looking at these small trees that are weeping pussy willows in the various display gardens. I asked about them and was told they were a grafted tree to get them to 'weep.' I thought that would be perfect for a spot in the front yard where I needed something like this.

At the very end at the very last booth, I spotted a booth selling these little pussy willows. Without turning around, I asked Phil, "Do you think I should buy one?" I felt his fingers running up my back in answer. Only when I turned, neither he nor anyone else was anywhere around!

So I smiled and asked, "What do you think, Mother?" I felt the same fingers run up my back and knew she was saying, "Yes, it will be lovely." I used to drive her crazy by running my fingers up her back when she was cooking.

Sue Purdy, Lancaster, PA

Bottom line: For Sue, this experience was bittersweet. She was excited and grateful that her mother had let her know she was there, yet sad that she was no longer physically with them. In the end, however, it was yet another validation that life goes on, on this side as well as the other.

****

Frogs, frogs and more frogs!

The saga of Gail and Phil amounts to an ongoing love story. The first message to Gail from her husband, Phil, was courtesy of a letter he'd written to her six months before his death, the second one delivered to Gail's sister, Debby, to pass along to Gail. Since then he's been a busy and imaginative messenger, his reminders of his continued existence amounting to croaking, good fun!

At least ten years before my husband, Phil, crossed over, he and I were decorating our Christmas tree. I didn't notice when he picked up a small, funny green toy frog and hung it on the tree. It was not a Christmas decoration. No one else in the family saw it for a few days. He claimed he was not hiding it. It looked silly and everyone laughed when they spotted it. Each year after that, he continued to hang that same frog. He claimed it as "his decoration." It became a family tradition to find the frog.

October 2001

My daughter, Valerie, called me on her lunch break from work to chat. Phil came up in our conversation several times, as he often does. She hung up and called back a few minutes later, laughing hard. She likes to play a word scramble called "Text Twist" during lunch. The aim of the game is to make as many words as you can out of the seven letters given and win if you get the word. She put in the word "FROGGED" and was startled to see it was the correct seven-letter word. She had never seen the word before. I looked it up and it means adorned or bedecked with frogs. She had just become a medium for me.

Gail Ingson

****

More frogs – on line.

<u>April 2003</u>

My uncle, my mother's brother, got married this past weekend. The week prior, both my mom and I were missing my dad more intensely than usual. Special occasions and holidays – they are still so difficult. In particular Mom and I had gotten together Thursday evening and had talked at length about the upcoming wedding and how much we wanted Dad to be there.

The week before I'd been in a training class in another city. I hadn't met any of my fellow students until the first day of class, and hadn't told any of them about our frogs. The computer network we were using had four standard login profiles set up. All four profiles were named after basketball stars. Friday morning, the day before the wedding, as I began to log in, the woman next to me suddenly said, "Frog?" I looked over at her machine, and there was a mysterious new fifth profile set up. It was highlighted as the default session and was called – you guessed it – "frog." In addition to being highlighted, it was in lower case letters, whereas the other four sessions were in full upper case.

I checked my own login sessions and still had only four. I began to laugh and told her I didn't know what was going on, but my machine didn't have it. A few minutes later another woman two seats over from me came in and began to log in. Suddenly I heard her exclaim, "Frog? Frog? What's this frog thing?" It had appeared on her screen as well. I started to laugh again, this time louder and louder.

About the same time, a third person in the row ahead of me, about two seats down exclaimed, "I've got a frog, too!" By then I was nearly hysterical with laughter, trying desperately to tone it down, because these people had no idea why I thought this was so funny! I managed to quiet myself to a chuckle and silently thanked my dad for his wonderful validation that really lifted me up and made my day.

Valerie Ingson

****

August 2005

My daughter, Valerie, and I took my grandson, Joey, to Hershey Park, PA. It was a favorite place for my husband and me to take her and my son when they were little. Because of that, Phil was on both our minds and we were pretty sure he would go with us.

It had been months since I'd heard the songs we associate the most with Phil. There are three at the top of our list. On the way up to Pennsylvania, the first came on the radio: "Because You Loved Me" by Celine Dion. The words in the song say many of the things Phil often told me. Valerie said we needed to hear another one to consider it to be anything special.

We were walking past an area where people were singing karaoke sings inside and they were being shown on an outside television screen. Valerie stopped and laughed as she saw a young woman singing my song #2, "I Hope You Dance," by Lee Ann Womack. It's been known to inspire me to do things at times.

We were tired on the way home and only halfway listening to the radio. Valerie reached over and turned it up as song #3 came on, her BIG ADC song, "You'll Be in My Heart," by Phil Collins. This song has played on her car radio so many times just when she needed it the most. Joey was asleep in the back seat and Valerie and I just enjoyed the warm smiles and feeling we had. We both said "thank you" because we feel it's always important to do that.

Gail Ingson

****

An anniversary ADC related by Valerie:
Mom had admitted that although she loved the frog validations
as evidence of Phil's continued existence, she'd begun to feel that
she would like other types, to validate the validations, so to speak.
She got them.

I stopped at my mom's house and the first thing she wanted to
do was show me a book she'd brought home for my son. I started
toward the table to see the book when I suddenly felt very thirsty –
and I mean <u>extremely</u> thirsty. All I could think of was that I needed
a drink of water.

I literally did an about-face and walked over to the sink. I
grabbed a paper cup from the dispenser, and paused when I saw
it. The design on the cup featured bowling pins. My dad, after he
retired and before he knew he was sick, became very involved with
bowling. He was an excellent bowler, winning awards and a little
notoriety in the local bowling scene.

I was confused, thinking to myself that bowling had been my
dad's thing, not my mom's. I asked Mom why she'd bought these
cups, if maybe she bought them because they reminded her of Dad.
She gave me a brief, blank look and then burst into a big smile. No,
she hadn't bought them on purpose. She didn't have a choice because
the store only had this one type when she'd last brought cups. She
didn't even realize there was a bowling design on some of the cups.
As a matter of fact, when we looked closer at them, actually taking
the whole stack out of the dispenser, we found the vast majority of
the cups were of other sports – basketball, baseball, soccer, football,
etc. We left the house with big smiles on our faces and warmth in
our hearts from his non-frog validation from my dad.

There is a certain song my mom feels my dad "sends" her on
occasion. While we were driving to the movies, we were at a stoplight
when I said to my mom, "I'll bet your song comes on some time
between here and the mall." She replied that she hadn't heard it in a

long time; she'd only heard mine – a different one I feel my dad sent me on occasion – so she doubted it would happen.

There was a song on the radio and I remember thinking *Hurry up, let this song be over so my mom can hear her song* I felt very impatient. The current song ended and the strains of the next song began. IT WAS HER SONG!!! "I Hope You Dance!"

Next, during the previews before the movie, my mom leaned over and said, "I think if we could get another bowling or frog validation between now and the end of the movie, it would be great. That would really confirm all the other validations for me." A few minutes later, there was a cartoon advertisement that began with a father calling out to his kids," Hey, kids, what do you want to do tonight?" To which his daughter replied, "How about bowling?" The ad continued but my mom and I didn't hear anything after that, too busy being amazed that, once again, Dad came through. With those three validations, combined with the cardinals my mom saw in the morning, I'd say she got her wish in a big way – lots of non-frog validations from Dad on their anniversary.

Valerie Ingson

****

Totally frogged:

As it turned out one year the best day for me to have my son's sixth birthday party just happened to be on my own birthday. I hired a magician for my son's party. At one point in the show, the magician called my son up to help and gave him is very own birthday magic wand. My son waved the wand at the crowd of kids watching the show, and the magician warned, "Be careful. Don't turn them all into frogs!" I smiled and thought, "Hello, Dad." Frogging #1.

A little later the magician started making balloon animals to hand out to the kids. He went through a list of what he could make and, of course, a frog was on the list. Frogging #2. He went around the room and made balloon animals for the kids. One of the last kids he went to requested and received – you guessed it – a frog! Frogging #3. Later, as we were opening gifts, one of the first gift bags handed to me was a frog gift bag. Frogging #4. (Keep in mind that no one at this party except my mom, me and one other friend knew about our frog experiences.)

After the party I was reading to my son, as I do every evening. He'd recently received a bunch of new beginner-reading books, so I hadn't read any of them to him yet. He chose four books out of the pile for me to read. The second book had – you guessed it again – a frog reference. Frogging #5.

Finally my son was in bed, everything was cleaned up from the party and I thought I'd log on and check my e-mail. I turned on the TV because I like to have background noise. Nickelodeon was on, so I flipped to ABC looking for something more for my age group. Lilo & Stitch was on but I thought, *Well, it's just for background noise. Guess I'll leave it on this station.*

I logged on and began my e-mails, only vaguely aware of Lilo and Stitch ending and America's Funniest Home Videos starting. What finally got my attention was the sound of Kermit the frog and Miss Piggy talking. Frogging #6. I turned around just in time to see that the video segment was all about FROGS, three different ones, including one in which a toddler was picking up frogs and putting them in her diaper, then taking them out again. Froggings #7, 8 and 9!

I commented to my mom that I felt my birthday froggings were signficant in the fact that there were so many of them. I've had four birthdays since my dad crossed over. Although I usually "hear" from him on my birthday, it's usually one, not multiples. My comment reminded my mom that the night before she'd spoken aloud to my dad and my grandmother and had asked them to do something special for my birthday. I'd say they more than met her request.

Valerie Ingson

****

Florida frogs:

When Gail came to visit, she asked if I had any frogs in the house. I told her I was not aware of any. Later when she went to get a drink of water, she saw a frog scrubbie someone had given me as a gift.

The following day at a Hallmark store I found a frog, but Gail told me it didn't count, that she had to see them without looking for them. As we were leaving, there was a big frog on top of some stuffed animals looking right at her. We went into the grocery store and there was a big display of wind chimes in front of us, fifty percent with lots of frogs hanging on them. At the checkout, the cashier pointed out a big picture of a frog at the checkout in the center of the store.

Things got even more interesting at Animal Kingdom at Disney World. Admittedly there are several frogs at the Animal Kingdom, but even there, we had unusual frog validations. We walked by a souvenir store and there was a man standing in front holding a huge kite with a frog on it. At the Rainforest Cafe's souvenir shop there were frogs everywhere – stuffed, on shirts, hanging from the ceiling. When they sat us at our table, it was covered with frogs. Even the ladies' room had a large picture of a frog on the inside door.

We watched the parade after lunch and were still surprised as a giant frog float went by. When we stopped at a restroom on the way out of the park, there were frog tiles all over the floor. As we were heading toward the exit of the park, there was a man holding a stuffed frog under his arm.

When we got into our car, Gail challenged "them" to come up with one more frog before we got home, pretty positive it couldn't be done. As we drove onto the highway, we couldn't believe our eyes when we saw a McDonalds with a HUGE statue of a frog on the roof. Gail thanked them for outdoing themselves.

When Gail left, I wondered if the frogs would be going with her, because I had had more than my share of them for a while.

Debra John

Followup: Gail remembers that incidents involving frogs began only a few weeks after Phil's death and considers them his choice because they are a true symbol of new life. They begin as tadpoles confined to the liquid density of water, then evolve into frogs, free of their previous confinement, able to live aboveground and free to return to the water if they so choose. For Gail it is much

like living in our dense physical form in this life and evolving into our spiritual form over "there."

Gail says she and her family were grieving when the frogs made their first appearance. They made them all laugh out loud. "It's hard to grieve and laugh at the same time," Gail responds. "Laughing is better and we know it is what our loved ones want us to do."

The frog stories have been shared with all of Gail's family and friends. It hasn't mattered to her if they believe or not. It has made them laugh. "The frogs have made a huge difference for the better in the quality of our lives. I can't imagine how sad and lonely these past ten years would have been if I hadn't been constantly reminded that Phil still loves me, sees me, hears me, and likes to make me laugh. I love it and live in a constant state of wonder."

So I say, "Let's hear it for the frogs!"

****

Birds and butterflies, feathers, flowers and frogs, silver and symphonies, all in their separate ways reminders of someone on the Other Side. We dishonor them when we fail to pay attention, when we fail to believe. Don't be so quick to dismiss such an experience. It's a precious moment, a symbol of their love for us. And love is the most precious specie of all.

C.W.

CHAPTER EIGHT - WHEN THE MEDIUM BRINGS THE MESSAGE - PART IV

JOHN HOLLAND

Not all readings with mediums are conducted face to face. This one was done by telephone. The dynamics, however, are the same.

In this transcript of the hour-long reading, Gail's explanations are in parenthesis. It is included in its entirety to demonstrate how intensive and extensive such a personal reading can be. For further clarification, John frequently talks back to those coming through to assure them that he is getting the message and understands. Those comments are underlined.

JH: Gail, before I start, I wanted to call you ten minutes ago. Your father, he was impatient. He wants to open this up.

GI: I talked to him today and asked him to come through. I looked at the clock at ten minutes to one.

JH: He wants to open this up. Here we go. He makes me aware, Gail, he says he's been gone more than five years, please, yes? I feel like he's one of the organizers. He's been there a long time, Gail. Am I right? It's been fifteen years?

GI: Yes. (It's been twenty-two years since he crossed. I wanted to hear from him because he seldom showed us his love while he was here. He was a good provider, but not a warm man.)

JH: He says add on more years to the five. He's also making me aware, Gail, did you lose your brother, Gail?

GI: No.

JH: Son?

GI: No.

JH: He has a younger man coming through, but I feel it's part of the family. I don't do "above, below" like John (Edward). I feel a younger male there, but I'll ask them. <u>Come on, guys, you've got to confirm who you are.</u>

GI: Would a son-in-law count?

JH: Absolute, absolutely. 'Cause I'm hearing the word 'son.' So you lost a son-in-law? So this will be your daughter's husband?

GI: Yes.

JH: Let him do his thing. It's very strange. One person I'm not getting is your mother. Mom still here?

GI: No.

JH: I'm not picking her up, so let's see if she comes in. I've got the two guys here. <u>Yeah, I understand that.</u> One of the gentlemen here is Michael. Significant, please? If I give you a name, it doesn't have to be someone who passed. Could be still living and I will hear, see, and feel information as it comes through. Mike or Michael.

GI: Phil's nephew, who is here. (Michael is the same age as my daughter and went to school with her.)

JH: If I'm wrong, Gail, trust me, they do correct me. Yeah. The gentleman who is your son-in-law, did this happen more than two years ago, please?

GI: No.

JH: Okay, it's recent. It's funny how I'm getting this, Gail. Your dad, even though he passes years ago, is there more of a faster passing with the son-in-law than with the Dad? I feel that the dad might have known he was going to pass. I feel the son-in-law goes much faster than him. There would be, I don't know, what connection to him, nothing really.

GI: (My dad crossed 22 years ago from colon cancer. He knew it was fatal and had six months to prepare to go.)

JH: But I feel that your son-in-law goes much faster, okay, than he does. <u>I understand that, my friend. Yeah, yeah, yeah.</u> Gail, the son-in-law, until they start popping in with their names, would he have a son here, please?

GI: Yes.

JH: It is just the one?

GI: Yes.

JH: I don't know if there are more kids there, so just let me do this. He says please acknowledge my son, my son, my son over and over. I'm supposed to say from one of the gentlemen, because they are coming through together. Gail, is this a birthday month for someone, please? Going into February?

GI: Yes.

JH: Whose birthday, because this is a big Happy Birthday to say hello to.

GI: It's my son's birthday.

JH: Happy birthday. When is it, February?

GI: January 30th.

JH: Oh, it hasn't happened. If you had said May or June, I would say no, you tried to make it fit. It's a big number for him, or they want me to emphasize it. Is Margaret connected to you, Gail?

GI: I'll have to write that down.

JH: It's either Margaret, Margie, Mary. I hate to give Marys because we all have them in our family. Is Margie passed, please? Because I feel Margie, Marge, Margie. It's not like it's Doris. Mar... Mar...

GI: (Margie was the much loved wife of Phil's favorite uncle, Vince. He crossed over earlier in their marriage. He continued to see and talk to her. She was the love of his life and a very good, wonderful and loving woman.)

JH: <u>Um-hum, I understand.</u> Gail, where is your husband, please?

GI: He's on the other side.

JH: Because I'm looking for him in your space here and I don't see him, which means he is passed or separated and way out of state. So you lost your husband also. You've got all the guys. Mom is most likely taking a back seat here.

GI: Yes, she would do that.

JH: Is your husband the one who had his own business, please?

GI: No, he did not.

JH: Okay, who had his own business? What male figure has their own business?

GI: My son-in-law.

JH: Would he work with his hands, please?

GI: Yes.

JH: Okay, because when I see some oil on people's hands, it always means to me that someone had some type of business.

GI: (Not long after they were married, my son-in-law, who worked for an alarm company, formed his own, one-man business installing alarm systems. He was proud of it, but eventually sold it because it was to difficult to keep it up.)

JH: Am I right in saying he also has a daughter? Does she go on to have another child? He acknowledges two kids, not just his own.

GI: Not that I'm aware of. (It's possible he did have another child. He wasn't faithful during his marriage and one girlfriend said she was going to keep his child.)

JH: It could be a nephew. He is acknowledging another connection to a kid.

GI: (Keven had a young nephew who had no father. He treated him like a son. The boy cried at Keven's funeral as if he also lost a father.)

JH: Is Joseph connected to here, too?

GI: Yes, that's his son.

JH: Yes! See? Bang! And that's not me doing it. They called him Joe, Joseph, Joey, but Gail, has your son-in-law been gone a year?

GI: Less than a year.

JH: Yeah, I understand that, and you understand. His wife has not met someone else, please?

GI: No, and I wish she would.

JH: It's going to happen, Gail.

GI: I'm so pleased!

JH: Sometimes they have something to do with it on the other side and he wants to say his wife will move on when she's ready. He wants to emphasize Joe, but there's another kid he wants to acknowledge. Okay, one second. Hmmmm. What state? You're in Maryland. Does Dad pass out of state?

GI: My dad, no, he passed in Maryland.

JH: It seems one of these guys passed out of your state.

GI: (Smacks herself.) My son-in-law!

JH: Okay, yup. You know what I keep getting Gail, very strong? Who's the Victoria, Virginia, Vivienne, big V name?

GI: Vince, there's a Vince.

JH: Absolutely! Because V always...who's Vincent, please? So is Vince gone now, please, because the V keeps coming in, keeps floating. I want to talk about the V guy. Definitely wants to keep coming in. Really, really strong, like the Big V.

GI: As he was ready to go, he was able to talk to the other side and give my daughter some messages.

JH: Absolutely! I want to call him, with the greatest respect, the Big V. So this is big in person, big in power, you know. Got to tell you, with his energy, I like what I'm feeling. This is someone I could laugh with, a kind person, and still is.

GI: (John described Uncle Vince very well. He lived until 81, was the patriarch of the whole family. Vince was loved by everyone, and never got over himself outliving my husband.)

JH: I understand you've got a lot of people, Gail.

GI: I know. (Laughing)

JH: You've got a lot of people there!

GI: Well, I AM getting older.

JH: Would you have one sister, please?

GI: My one of two sisters is very close to me, the other is not.

JH: Living?

GI: Yes.

JH: Just the one, please?

GI: Two

JH: Because Dad, I'm going to jump around with these guys, the father wants to acknowledge his girls. That's how I know there is more than you, and I'm sure there are boys. I'm also feeling tightness in the chest. Gail, I'm curious where the lung cancer was, emphysema?

GI: My husband died of lung cancer.

JH: Absolutely! There is also a folding of the flag, Gail, which always means to me someone had the military funeral.

GI: My husband did, Uncle Vince, Keven.

JH: Gail, you were together when he passed, correct?

GI: Yes.

JH: I don't know if he was your only man or if the two of you go way back because...he's here. <u>Yeah, yeah, I hear you.</u> He's making me – bless him – he's making me aware of "My Only Love." I'm hearing that song from Diana Ross, "My Endless Love."

GI: (Phil signed all of the cards he bought in the last few months with words like 'Forever,' 'Eternally.')

JH: Do you two go way back?

GI: Thirty-six years.

JH: Absolutely, darling. Absolutely. I understand. What did you do for him besides Christmas? There's a special dedication, which means you put a tree at the grave?

GI: Christmas and a tree is something that happens to me that is an ongoing ADC for us.

JH: From your husband?

GI: Yes.

JH: Absolutely, because he keeps... They know there is something about Christmas, but Christmas is so common to everyone. This has to be more than just Christmas.

GI: My daughter had it verified with a vision from his mother saying what we thought were ADCs were really from him, and they all think it's hilarious. It's a story with a frog.

JH: Okay, good. As long as you understand that, because it is a connection to Christmas, some confirmation. He's also making me aware, and I know I'm going fast, but this is all recorded anyway, so don't you worry. You'll be able to listen again, but it's just that I'm on a roll with you.

GI: I'm really from New York, so... (I was going to say I'm used to fast talking.)

JH: Alright, Gail, so you just gave it away. I was just going to ask why is your husband talking about New York. Gail, let's go back to the son-in-law. Did your daughter know you were going to have this conversation with me?

GI: Yes.

JH: Alright, okay. Gail, let's stick with him for a second, cause this is important for your daughter. <u>Alright, hmmmm.</u>

GI: She thought he would come through.

JH: Yes, is his boy older than eight?

GI: He's seven.

JH: Okay, because I don't know how old you are, how old the daughter is, but I do feel eight years old with his kid. He is very connected to his kid. Either the kid is dreaming of, and I know what he is going through, but with his passing, this was unexpected?

GI: Yes.

JH: Yeah, because, Gail, this is very strange. I'm getting a lot of question marks about his passing.

GI: There are.

JH: And he's not really talking about it. Gail, I don't want to make it fit, but can he take on some of the responsibility for his passing?

GI: Yes, he can.

JH: Alright, Gail you know where I'm going with that.

GI: Yes.

JH: So did he take his own life?

GI: Yes.

JH: Yeah, so if you were sitting here, I've got like fifteen question marks on my page. It's always a sign that they took their own life here. You know who's helping him out, Gail? It's your husband. Okay, I really feel, really feel it's your husband, and he's with the guys. You tell your daughter he's in the "Boys Club." Not a lot of confirmation here from him, because I think when someone takes their life, this is what just seems to work with me, people who take their lives are in the process of healing. So others come forward to help with the communication. Am I right in saying, Gail, that your son-in-law passes---- Is David connected, please, living or passed?

GI: My brother, David, living.

JH: Uh, I understand this. With your son-in-law, Gail is his head affected at all with the passing?

GI: Yes. You want to know what happened?

JH: ....was it a hanging?

GI: You got it.

JH: Hanging. Yes, hanging. He is taking responsibility for this, Gail. Sometimes I feel he tried to pull away at the last minute, or he tried to, but I do think he is taking on some responsibility. But I've got to tell you he is going through the healing process with the gentlemen over there. All your guys – not guides – on the other side. <u>Yeah, I understand that. Um-hum</u>

GI: I have chills going up and down me. (Keven was talking illegal drugs and was drinking when he hanged himself.)

JH: Is he also – your daughter, what is your daughter's name?

GI: Valerie.

JH: Oh. Remember I kept saying V? Okay, this is interesting, because V is not a common letter, like M or B. You know what I mean. Okay, there's the V. Probably. Do you know if Valerie, <u>yeah, I understand that</u>, she's in Maryland.

GI: Yes.

JH: Because he's saying "close to mom, close to mom."

GI: Fifteen minutes.

JH: Oh, that's close. And he's also making me aware – I usually don't like to do flowers, Gail, right? But do you know if his wife – your daughter, Valerie – planted a rose bush for him?

GI: I don't think she did. (Later there is a huge validation of another planting for him.)

JH: Okay, there is something about a flowering bush. When I get flowers, I don't like to do that, Gail, because we always get that and jewelry from people on the other side. There's something about the rose, unless there is a name, Rose. There's something about the rose and I also want Valerie to watch for blooming flowers, although this weather, it's been global warming, watch for the flowers. How long has he been gone?

GI: Less than a year.

JH: I want her not to just sit and watch for twenty-four hours, but about the blooming flower when it's not supposed to. It's almost like a rose blooming in December. That kind of feeling. See if that can be placed.

GI: (So far that doesn't strike a bell with us. It might be something coming up.)

JH: Gail, with your last name, and I don't like to look at a name, is there Italian blood?

GI: There is Italian blood in relatives, but not on my husband's side.

JH: Okay, the reason why I'm getting it is because I got the Vincent.

GI: He was always being mistaken for Italian. He was Lithuanian.

JH: Vinnie, Vincent is Italian to me, but is Anthony connected to you?

GI: Anthony, Tony, is Vince's brother.

JH: Absolutely! Okay, absolutely! Because I keep hearing Tony and – wait a minute – those are Italian names!

GI: Lithuanian.

JH: But really okay, me being half Italian. Vinnie, Tony, okay, that's fine. So Anthony is being acknowledged, also the name. I understand that. Yes! I hate to give the name John, but I'm getting it.

GI: My sister is married to a John. (I can't think of a John right now. Don't think it is connected to my brother-in-law.)

JH: Okay, that's alright. Gail, hmmm, your husband, gone more than two years?

GI: Yes.

JH: Are you still wearing the ring, please?

GI: You are seeing a ring?

JH: He's showing me a ring?

GI: (This part of the reading doesn't go anywhere, but I'll cut and paste the "Aha!" story about the ring.)

JH: Okay, because he's saying, mention the ring. I don't like when they give me that as evidence, because it's common and general, but he mentions the ring, the ring.

GI: I took his off in the hospital and wrapped it in a tissue and must have thrown it away with them.

JH: Okay, don't worry about it. It's more you than them suffering about it. They could give a toss. Okay, one second, Gail, is there a ring that you have, please, of your mother's with a missing stone? Just prongs.

GI: Hmmm. No, I don't.

JH: I'm hearing 'mention the ring with no stone.'

GI: There's one that I bought that is missing a stone.

JH: Okay, that's okay. That's alright.

GI: (I'm going to insert the story here about the ring with the missing stone. John Holland is an incredible, powerful medium and a very nice person. At one point he kept talking about me having a ring, given to me, that has a missing stone in it. He mentioned birth stone, engagement, etc. My mind went blank, and all I could remember is I do have a ring without a stone in my jewelry box. That wasn't it, and John moved on. That night I couldn't fall asleep. My body felt electrified and tense. About an hour later of not being able to relax, I received my "Aha!" moment. My body finally relaxed. About fifteen years ago I was sitting at my kitchen table chatting with my brother. I happened to glance at my engagement ring, and the diamond was missing! It was around Christmas time and I had been to several different stores. My brother helped me search my entire house, and took me to the stores. No stone anywhere. I went out to my car and checked everywhere I could see. It wasn't there. I felt devastated. My husband took me back to the store it came from and had another diamond put in it. The ring just didn't look or feel the same any more. Six months later I was vacuuming out my car and getting it ready to sell. Fate made me see something sparkle as it went into the bag. I took out the bag and dumped everything onto a paper. Yes, it was my diamond. My husband and I took the ring back to the store and had it mounted back in. The other diamond was traded for some very nice jewelry.)

JH: Gail, you are still in the house that you and your husband lived in, please?

GI: Yes, I am.

JH: Yes, because I'm saying to him a thousand times, did she move? He's making me aware, she's still in the house. <u>Okay, one second. Yes.</u> Your husband makes me aware, and I hope he pops in his name, makes me aware he was ready to go. Do you understand that?

GI: Yes.

JH: Yeah, I feel like he fought it. This is the gentleman with the lung cancer, correct?

GI: Yes.

JH: Fought it for awhile. Gail, when he was in his youth, was he a big boy?

GI: He was about 6'1", always slender.

JH: Right, okay, more taller than big. <u>Okay, one second.</u> Thank you, Gail. He passes in the house?

GI: No, he—

JH: That's okay, Gail. He was more home than in a hospice or hospital.

GI: Yes.

JH: That's okay, because when someone is convalescing, three months, four months, it's almost like he passes at home, because he spends more time at home before he goes. But he's making me aware – <u>yeah, I see you</u> – he's making me aware you were there when he passed, correct?

GI: Yes, we held hands and prayed—

JH: Okay, let him do his thing. Gail, he's making me aware because I'm saying "Talk about when you passed here." I'm getting him gently going, but he is making me aware – and I always get this, Gail – and this is what I am hearing. "Thank you for letting me go." Okay, so I don't know.

GI: That's a relief, because I had to make the decision.

JH: I feel like you talked him right to the other side. He followed your voice, went over, went, went.

GI: (I did tell him, after he fell into a coma, to go into the light. The Gemini in me couldn't help noticing he was staring at the television. "I said, "But not into the television." He would appreciate some humor.)

JH: He met up with Ann, Andrew, Andrea. 'I met up with Ann,' and I feel like it may go back now with you. I don't know if it's an old neighbor, and you've got this all written down.

GI: (I do have a book of family history written in it. Anthony, mentioned before, is the only person I can think of who would meet him.)

JH: <u>I understand.</u> Gail, how is your thyroid now?

GI: Hmmm, nothing that I know of, nothing.

JH: Do you have, Gail, remember this is not a prediction, do you have any throat issue going on, please?

GI: I have allergies all the time. There's always a problem with my throat.

JH: Would there be – I don't have allergies – can that affect the throat area? Oh, no, he's shaking his head. Don't go there. Someone in the family connected to him. This is husband. I don't know if someone has a scar on his throat or has had their thyroid taken out, or their thyroid looked at. Female. Is his sister still here?

GI: He has no sister, he has a cousin that is like a sister.

JH: Still here?

GI: Yes.

JH: Are you in touch with this woman?

GI: Yes.

JH: Just, you don't have to freak her out, just – Gail, has she had any, has she had her thyroid looked at? Is there any issue? Is she gaining an unbelievable amount of weight? Is there a weight fluctuation? Just see if that—

GI: Her name is Rose.

JH: Okay, cool, and that was like his sister?

GI: Yes.

JH: And see if the thyroid thing, and if she knows you are into this stuff, maybe she's not going to be freaked out. Just go slowly how you give the information. In other words, he's keeping an eye on her, okay?

GI: Is this a warning for her?

JH: More of a head's up. More of a caution, a warning is too graphic. <u>I understand.</u> Is Catherine his mother?

GI: (I checked with my brother-in-law, and yes, Rose has problems with her thyroid.) Catherine? Let me write down Catherine.

JH: It's either Caitlyn or Catherine, but on the other side. There's a lot of people between your husband, the uncle, it's like a family reunion. <u>One second....</u> You tell your daughter, Valerie, he knows, the son-in-law, the husband, this is not her fault. Gail, Okay, he knows it, but Gail, you know what – was there a separation between the two of them before this happened?

GI: Oh, yes, they had recently gotten divorced.

JH: Because I see an arrow going one way and an arrow going another way which means to me, you know, but this is not her going. This, I feel like this was planned out by him, and not for a long time. It was his choice. He takes responsibility and he is the one to deal with it now. It's nothing to do with her or the son. She is going to meet someone else, Gail, I'm telling you, and your grandson will have a father in his life.

GI: Oh, I am so happy to hear that.

JH: I really do feel that and I always like to back things up like that. A very strong Henry, Helen, Hank, big H, almost like up with the big V. That doesn't mean who it is, the H. It could still be a communication from the other side.

GI: (The H has to be Phil's mom. Her first name is Mary, second name Helen. She is powerful enough that she is the one who showed herself to my daughter and verified our frog ADCs are real.)

JH: Gail, are you a church goer?

GI: Yes, I am.

JH: Because your husband said, "I see her in church." I said, "Give me something more." Now are you a once-a-week church go-er?

GI: Once a week but also an EM, a Eucharist Minister and a hospital visitor.

JH: The reason why I'm saying that is when I get a really churchy church feeling, I want to say you are a church goer. A lot of people aren't, and that means to me you are involved in the church. And I know, after the fact, you told me the minister, but he makes me aware I have to put the whole church situation around you. Gail, is your husband – no, this could be the dad coming in here now. Is your dad or your husband the one with the hat? Dad or the husband wore the hat. Not baseball cap. It's more of a hat.

GI: Phil wore hats. He had a hat collection.

JH: Phil is who? Your husband?

GI: Okay, I gave you—

JH: That's okay, that's okay, because he kept tipping his hat to me. That means not baseball cap, but if he had a hat collection with the brims.

GI: He had a hat collection with the old fashioned brims. (Phil did collect baseball caps, but they were always the old square-looking style with a large brim.)

JH: A fedora thing, because he keeps tipping his hat. This is just more validation. <u>I understand that.</u> He wants to make me aware, he's not just your husband. I feel like a best friend with this guy.

GI: We were.

JH: And I'm not saying you were. You still are. Gail, now you sound pretty young to me, alright. But don't give me your age. Why is he concerned about your legs, or your foot, please?

GI: I'm not young, but I don't know.

JH: You're not having any circulation problem with, Gail, with something with your legs, or ankle, or something?

GI: Not that I'm aware of.

JH: Alright, don't freak out if you see something, just be forewarned, is to be forearmed. Wait a second. Make sure the tape is still going.... lovely. Hmmm, right so you and your husband met in New York?

GI: No, we didn't.

JH: No?

GI: Right here in Maryland.

JH: Would your – there's another New York connection that I'm supposed to talk about besides you being from there. Okay. Do you still have relatives there, Gail?

GI: I do have relatives there.

JH: Okay, Gail, I dunno, he's getting a – yeah, yeah. How long has he been gone, please?

GI: 2001.

JH: Has your daughter been to New York since he's passed, please?

GI: We've been up to New York several times.

JH: Yes, okay, 'cause he's saying to me, this is your husband, okay he's clear and to the point, okay, I don't feel like I can fool around with him, but I feel like he wants me to say exactly like he's giving it to me. He's saying no. 'Since I've been gone,' I saw at least your daughter in N.Y., okay, or the trip or trips to NY, okay. Oh! Did you catch the show, too? Did you catch a show while you were in NY?

GI: We went to see John Edward several times and I have a friend on Long Island.

JH: Okay, okay, that's fine.

GI: Oh, yes, we did go see a show, the Rockettes!

JH: 'Cause they said they caught a show. Alright, that's not so great evidence, Gail, because it is New York, but I do feel like you probably had an extra seat there, your husband right behind, watching.

GI: (New York City is where we spent our honeymoon at the World's Fair in 1965. My mother, father, one brother, myself, and two grandparents were born in New York.)

JH: <u>Yeah, I understand. Ah, really?</u> Hmmm, Gail, would your husband have loved babies.

GI: Oh, yes!

JH: Most guys are like, they can't deal with it, but he's making me feel—

GI: He had his grandson and loved him dearly.

JH: Somebody, he has a baby there with him, Gail. I think it might have been a newborn or one who never made it here. Okay, he's got one in his arms and I'm thinking, why doesn't a woman have that, and he says, 'I'm good with kids.' And this may sound strange, Gail, but sometimes when they go over, they can teach, they can do whatever they want. I really feel your husband is somehow helping babies. I don't know why I'm getting it, but something about helping babies.

GI: My daughter miscarried several times.

JH: Okay, hold on Gail, let me flip this tape. I don't want to miss anything.

GI: I've been waiting four years.

JH: He makes me aware, he makes me aware, alright, okay, this is your husband. He's got all these guys, and I feel like, I don't feel the mother, but I can't validate her until she gives me something, but I just feel her energy in the back.

GI: She was like that. (I'm pretty sure John is not talking about my mother now, but Phil's mother. His mother has a lot of energy over there. This next part of the reading is astounding. I didn't know how much so until my daughter listened with me. It wasn't about who I thought it was.)

JH: Hmmm? <u>Really?</u> Now, I don't know if this is a dedication or, Gail, or this is something – was there any type, first of all just say yes or no, was there any type of tree planted for the husband?

GI: Uh, no.

JH: You know what he's giving me, Gail, was there any type of ceremony? I don't know if he was alive for this, was there any ceremony in memory of your husband or your son-in-law in a park, outdoors in nature? I feel like he is giving me trees. I don't, because, I don't want to. Just say yes or no to the dedication. I just feel like there was something done outdoors for him, but it was more like a memorial.

GI: He had a military funeral but I can't think of anything else.

JH: I just feel like, in Maryland, in Maryland, is there, where you live, a favorite park where you used to go for cookouts or something?

GI: I'm getting a blank here. Maybe when I hear the tape it will come back.

JH: Okay, I just feel like I'm here, Gail. Is MacArthur's Park in New York, like that song MacArthur's Park is melting in the snow. It's either MacArthur's Park, the name MacArthur, or he's just showing me the event at the park, but I feel it's a place with picnics, a picnic table. Where you could do the grill, and there might be a lake there, also, that's involved.

GI: I have a block on it right now.

JH: That's alright, okay.

GI: (Valerie and I listened to the tape together. This part had her crying. Joey loved going to a park near their home with his dad. John described the park exactly, including the lake. When Keven crossed over, Valerie's co-workers took up a collection and had some trees planted as a memorial to Keven, in that park. I believe they are near the lake.)

JH: Gail, are you working?

GI: No, not at this time. I recently retired and worked for many years.

JH: Okay. He still – to me – he's saying you are still working. That could be how busy you are, but, Gail, who was the – this could be your daughter, I'm not sure – did someone have a supermarket connection? Supermarket. Did anyone work out like a checkout person or something?

GI: My son.

JH: Yeah, because I'm seeing ca-ching, ching. You know, where they do the checkout and that means supermarket. So wherever this is, your son was a checkout person.

GI: He started out that way.

JH: That's right and your son is still there.

GI: (My son worked in a large grocery store while he went to college. He worked his way up into management and later into a nice government position.)

JH: That's right and your son is still here. <u>Yeah, uh hm. Lovely. Yeah, yeah, yeah, I understand that.</u> Your son has children, Gail, correct?

147

GI: Yes.

JH: Yeah, will you please tell your son, he knows he's a grandfather again.

GI: Thank you. I will tell him.

JH: I get 50/50 on this. Was it a boy, the second one?

GI: No, the first one.

JH: Okay, as long as you know. Please tell your son. Is that Steven?

GI: No.

JH: Okay, there's a Scott or a Steven I'm supposed to acknowledge.

GI: That's the nephew's name that Keven treated like another son.

JH: Are you still doing the crossword puzzles?

GI: Occasionally. He (Phil) was the crossword puzzle person.

JH: Okay, okay, because the crossword puzzle, I don't do those, Gail. I can do Tic Tac Toe, but I — He's talking about crossword puzzles, so I – it's almost like you looking over his shoulder or him looking over yours, because that is what he is giving me. Umm, I understand that, clever man. He makes me aware, too, Gail, would he have known how to handle a deck of cards?

GI: Ohhhh, cards are HUGE.

JH: Yes, because he's saying – he's quite cocky, alright. He is a love though, Gail. I've got to tell you this, this is the kind of guy you could have a beer with or a cup of tea or coffee, but he is making me aware and says, "I'm awfully good with cards." So I say okay, that's cool, that's cool, and you know what I keep getting, Gail, over and over again? This is a different kind of name. Is somebody called Gus or Gussie?

GI: (Like I said, cards are huge. Most of that group over there got together frequenty to play penny ante poker from the time I met Phil. They also loved pinochle. One by one they crossed over until just Phil, his Uncle Vince and brother, Ted, were left. They continued playing until Phil was no longer able to. The name Gus is driving me crazy because I feel I should know who it is. It's just hiding somewhere in my memory.) That's alright.

JH: That's okay, Gail. Did he take you to California?

GI: Yes, he did.

JH: Because he's making me aware, remember our trip to California. I don't know if this was business or pleasure. Yeah, because you are in Maryland, he's making me draw the map of California. Oh, did you? Did you also go to Arizona in the same trip?

GI: The same trip we went to Las Vegas.

JH: Okay, Las Vegas, Nevada. 'Cause he's making me aware, and I never know, Gail, is Las Vegas considered Arizona or Nevada?

GI: Nevada.

JH: It is Nevada, it is, but he is taking me to two locations, California and I said Arizona. No, no, no. Oh, clever, sorry, my correction. I love when they correct me. Have you done Sedona?

GI: Yes.

JH: Sorry, he's telling me, this is your husband, "I took her to California. Now, I didn't say Vegas, I told you to go to Arizona." Alright, then he showed me the red rocks, which means to me Sedona, which I've never been to. Did you go there without him, though?

GI: No, we went together.

JH: Okay, that's cool. See, so he took you to California, nice guy, then, Gail. Takes you to California and Sedona. Oh, you went together. Who else went with you, please?

GI: We went, we did a lot of trips. California was our last vacation.

JH: Okay, see, Gail, they take that with them.

GI: He was going through all our vacations, just before he went.

JH: Looking at all the pictures, which is beautiful.

GI: (John asked who went with us. I remembered the trips were bus tours and a lot of people went with us.)

JH: Gail, in your house, where is the rainbow prism thing?

GI: (John goes on awhile trying to get the rainbow connection to me, but I couldn't connect with it. There IS a big rainbow connection to my son's father-in-law, who died a month before Phil did. Rainbows were showing up often and everywhere. I would get calls and hear stories about the rainbows showing up.)

JH: Either he sent a rainbow when you asked for it, but there is a definite rainbow connection, and I don't do rainbows, butterflies or foofoo, unless there is a Dorothy or Judy in your family. Then I would get the Wizard of Oz.

GI: There is a rainbow connection with my son and father-in-law.

JH: As long as you know I'm not just throwing it out there. You say, well, I used to have those (prisms), it's easy for me to say, that's it. No, they are making it bigger than that. You know what he's' making me aware of, too – this is your husband now taking over Gail. Okay? <u>Ah. Yeah.</u> What is his name, please?

GI: Philip.

JH: Ah, Philip, that's right, you said that. Gail, he makes me aware, one of the choices of deciding to leave, they always do this, Gail, and I'm supposed to reiterate this. When they can't be the husband, the father, the grandfather to the best of their ability, usually it's a man thing. Some women can last sickly much longer, but when he couldn't be the man, the husband, the father in the way he wanted to be, that's when he knew it was time to go. He can do more there physically than you know. He can appear physically. Do you understand that?

GI: Yes, I know exactly what you mean.

JH: Yup, you know what he is making me aware, Gail, you'll say no to this but did you go to the UK?

GI: UK? Yes, we went to the UK.

JH: Okay, he is showing me Big Ben. Alright, that always means to me, going to the UK. Did you go just once?

GI: England itself, only once.

JH: He makes me aware, I don't know if you loved it so much you wanted to go back, but he is giving me the Big Ben sign, which means to me there is some connection to the UK. So that's good the two of you did this travel.

GI: We loved traveling when we could afford it.

JH: You know what I'm getting, too, Gail? In my room, currently I have a candle lit here. Who's the cigar smoker? Or pipe, this is not cigarettes. I got kind of a lightness smell, so I know it's not cigarettes. There's definitely a cigar sweet Tobacco.

GI: His father was a cigar and pipe smoker.

JH: Big time! Yeah. Also I like the way your husband works, good communicator. Gail, that means you, too. Sometimes they're quieter here, but they get louder there. But sometimes I like it when I think they are a good communicator. He's telling me to go to my middle name and to just use it. Albert.

GI: Yes, I just heard about your middle name.

JH: There's an Albert connection, or an Al, or Allen, or Alice.

GI: (I couldn't think of it right the, but there are several men named Vince there. The big V - Vince's middle name is Albert.)

JH: Okay, Gail, I know you said you were older, but you don't sound it to me, darling, neither does your spirit. I feel it here. <u>I understand.</u> You know the son-in-law, Gail, does this happen in the garage?

GI: Yes.

JH: Because I'm saying back to you, my friend. What else? Because when I talk to you, I'm talking to your husband. I'm talking to him like you shout it out on different wave lengths, I'm saying, where did this happen? Give me more validations. Give me more validations. I said, 'did you do this in the house?' He makes me aware, in the garage, in the garage. I also have to say, Gail, I don't want to pop in another name, but is Robert connected to you? Or Bobby? You know, when I get RT, it always means Ruth or Robert. There's an RT connection I need to give you. <u>One second...</u> You know, Gail, too, about your son-in-law. Sometimes, Gail, when someone takes their own life, there are signs of it like they had mental illness. Am I right there were no signs of this?

GI: No, there were plenty. He was bipolar.

JH: Alright, was he okay for a while?

GI: Yes, when he was good, he was wonderful.

JH: Because I feel like, I just feel like, I know he's bipolar, you are telling me, but I feel surprised when this happened. It is a surprise when someone passes tragically, this way, but sometimes it is expected. I don't expect this from him.

GI: You know, we didn't.

JH: Like someone who's not threatening it at all, but someone who is threatening it all the time, you say, yeah, they used to say it. That goes back to her thing, this is not her fault. <u>Yes, I understand that.</u> I forgot to tell you, because this is adamant, he's been gone almost a year. The dog has passed since he's been gone?

GI: The dog? My dog?

JH: Yes, okay. You lost your dog, because he's saying, "I've got the dog that passed," which means that the dog is with me. It has to be the dog joined him afterwards, or joined the family after his passing.

GI: Yes. (Has to be Gizmo.)

JH: Talk to Valerie about Niagara Falls. He's mentioning the falls. Could be Niagara or some other nice beautiful place where there are falls. Valerie, remember the falls.

GI: (Our whole family visited Niagara Falls and stayed on the Canadian side. They were beautiful and inspiring. Valerie could not think of a place she and Keven went to that had falls.)

JH: I've never been to Niagara Falls. Niagara Falls means nothing to me, so I've got to give it just as I'm getting it.

GI: You should go. It's nice.

JH: Oh, <u>um hmmm, one second.</u> Yes, is Valerie in a condo?

GI: No.

JH: Is she in the same house? Has she moved, 'cause I know you said that separation. Has she moved?

GI: No.

JH: Okay, that's fine. I got a condo. I moved from a house to a condo. So she's moved since he passed. Good thing. This is a good thing.

GI: (Valerie bought her house while Keven was still alive. He had a chance to see it, but not often because you didn't know if he would have a bad personality change. She made sure he had no key.)

JH: He talks about the nurse, the nurse, the nurse. There is a nurse, but I don't think he knew her as well. Who is the nurse, Gail?

GI: My brother is married to a nurse.

JH: Living?

GI: Yes.

JH: That's fine. I have to emphasize that nurse here. There's a hello to the nurse. May not be coming from him, but I got to acknowledge the nurse.

GI: Wonderful nurse.

JH: Wait, wait, wait, is she more than an RN, please?

GI: Yes.

JH: Okay. That's her, because I don't want you to feed that to me, because I'm saying quick, and he says to advance her, which means to me head nurse, specialized in something, not just an RN. Okay, what does she do?

GI: She is a head nurse.

JH: Okay, it's almost like a RN with stripes. Like the sergeant. Okay.

GI: (My brother finally married the nurse he has loved for thirty years. She was at my husband's side on the day he crossed, and called us over to say he was going. Phil and all of us love her.

John goes on here talking about the people Phil is hanging out with. Phil mentions me knowing a judge or someone on the Supreme Court. John is sure of it, but I don't think I do. At least at this time.)

JH: How old are you, Gail?

GI: 62.

JH: God! You're old! Right! If you had said 92, I'd say, okay, well, but he talks about meeting up with the judge. I feel like your husband is a communicator for other people.

GI: (John talks more about the people Phil is with. He says, 'just like you're in Pam's group – FriendsCommunities – I feel like he may be part of the group, too.' John talks about Phil being goofy with him. Yes, my dear husband could be goofy; otherwise he couldn't have survived living with me.)

JH: He's goofy with me, too. He's showing me, Elvis, Elvis.

GI: He was told he looked like Elvis all the time.

JH: At your house in Maryland, do you have a nice sized yard, please?

GI: Yes, he loved his yard.

JH: 'Cause he's taking me to the yard. He's talking about.... I don't know if this is significant. While he was here, or you did it afterwards, did you have to cut down the tree?

GI: Ah, yes.

JH: Okay, what is that, Gail? Why does it happen? The reason I'm asking is I just want to see how he is validating. Does it happen because it's a dead tree? Gave too much shade? Does it happen after he passes?

GI: It happens after he passes. It died.

JH: Okay, I feel like that's a sad thing. Okay. I feel not that he is sad about it, but like, we had to cut down the tree. So did the tree have some age to it?

GI: It was one he planted.

JH: That would be it. Yes, that would be it. Okay. And this tree is in the yard, yes? 'Cause he's saying, go to the yard, tell her I know about the chopping down of the tree.

GI: It was in the front yard and was a beautiful blue spruce.

JH: That's nice. That's okay.

GI: I killed it.

JH: What did you say it was, a spruce goose blue?

GI: It's an evergreen tree and they call it a blue spruce because it has a blue color to it. I killed some weeds.

JH: And you took the tree with it.

GI: I didn't mean to kill the tree.

JH: (Laughing audibly.) That's okay. Don't worry about it. Don't worry about it. Trust me, you are the one that's here, that's still here with this. I understand. With the greatest respect, darling, although it's still winter, I know you're in Maryland, are you having a squirrel issue?

GI: Oh, lots and lots of squirrels, but it's my fault. I'm feeding them.

JH: Okay, because he's (laughing), Gail, you know what he's saying. This is what I'm getting from him. "What are you doing?" When you were here would you still feed the squirrels? He would say something or he is just commenting on the squirrels because this happened after he passes.

GI: He may be commenting on the squirrels. He would put up little barriers for the squirrels.

JH: Yes, yes, to keep them from eating bird seed or something, and you are feeding them?

GI: I'm feeding the birds.

JH: Alright, this is just validation.

GI: (It's impossible to try feeding just the birds. Squirrels are smart and get past most barriers.)

JH: Gail, he's a bit of a romantic, by the way.

GI: I know.

JH: Okay, let me see if I'm right with this. I'm hoping you say yes, 'cause this would be beautiful. Did you go to Paris?

GI: Yes, we did.

JH: LOVELY! Because he's showing me, because he's making me aware he's such a lady's man with you, such a romantic, and he shows me the Eiffel Tower.

GI: Yes, we went up the Eiffel Tower.

JH: Absolutely! Who knows, you probably kissed up there, too. He's making me aware he wanted to give you the best in life, okay, because of what you gave him. Alright, and he's making me aware of the romance and the love still between the two of you. It's like, look, you went to Paris. You can't be any more romantic than the city of Paris.

GI: (Our son and daughter went with us and we walked all over the city. It was a wonderful experience. This next part does not apply to us but could apply to my daughter and Keven, or my son and daughter-in-law.)

JH: Really! God, you have traveled, Gail. You did New Orleans, Mardi Gras?

GI: No, we haven't done Mardi Gras.

JH: Is there any tie to the south of New Orleans?

GI: No.

JH: I feel very southern with you, or some people.

GI: Florida?

JH: Florida is different for me. I get that when ah start tawking laack this. New Orleans, Georgia, Mississippi. I want you to remember that.

GI: Okay.

JH: Something about the south, but it's not like watching a TV program, Gail, it has to be more significant, and it could be a trip coming up. As you know, as you know, doesn't mean for you to make it happen.

GI: I'm going on a Caribbean cruise with you.

JH: Well, yeah, that's the Caribbean and that's south, but when I start tawking laack this, this means to me it's on the southern connection – but on a side note, Gail, what I'm also getting, ummm, and this comes up, but I don't think, I don't believe it's your husband. Who's the alcoholic?

GI: My father. (My son-in-law, who committed suicide, was also an alcoholic. I do not drink alcohol, because I'm afraid I will like it too much.)

JH: Okay, because that kept coming in and I'm like, I'm not going to that yet, because this reading is so positive, so positive – not that the alcohol can be a negative, but I keep getting that alcohol condition. If your dad was an alcoholic, or is, then that would come up here. But you are in a process, Gail, too. This is coming to me in an intuitive level. You've got a lot of endings and starts this year, like God, that's ending. Not every ending, Gail, means a door closes, it means watch for the window that's going to open. I've got a lot of doors closing, but a lot of them opening. Some people are always stuck in a nothing happening. I don't feel that way with you. Doors closing and other doors opening, constantly, one after the other.

GI: (John gives me an intuitive warning about some personal problems.)

End of transcript

CHAPTER NINE - SYNCHRONICITY

Merriam-Webster defines synchronicity as "the coincidental occurrence of events and especially psychic events (as similar thoughts in widely separated persons or a mental image of an unexpected event before it happens) that seem related but are not explained by conventional mechanisms of causality – used especially in the psychology of C. G. Jung." Then there's coincidence – "the occurrence of events that happen at the same time by accident but seem to have some connection: *also;* any of these occurrences." I'm willing to bet that we toss off as coincidence instances of contact from the other side. Some may consider the following as just that. In my opinion, the determining factor is whether it happens to <u>you</u>.

****

Paper or plastic? No question this time:

My dad, Timothy Mitchell, passed in 1998 from an unexpected massive heart attack. He was only 48 years old. My husband and I were expecting our second son in July and Dad's death was devastating. He had held our family together. He was our rock. I remember waking up the morning after he passed and feeling as though I'd been punched in the stomach, truly feeling physical pain, and then just sobbing uncontrollably the whole day. Never in my life had I felt so empty, despite the precious new life growing in my belly.

Time passed and it did get easier to function. I started following the work of well-known mediums, meditating regularly and becoming more spiritual. It became my quest to find out if my dad was alright, and if he was, then where was he and why wasn't he communicating with me?

One evening while I was washing dishes after dinner, I was talking to my dad, asking him if he could please send me some kind of concrete, tangible sign that I could not dispute, to tell me that he was okay, and that I was on the right spiritual path. I was at a point where I wanted badly to believe that there was an afterlife, and that Dad did really see what was happening, while at the same time really questioning it all.

I finished the dishes and made my husband's lunch for work the next day. His lunch bag was nowhere to be found, so I grabbed a plastic grocery bag, put his lunch in it and placed it in the refrigerator.

Later that night I returned to the fridge to get something else out. I gasped as I glanced at the bag containing my husband's lunch. There, printed in bright red, bold capital letters, was TIMOTHY MITCHELL, my father's name! This was not something in someone's handwriting, but printed by a commercial printer. This was my tangible sign! Dad gave me his seal of approval, alright!

Dawn Jones

Followup: This is one of those times when someone with a skeptical bent might pronounce this pure coincidence. I beg to differ.

****

Snapshots in time:

Since my mother-in-law passed, the first Thanksgiving without her physical presence was hard for all of us, my husband Mark, especially. Each and every day since she passed, as he heads out the door to work, Mark's first morning ritual is to look to the sky and say, "Good morning, Mom." The only people who know this are Mark and myself, and we have never talked about it in front of the kids.

A few weeks before, my father-in-law gave us a beautiful pewter Christmas ornament with two angels on the sides with her picture inside it. On Thanksgiving morning I reminded Mark to hang it on the tree before my father-in-law came over. He asked me to do it, but I didn't because I felt like he had to do this himself. So I set it aside and continued preparing our meal, and turned up the radio as I worked.

A while later, Mark came downstairs and took the ornament from its box. He had it in his hand, ready to hang on the tree, and at that exact moment, we hear, "I need a sign to let me know you're here," – the song, "Calling All Angels," by Train, playing on the radio. We had goose bumps. As we stood there in awe of the moment, Justin, our five-year-old son, comes happily running up and in a sing-song voice says, "Dad, Grandma is saying something to me in my head. She says 'Good morning, Mark.'"

As we talked about this and had a moment to process what had happened, and after thanking my mother-in-law, Connie, for that wonderful message, I gently asked my father, who had passed years before, "Hey, Dad, I know you're okay, but can you say hello to us today and let us know you're around?"

Later when John, my father-in-law, came over, he surprised us with another angel ornament. My dad's photo was in it this time. Unknown to John, the photos in both ornaments were taken on the same day at the same party, and this just happened to be my favorite photo of my dad. So I guess they are still at the same party.

Dawn Jones

Holidays, especially the first after the loss of a loved one, can be difficult, to say the least. But considering even the remote possibility that those loved ones are still with us, still concerned for us, it is that much more important that we continue our holiday traditions, perhaps set a place for them at the table,

drink a toast to them or simply remember previous holidays and good times with them. They'll be celebrating the event along with us. Believe it. Know it.

****

Directing from the wings:

My mother-in-law passed away in 2004. My sister-in-law believes in after death signs, but we decided to test it. We asked my mother-in-law to give us a sign. Her favorite song was "How Great Thou Art," so we asked her to have that song played somewhere to show us she was around. Since neither of us really attended church, we thought it would be interesting to see how she would make that happen.

We were at our niece's wedding months later and one of the songs she picked was "How Great Thou Art." This niece does not live near me and had no knowledge of the significance of the song. Also it's not a typical wedding song. We even asked her if she knew that was Grandma's favorite song, and she said no, she just liked it. We both figured it was my mother-in-law's way of saying she was at her granddaughter's wedding. The interesting thing is that she also made sure both her daughter and I were in the same place when the song was played.

Deb Tanner

Bottom line: It takes a certain amount of moxy to test the belief in communication from beyond life. Even then, should we get the results we demanded, our first reaction is usually to rationalize, squeeze it into one of the boxes with which we're more familiar and call it a coincidence or pure happenstance. Deb and her sister-in-law did neither. They asked for a mini-miracle and they got it. As far as they were concerned, they received the proof they'd requested.

****

Kelly Alaska had always had a feeling that her grandmother was "out there" watching over her, but had never really looked for signs or any sort of validation. Like many of us, she may have been straddling the line between a soft belief and a firm "knowing." So her grandmother gave her a gentle nudge.

I was having one of those bad days when life just caught up with me and I eventually gave in to a pity party for one. There I was, sitting in the middle of my bed well into twenty minutes of just letting it all out – worrying about everything, thinking too much, and sobbing like life was over.

And then all of a sudden, this calm came over me. It was odd because I really felt like I was deserving of this cry fest and wasn't doing anything to stop it. But this calm came over me and the tears stopped much more quickly than they'd started. I just sat there feeling giddy for a minute, and then realized I had been sitting with my chin resting on my fist and my thumb gently rubbing my lips. I thought *how odd. I've never made this gesture before in my life.* Normally I'm a nail biter.

Almost before I could get the thought to process in my brain, I got this picture in my head of my grandmother. My grandmother had passed away years before, but this image of her played in my mind of her driving me, in the back seat while I was thirteen. Her thumb was caressing the steering wheel. I hadn't thought of that gesture in years and years, but here I was mimicking that exact caress.

I know in my heart that Grandma was there with me, helping me, easing my soul. I didn't have any answers to my worries, but I was calm and wasn't worried about what tomorrow would bring. I felt relaxed and convinced that the future would unfold as it should with or without my pity party. Now I know this could be thought of as a self-indulged soothing act. But what's important is that I KNOW in my heart. How well I know me and the peace it brought to me in a much needed time of my life.

Kelly Alaska

Followup: With that simple gesture came so much: calm, peace and knowing. It was also a reminder to pay attention to signs Kelly would probably not have noticed before. And she kept it to herself for a while, not because of concern about what others might think. It was hers, her experience, her contact from her grandmother and too special to share. She eventually told a few members of her family and would later discuss it with others, some of whom reacted negatively. With her mother, a bond was created, their shared belief that Kelly's grandmother is still around. So as far as Kelly is concerned, she received far more than that one simple sign.

****

Licorice and love:

My sister and I went to Santa Fe to go shopping. Before coming home, we stopped in at Harry & David gourmet food store. I was looking at the bite-sized licorice and bought some. I told the clerk," My mom loved licorice, except she liked the long red strands."

On the drive home we talked about Mom a lot, reminiscing about our childhood. And we ate that licorice like there was no tomorrow.

When I dropped my sister off at her home, she went to open her door, then waved at me, reached down to pick something up, and came to the car. It was a dime, one of our signs from Mom. I told my sister, "She's telling us 'Hi.'"

This morning when I woke up I was thinking of my mom. My husband went outside. When he came back in, he asked, "Is this yours?" In his hand was a long, black strand of licorice. I asked, "Where did you get that?" He answered, "It was just laying there in the driveway."

I started laughing and said, "It's Mom, it's Mom, and she must be telling me good morning." I was more than excited, I was ecstatic.

Then to be honest, I started doubting. I thought, well, if it had been red, then I'd know for sure. Halloween was two weeks ago; maybe a kid dropped the licorice.

But this strand of licorice was as fresh as fresh could be and it wasn't <u>my</u> licorice because mine was small, fat, and bite-sized.

Thanks, Mom. I love you, too.

Kelly Kasza

Followup: This experience occurred more than a year and a half after her mother's transition, and Kelly can still remember feeling warm and fuzzy, as if her mom was still nearby. It had no great impact on her life, because Kelly was already firm in her belief in the survival of the soul. Over the years, she has had a number of messages from her mother, as well as her dad, who crossed over more recently, and has been able to share her experiences with the rest of her family, as well as close friends.

From Kelly: "If this particular ADC did anything, it was confirmation of my KNOWING that all who cross over can and will communicate if we are open to hearing/seeing." Her knowing has served her well.

****

Grandparents again, every bit as caring and committed as they had been when they were here. And every bit as imaginative. This one for a grandson:

My son was sad that all his grandparents died before he entered college. From 2002 to 2006 we had lost three parents. He felt that they never got to see how well he had done in high school or to know where he was accepted at college. He's a scientific kid and doesn't always accept signs. So <u>I</u> picked one. I told him a sign from the grandparents would be something relating to games they used to play with him. I picked Yahtzee or Skippo. If they knew what was going on with him, they would send him that sign.

We were driving him off to college and had borrowed my sister-in-law's van to accommodate all the stuff. She had cleaned it thoroughly before giving it to us. When we stopped on the way to get something to eat, my son said, "Now even <u>I</u> have to admit this is weird!" He held up a Yahtzee sheet he'd found on the floor of the van. My sister-in-law swears they took everything out of the van and cannot understand where than came from. I know where it came from!

Deb Tanner

Bottom line: It was Deb who selected a sign for her son. Of any number of things she could have chosen, she narrowed it down to games her son and his grandparents had played together. And that's precisely what her son received. Further proof that our loved ones pay attention and respond to something that's important to us. How about that!!

****

Another gran's very special gift:
A little less than twenty-four hours after my grandmother passed, my sister-in-law and I believe we received signs from her. My sister-in-law had cared for her for the last five years of her life and they were very close. My grandmother considered her another granddaughter.

My sister-in-law felt she received a gift from Grandmother by way of a phone call from a daughter she'd given up for adoption more than twenty-three years before. The phone call came just hours after Grandmother's passing on September 24th, which was also the birthday of my sister-in-law's daughter. Coincidence or synchronicity?

Lori Messer

Followup: As far as Lori's concerned, the timing of that landmark call leaves no doubt in her mind that her grandmother set that up. Even if her niece had her mom's phone number for a while, or had just received it, the fact that she called on her birthday and her great-grandmother's day of departure from this life Lori considers no coincidence. And I, for one, won't argue with her.

****

TAJ 25 in 2003:

My whole family had been spending a week on Cape Cod for about the last seventeen years. Last year was tough because my mom was so sick, and this year was tough because she'd no longer with us. She had passed away in October of 2002. This vacation was so important to her, because it was her whole family – my three brothers and their families, Mom, Dad when he was alive, and me – in one house for a week. We have a blast.

This year I was having a really tough time. Every time I attempted to do the things that Mom and I did, just the two of us, I just had no desire. This one day I decided enough was enough and I was going to go to some of our favorite shops while the others were all at the beach.

I got in my car and headed out. I came to the first shop and I just couldn't do it. I drove past it. I started thinking about Mom and talking to her, apologizing for not being able to do this yet. I promised her that I was okay and that I would be able to enjoy these things again some day. I was crying as I was "talking," and I just kept driving.

The next thing I realized, I was on the road to Rock Harbor, one of our favorite places. It's absolutely beautiful. I was like, "Oh, great!" but figured, what the heck. I drove into the parking lot and parked facing the water. I sat in my car and just let go. I let myself feel everything I had been fighting all week, all the loneliness, etc. When I was done, I composed myself and left. I drove to our favorite place for chowder, bought a cup, ate it in the car, and headed back to the house.

On my way I remembered that we needed a couple of things at the store, and stopped at the Eastham Superette, where we always shopped. The whole time my mom was still very much on my mind. When I got back into the car and pulled out onto the side road, waiting for the light, I looked at the car in front of me and the license place read "TAJ 25." My mom's favorite place in the whole world was the Taj Mahal in Atlantic City! I was blown away. It was something very special to us, and we always referred to it as the "Taj." We went several times a year for about as long as we'd been going to Cape

Cod. In fact, I took her to the Taj about a month before she passed that last fall.

I was really taken aback by this. I just knew it was a sign from Mom. When I read that John Edward was going to be in Atlantic City, I couldn't help but wonder if he would be at the Taj – I knew he'd been there before – and was Mom trying to tell me something more than just that she was with me.

Mary Ellen Gray

More about the Taj Mahal Mom:
A group of my friends that I met through the Taj Mahal casino site, and who all live out of town, had set up a bulletin board so we could get together and chat. The guy who maintained the site decided that it would be nice to add some images in dedication to my mom. They all knew her well. I signed on to check it out one morning and he had an image of a Celtic cross and some doves. The cross looked almost identical to one my mom had on her living room wall. A friend of my brother-in-law hand carves them and my brother and his wife had given it to my mother a couple of years before.

I asked my friend if he could tell me where he'd gotten the image. He sent me the link to the page where he'd found it. I clicked on it and, sure enough, it was the Web page of my brother-in-law's friend. I told my friend and it blew his mind. He said he just did a search for "Irish cross" and pulled up this guy's home page, out of all the hits there must be out there on the Web. As I told my friends, John Edward says, "There are no coincidences."

Mary Ellen Gray

Bottom line: The reaction of Mary Ellen's friends is a testament to her mother. She was clearly well-loved. And she was probably delighted to have one of the images she held closest to her heart among those included on the group's Taj Mahal casino Web site. Mary Ellen is right. There are no coincidences.

****

Sarah's dad comes through:

My father passed when I was eight and he's been sending me ADCs pretty much my whole life. It was Saturday afternoon and I decided to go grocery shopping instead of wasting my Sunday after church doing it, since it usually takes me three hours or so. The weather was fine when I left the house, but it was summer and as usual with the South and the heat, we can have a thunderstorm very quickly, usually in the late afternoon. While in the store, I heard the thunder and decided to get my umbrella out of my car before it started its downpour.

When I walked out and looked at those clouds, they made me nervous, they were so black. When I got back inside, the clouds opened up and the rain was coming down sideways! The power was fading in and out. The crackling of lightning was all around us. As luck would have it, I only had one more thing to get on my list or I would have stayed shopping through that storm. I am so glad I carry a golf-size umbrella because I really needed it. I barely got wet and was quickly in my car. When I started my car, I grabbed the rosary that my sister purchased for me at the Vatican and blessed for me by Pope Benedict, and a necklace my husband had gotten for me in Mexico that has a cross with a cherub holding a guitar, which reminds me of my father. I said a prayer and asked both of them to guide me home safely amid this storm.

I could barely see two inches in front of me and the lightning was striking within yards of my car. The hair on the back of my neck was beginning to stand up. From the grocery store to my house was less than a mile, but for the first time ever, I really thought I was not going to make it.

I asked my father was he going to protect me or be there if lightning struck my car. That's how scared I was. Within seconds, Psalm 23 started going over and over in my head: *yea, though I walk through the valley of the shadow of death, I shall fear no evil, for Thou art with me: Thy rod and Thy staff they comfort me.* With extreme caution I drove as fast as I could on rain-soaked roads, determined to get home.

I pulled in on my street and lightning still clashed all around me. I swore it hit a transformer above my car, but I was not going to stop. I could see my house and I was going to make it. I pulled into my driveway, opened my garage door, ran up to my bedroom, and cried for ten minutes straight. I was shaking from head to toe. My husband told me the power in the house came on just as I pulled into the driveway, which is why my garage door opener had worked, and went back out as I came in the house.

Psalm 23 was my father's favorite passage in the bible. I hadn't thought of that passage in years. I hadn't heard it said out loud since he read it to me. Before I was three years old, I could recite it word for word. He and I used to sit together and practice it. He always told me that whenever I needed anything from God, to think of this passage and I would find answers. That Saturday I found answers not only from God but from him as well.

Every February 1st I dread, as anyone can imagine. It's my dad's D-Day. This marked his twenty-second year of being on the other side. Every year I tell myself it's going to be better and sometimes it is and sometimes it's not. A week before the day I start to get knots in my stomach, so the hours before I go to choir practice, while I sit down for dinner with my family, I quietly ask my dad to start sending his signs to help me through this time. That night at church, my choir director brought out a song that we have sung a lot lately, but he says he was drawn to sing tonight: "How Beautiful Heaven Must Be." I smiled as tears started rolling down my face.

Another sign: that Sunday at church I was helping children make cards for people who were sick and a child I don't know asked if he could make one for his mom. Something just told me to tell him yes. He looked at me and told me his mom was in Heaven. I hugged him and told me my dad was, too, and his mommy would love his card.

That Wednesday came and it was D-Day. I woke up at 7:36 a.m. to the sound of a man's voice in my room. To me it didn't sound like my father's, but it had been so long I wouldn't know. My husband works out of town, so I know it wasn't him. I hope it was Dad.

When I took my daughter to school that day, I saw a repair truck next door that said, "DADS' Repair." That night was choir practice and again he comes through. We sang "Remember Him." This time I couldn't do it. I sang as much as I could, but basically just listened. I came home that night, and "O Brother, Where Art Thou?" was on TV (which I swear is about my dad's side of the family) and I thanked him for letting me know he's okay and that he still loves me. A father's love is unbreakable and he proves that to me every year.

When my dad passed, I not only lost him but his family, too, as it was a family member that shot him. I think it hurt them too much to see my brother or me, since we look just like my dad. I lost contact with them for a long time.

When I had my first child I realized how important it was for me and my son to have them in our lives. I swallowed my pain and started reaching out to them. I had only really been able to reach out to my grandmother and grandpa before he passed. I'd spoken a few times with my uncles and aunts.

Fast forward to a few weeks ago. John Edward was coming to Atlanta. I had great tickets meant for my husband and me. He couldn't go because of work, so my best friend drove down from Indiana to go with me. The show was on Sunday. The weeks leading up to this I had conversations (as I do) with my dad, letting him know (as if he didn't) that I was going to see John Edward.

On Wednesday I was taking a nap and my husband came to me with the phone. I asked him to take a message and he told me he couldn't and to please answer the phone. On the line was my aunt, my father's sister and the person who took his life. I almost dropped the phone. We spoke for nearly an hour and a half. She asked me if I hated her and I was able to tell her honestly for the first time, "NEVER." She tried to explain to me what had happened that night and the fear that she had for her older brother. It was a very healing conversation for both of us, probably more for her than me, since I'd been through counseling at least twelve to fourteen years to work through the issues. But it felt great to speak to her. I had tried many times to find her and no one knew where she was – her name is extremely common – or where I might find her.

I asked her why she decided to call me that day. She said she just "felt" she needed to. I asked her if she knew who John Edward was and told her that I was going to see him that Sunday. She asked me to call her after the show, in case my father showed up. I smiled and told her that he just did.

I knew in my heart that he had done this. I thanked him when I hung up the phone and felt so at peace – after I cried for a little while. I knew that was my gift that week. When anyone asked if I though my dad would come through that Sunday, I would tell them no, because he came directly to me.

Sarah Cook

Bottom line: It is not that uncommon for the departed to maneuver events in order to open our minds to new possibilities, or to repair wounded relationships. By the time she received the phone call from her aunt, Sarah was ready for it. And knew without a doubt that she had her father to thank for it.

****

The rose tattoo:

I have been thinking a lot about my best friend, Christy. In my heart I feel that she died on October 23, 2003, my birthday, but officially she died on October 22nd when they took her off life support. After I received the phone call, I drove from Portland to Reno where my dad lives, almost a halfway point and a good resting spot between Reno and Phoenix. My sister and I slept for a few hours, got up about midnight and planned to take off from there, so I could make up some time with no traffic.

It was very, very dark in that Nevada desert, seeing only a few cars here and there, and a coyote crossing the road every now and then. Around 4:00 a.m. my sister and I spotted this HUGE yellowish orange glow in the sky. We could not understand what it was. The moon? A UFO? We couldn't see well enough to know. But as time passed, it got further up in the sky and we could tell it was the moon, but it was HUGE!!

As we were staring at the moon, out of the sky comes this meteor. We watched it as it fell. We SAW it catch on fire and LAND in the desert! I couldn't speak, and my sister was yelling "Did you see that?" I pulled over and caught my breath. This was about ten hours before they took my best friend off life support. Somehow I think this was telling me she was actually leaving her body and moving on. I have never seen anything like this again, but I still vividly remember that night/morning!

I traveled two days to get to Christy, but by the time I arrived it was too late. I missed her passing by two hours. She died of leakage from her intestines and that lead to cardiac arrest. She had gone in for a gastric bypass procedure, but it turned drastically wrong. When she died, I felt like a piece of me died with her.

I went back to Phoenix in August, and my husband and I went to her grave. I looked at her headstone and read what was inscribed. But to the right of it, I noticed this design: a butterfly landing on a rose! This is the SAME tattoo I have on my shoulder!! I'd gotten it the previous year on my birthday, when my best friend was dying in the hospital. (I hadn't gotten the phone call yet and didn't know.)

What made this coincidence even more extraordinary is that when I went in to get my tattoo, all I wanted was the rose. The guy messed it up and could not complete it. I went to another location about a month later and the tattoo artist fixed the rose, but also freehanded a butterfly on it. So this wasn't just a picture you pick out of a book. My tattoo was actually one of a kind. So for it to be on her headstone was a shock and I just cried. I called my husband over and he couldn't believe his eyes. It's the exact design, except for being a mirror image of mine, in that the butterfly is on the opposite side.

My husband, my boys and I just moved to Alaska. Since being in our new home, my TV turns itself on and off all the time. This is a TV we have had for years and it has never done this. I have not had a dream with Christy in it, but I think that the design on her grave, and my TV are somehow connected to her. I look around at all the things she has given me over the years, all the e-mails we have shared, and felt that somehow she WAS my soul mate.

Nikki Canada.

Followup: It's clear how badly Nikki felt that she hadn't been there before her dear friend died. But in retrospect, she firmly believes that Christy bade her farewell the day before her actual death. Their bond was such that Nikki feels she is around somewhere. She still talks to and about Christy, and hopes Christy hears her. I would hazard a guess that Christy hears every word.

****

Cookie Monster, bless his (its?) heart:

My daughter, Jaymie, was six when she had to go into the Children's Hospital here in Ottawa for day surgery, a hernia operation. The date for this operation fell on the same week my infant daughter, Robyn, had passed away fifteen years before, and on the same floor of the hospital. I knew in my heart, however, that my little Jaymie was in good hands and would be fine.

While she was having her operation I went into the pray room, the same pray room I had entered fifteen years prior almost to the day. I went in to tell Robyn I missed her every day and would love to hear from her. I felt at great peace while I was there.

Within a few hours my little Jaymie was ready to come home. The next morning we were sitting on the couch watching Sesame Street. Jaymie was about to change the channel because there was a segment where this woman had a really high-pitched voice and it was getting on our nerves. Just as she was about to click the button, Cookie Monster came on and I said, "Oh, no, don't change it. It's Cookie Monster." He was doing his LETTER OF THE DAY.

Just as I said this my eye catches the newspaper placed on the footstool by my husband. I had yet to read it. It was closed, but a part of it was folded back on a section in the paper called "Comments." In this section are letters to the editor and LETTER OF THE DAY where people write in and give their opinion. This particular letter was about hockey. All my eye could see was the title, "Letter of the Day,." I started laughing, grabbed the paper and started reading.

I read each word in this letter, careful not to jump ahead and the whole time thinking *there is nothing here. It's all about some guy telling another guy he knows squat about hockey* and then the article ended with the person's name who had written the article. Guess what the name was? It was Robin! I know the spelling was different, but to me this was unimportant. To me this was the sign I had asked for less than twenty-four hours before. Amazing. Truly amazing!

I am so blessed to have been given this message from the one and only Cookie Monster, better known as "my angel in the sky!!"

Leigh Brown

Followup: This ADC touched Leigh deeply because, as she puts it, "It set my beliefs in stone. That is because with this ADC I had asked for a sign and had received what I had prayed for which such great intent. The feeling that came over me lasted for hours that day. I remember feeling such joy!"

Each ADC has had that same effect, leaving Leigh giddy and comforted. She was able to share the event with her on-line Friends, which made it even more special. She has no doubt that Robyn heard her and was with her in that prayer room.

****

A brother's acknowledgment:

I worked night shift in the county jail as a correctional officer. Often I transported inmates to and from jails. As many of us do, sometimes alone while driving, I wondered if my brother, Karl, was sitting next to me. Karl was injured in a skydiving accident and never fully recovered. In response to questions, he would sometimes communicate by blinking his eyes once for yes and twice for no. I asked him if he wanted to see a picture of me in uniform, and he blinked his eyes once for yes. I told him I would send him one. I never did send that picture before he died, but I felt he could see me now.

While returning from a transport, a car with the license plate, ECK 098, caught my eye as it was passing me. ECK are the first three letters of our last name – my maiden name. Not a common surname, I wondered if the numbers 098 had any meaning. Figuring in my head, I realized '98 was the year Karl had his accident. There was a computer in booking where you could get driver info from a license plate number. I decided to enter this license plate number the next time I was stationed in booking. Will there be something related to Karl in the driver's information? I wondered.

My chance came a few days later when I was stationed in booking. As soon as I was alone, I input the license plate number. I took a breath when I saw the registered owner's last name, Carlson. Also interesting, the driver's address was in a town called Solway, pronounced "soul way?"

This isn't the end of the story. A few nights later while stationed in one of the housing units, an inmate commented on a book I was reading, a book by psychic John Edward.

"You don't believe that stuff, do you?" he said.

"Let me tell you a story," I said, and I proceeded to tell him what had happened days earlier with the license plate numbers. His eyes widened and he told me I had to play those numbers - 098 - in the Daily Three, a lottery in Minnesota.

I told him these things don't happen so we can get money, but as a way for a loved one to communicate with us. He wasn't deterred. He excitedly found a newspaper, showed me the winning numbers from the previous day, and explained how it was played. I hadn't heard of the Daily Three before, but he was so insistent that I bought a ticket at the local gas station, and you can guess what happened. Those numbers came up, and I won $50. Not a fortune, but I was awed.

Winning $50 underscored the experience. I think that is why these things happen, to grab our attention and let us know that our loved ones are there, that we're not alone. I still have the license plate computer printout and the winning lottery ticket stub. I've had other like things happen since, some spectacular, some less so, all amazing to me nevertheless.

Suzanne Davies

Bottom line: Most would never have made all the connections or, at most, would have considered the connections a reach.

But add up the most pertinent items: 1) while driving, Suzanne frequently thought of her brother, wondered if he might be riding with her; 2) during a drive, the license plate with the first three letters of her maiden name; 3) the number on the plate was the year of her brother's accident; 4) the name of the owner of the car was similar to her brother, Karl's name; 5) playing the numbers on the license, Suzanne came out a winner. Okay, sometimes signs aren't as nice and neat as we'd like. The departed use whatever they can and hope we'll catch on. Suzanne did and became a winner in more ways than one.

****

Winged approval from beyond:

Two promises I made about things I would do when I got a car was to: 1) go down to the beach more often and take pictures of the sunset; and 2) visit the cemetery. I used to go with my mom to visit her mom and dad on such occasions as birthdays, Mother's and Father's Day. I never felt exactly right going because I couldn't have my OWN time with them, especially if my brother tagged along. So I finally went and there wasn't a living human in the whole cemetery.

I had no trouble finding the grave marker. I sat down in the cool grass because even though it was fall, the sun was hot. I cleaned off the grave, removed the grass clippings and sat there and talked with both Nana and Papa. I know they aren't really there still in their boxes; it just felt right to visit them there. I talked some, and while I was talking, a little white moth flew directly over my head and rested on my Papa's WWII flag holder for a second, then flew off. How sweet. It actually came to visit right after I had finished singing "Amazing Grace" to Papa. That little white moth reminded me that he heard me and was proud.

I got up and went over to my Nana's sister's grave marker, which is over by the only tree in the cemetery. The following day would be the anniversary of her husband's passing five years after she died. I didn't know this and was surprised when I sat down and saw the dates on her marker. I gave them my well wishes and headed back towards Nana's grave. When I arrived, a Monarch butterfly flew over in front of me and headed towards my car. It actually flew over my car as well, and paused. I guess both Nana and Papa saw my new car. It was nice hearing from them even in this small way. This was my ADC. It's small, but I hope it provides some comfort in knowing that our loved ones can reach out with anything to grab your attention and say, "Hey! I'm here watching over you."

Stephanie Kazmierczak

Followup: When one thinks about it, there's something symbolic about winged creatures as bearers of messages from the departed. In checking old journals to see if her after death experience had occurred at some critical point in her life, Stephanie was reminded that just prior to it, she and her mom had been going through a difficult period. Also she was finally out on her own and had a brand new car. So for her, one tiny white moth and a Monarch butterfly were more than enough to assure her that her grandparents were still listening and sharing in her pride at what she had accomplished. They were celebrating her new freedom along with her.

Stephanie shared her experience with close friends, in the process, opening them to the possibility that their loved ones could come through for them as well. A pair of tiny winged messengers may have made a difference in many lives.

CHAPTER TEN - WHEN THE MEDIUM IS THE MESSAGE - PART V

JOHN EDWARD

A "Me, too" happens quite frequently during group readings, where information being given to someone fits another person or family like a glove. In this instance, the gloves were Adrienne's, this recount courtesy of notes taken at the time.

Tara invited me to attend a (*Crossing Over with John Edward*) gallery show, though Tara and I had never met. My husband took me to New York and ended up being able to get in through divine intervention, I guess. We were taken to our seats and we all, my husband and Tara and her husband, were seated next to each other, Tara beside me.

John did a little explaining and then started doing his thing. Then John stepped back and said, "I am coming over here," and he pointed to our section. We were sitting in the second to last row. He said, "I am coming to the last row, no, the row before it, no, the back row, no, to the girl with the light hair and the scarf." That was Tara. There were so many "me-too's" - readings for someone else that also apply to a second person in attendance — that I deleted most of her comments and added where my "me-too's" were. John spoke to the fact that everyone who gets the reading is supposed to.

JE: Something regarding red, white and blue, and maybe a dog's death around that, the dog that died on a birthday or a significant day and that was intubated.

AB: (My Doberman, Asia, was at the Emergency Vets on Memorial Day weekend with tubes all over her and I had her put to sleep the Monday after.)

JE: Is October significant?

AB: (October 25th was the birthday of my sister, who's passed over.)

JE: Did someone lose a bird?

AB: (I had many birds, even had an aviary. But it was particularly painful when my Cuddles, a parakeet, died in my hands.)

JE: ....seeing yellow, flashing yellow. (This means caution to him. Then he asked about Tara's house and the stairs going to the basement.)

AB: (Although this had not happened at the time, I since fell from the basement stairs onto the cold basement floor. I also fell down the stairs from the bedrooms and broke my leg, then lost my balance at the top step from the basement and injured my rotator cuff.)

JE: This would be a first, did someone lose a duck? I am seeing the Aflac duck, could be insurance linked.

AB: (I think he asked about a father figure around this as well. My father had his own independent insurance company. He died in 1975 at 75 years of age.)

Adrienne Baumgardner

****

Peggy Smith's experience at a John Edward seminar also fits the definition of what John calls a "Me, too."

On July 13, 2003 my husband and I went to a John Edward seminar in Charlotte, N.C. We hoped to get a reading but were not singled out. Then during the last reading of the day, John started saying things that we could validate. Since we were not in the area he was pointing to, we believe it was a "Me, too!" reading.

We were able to validate everything John was saying, e.g., someone went by a "sweet" name. I was nicknamed Pixie because I loved a candy called Pixie Sticks. John was given the number 12 or December, also the number 17. Both my husband's and older sister's birth month is December, and the number 17 is the day of the month my sister was born and the day my father died.

Two days later I called my sister to tell her what happened. No sooner had I begun when my sister said she heard something fall into a box on the table at which she was sitting. When she looked in the box, which had been empty before my call, there was a blue marble in the box. When I told my sister the date and time of the seminar, she told me that she had had an <u>overwhelming</u> urge to go to a Saturday mass which, coincidentally, had started the same time as the John Edward seminar. My sister and her family have <u>always</u> gone to mass on Sundays. Because of this, my husband, sister and I are positive that we had a "Me, too!" reading at the seminar.

Peg Smith

Followup: As far as Peggy's concerned, the timing of this incident was no coincidence, since the day she discovered that John Edward would be in Charlotte was her birthday. The "Me, too" reading was also significant for Peggy's sister, Debbie, who had been having a hard time. Finding the blue marble in the box served as proof to her that her family on the other side were sending a message and watching over them both. They take great comfort in knowing that they continue to offer their support, regardless of the distance between them all.

CHAPTER ELEVEN - THE INEXPLICABLE AND OTHER MIRACLES

Some ADC experiences straddle the admittedly arbitrary categories I've used. They are still, however, no less valid or of less impact to those it happened. The first of these inexplicables is mine.

****

He touched me:

The first time I felt Bob West's touch was not long after I'd heard his voice, so I was still trying to process the full implications of the phenomenon. I freely admit I'm not a morning person. Between the time I wake up and get up I may blow a good fifteen minutes indulging in a round of internal pep talk which typically involves all the reasons for getting on with the day. That's what I was doing and also watching a sunbeam paint a stripe across the ceiling when I felt a firm grip across the instep of my left foot. I hit the floor a quarter of a heartbeat later, the covers trailing after me. No one there and no cats in sight, either. Yet I'd felt it. I had no explanation and convinced myself that there was undoubtedly a medical term for it involving muscles and tendons or some such.

By the second experience, I could connect the dots. It was a typical day – in other words, I was in my office at the computer working on something or other when, once again I felt a firm grip on my right arm just above the elbow. Scared me spitless. This nut-brown woman turned the color of the paper on which these words are printed. My office door was closed, as cats and keyboards don't mix when I'm up against a deadline. I cased the rest of the rooms, checked other doors and locks. Then it clicked. Bob West. I wish I could say I accepted the evidence of his presence gracefully. I didn't. I let him know in no uncertain and unlady-like terms that even though he was still the love of my life, any further touchy-feely was off-limits. For heaven's sake, I take blood pressure medication for a reason!

Any doubts that he'd been the culprit, which I really didn't have, were laid to rest several years later when, during a group reading with Suzanne Northrup, Bob West came through. He described several unique items and their precise locations in my office, a room that had previously served as his home office but which is now configured differently and in whom only the ladies from Merry Maids are permitted.

Welcome or not, I consider feeling his touch a miracle and now years after the fact, remember it with a smile of gratitude.

Chassie West

Followup: The "reach out and touch" phenomenon hasn't happened since that last episode. And I smile in gratitude that it hasn't. I have to assume he got the message.

****

Time for pay-back:
In March of 2005 I had a packet of paper in an envelope I had placed on my desk at work. They were solidly on the desk, mind you. I was having a bit of a rough start to the day – you know, one of those when everything seems to be going a bit off and you are just a tad irritable?

I was at the file cabinet and heard a THUMP. There was the packet of papers – on the floor. I thought it was strange, because I was sure they weren't hanging off. The 9.5" x 12" envelope was flat and heavy enough that no normal air current was going to move them. I wasn't anywhere near them when they fell. I put them back.

A few minutes later I was typing, again not near the papers. THUMP. They were on the floor. I thought O*kay. Who is messing with me?* I put them back.

You guessed it. Third time. THUMP, on the floor. I picked them up and said out loud: "I don't know who you are, but I am really not up for this this morning. So if you could find another way to say 'hi,' I'd appreciate it. Thanks for coming and saying hello. And who are you anyway?" Obviously, I didn't get an answer – yet – and the packet stayed put the rest of the day. I kept telling folks about it through the day and telling them that this pack of papers must have been possessed!

After I got home I got a phone call about Uncle Carl's early morning passing. I couldn't help but wonder if he hadn't stopped by to say 'hi' and give a little payback. When I was little, I used to take his newspaper off his lap and throw it on the floor next to him. He would pick it up and I would do it again. This was repeated until there were peals of laughter. He would think it was amusing for a while, and then he'd tell me to find another way to have fun.

I can't be 100% sure, but I am 99% sure that Uncle Carl said goodbye a little mischievously in the morning shortly after he passed. And I admit that before I connected the dots, I was irritated by his antics. Still, it was funny, and in retrospect, a little bittersweet. Coming as it did hours prior to hearing about his death, in a way it prepared me for the news and reassured me that Uncle Carl was well on his way to an easy transition.

I think many people enjoyed this bit of mischievousness from Uncle Carl. For some it was their first introduction to this wonderful man. I sometimes think that people are frightened of ADC's but this one shows that the true nature of a person continues even after they leave this plane.

Sue Purdy, Lancaster, PA

Bottom line: Isn't it reassuring to know that the things we loved about those who have made their transition don't change? Sue's Uncle Carl certainly hadn't. And Sue could take great comfort in that.

****

There is nothing that brings more anguish than seeing someone we love begin the long goodbye as dementia takes over their lives. And ours. It consumes those it affects as well as everyone around them. Yet on occasion, we're left with invaluable gifts of love.

I had not had "my mother," for over five years due to dementia. I missed her, our talks, her advice, her sarcasm. Finally after what felt like interminable years of struggling with her dementia, my mother seemed to make a choice to leave this life. She stopped eating, then drinking. During her last five days, my siblings and I took turns staying with her 24/7. I had been caring for her during the last year and a half of her life. Thus, during those last days I was with her as much as possible. I did the night shift, slept a few hours, and went back. She was living at a wonderful assisted living home. Her room had all of her own bedroom furniture and knick knacks. It was home to her. So this is where she wanted to die.

At 7:00 a.m. on March 29, 2005, I knew her time was drawing to an end. I lay on her bed right beside her, holding her hand, assuring her the angels would take wonderful care of her and it was okay for her to move on. At 11:00 a.m. she took her last breath in this world.

She chose to give me the most wonderful gift a mother could give a daughter. She gave me her peace. At her death I literally felt her soul pass through my body, stop for a moment to envelope me with her pure essence. It was an overwhelming feeling of joy. Her joy. I felt "my mother," the person she had always been to me, the one I knew, the one who loved me. I knew she was free of illness and full of joy and peace. I carry that gift each day and my grief was short-lived and tempered with happiness for her. I knew she was happy and she wanted me to be happy, too. When I think of her,

I feel warm and safe, not sad and lonely. And I truly know there is more beyond this world because I felt it. My mother shared it with me so I would not fear for her or myself. My conviction of this gift was so strong that as I prepared her eulogy, I included it for all those who loved and knew my mother, in order to share this gift. To my surprise, it was received by many as a gift to them. Perhaps the depth of my feelings allowed others to appreciate and feel the depth of her gift for themselves.

Several months after my mother's death, she gave me another wonderful gift. I had been doing some personal work on allowing myself to feel more deeply and was struggling with just letting it happen. My mom always had a cabinet with her antiques and things all five of her children had given her. They were far from antiques in the literal sense, just memories Mom cherished. In that cabinet was a nut. I don't know which of us gave her this treasure some forty years ago, but it sat in that cabinet with the rocks that looked like ice cream cones and teapots.

After her death I came across the nut in her belongings. She had kept it with her long after the cabinet had moved on. I placed the nut on my bookshelf, taking notice when I dusted. One Saturday morning I glanced at the nut and, to my amazement, it had opened and looked like the most perfect and beautiful flower with a very petrified nut resting upon one of the petals. The moment I saw it I knew Mom had had something to do with this miracle, and my heart opened wide.

A friend who is an intuitive was coming over for dinner that night, so I decided to tell her about what had happened to the nut. She asked if I wanted to talk to Mom and I said yes. Mom would always wait to be asked for advice. She also struggled with showing her feelings. Mom simply told me that I, too, could open up to my feelings with the same ease with which the forty-year-old nut had opened, to just let it happen. Her gift to me this time was subtle but hit directly to my heart, as she knew it would. Over the years, she and I had many conversations, but as the words of those talks fade, the experience of the opening nut will with be me forever. Thanks, Mom.

During that same reading with the intuitive, my dad came to talk, a surprise, since Dad was always a doer, not a talker, and felt that his love could best be shown by taking care of his family, which he did well. He told me he wished he had a way to let me know he was watching over me and would always be with me. He had died thirteen years before my mom, and I had grieved long and hard over his death, my heart literally hurting for months and months.

A few weeks later I was on a trip and had a rental car. I hit a curb with the front bumper, putting a large dent in the passenger side, along with scratches. I decided not to worry about it and just deal with it when I returned the car.

One morning a few days later I went out to the car to get something and decided to take a closer look at the dent. It wasn't there. I felt a bit dis-oriented, and walked around the car a few times, even checking inside to be sure I had not somehow gotten the wrong car. It was the right car, just no dent.

I went in the hotel to get my companion. She came out laughing – until she looked at the bumper. No dent, no scratches, just a small yellow line from the yellow curb I had hit. Then I realized it was Dad. He wanted to let me know he was watching. You see, he had been a car body man. He spent countless hours fixing our cars, our houses and anything else that needed fixing. His single action of fixing that car brought him closer to my heart. I felt safe again. Thanks, Dad.

Lorraine Peck

Bottom line: There are no words to put into perspective the gift with which Lorraine's mother left her: the sharing of her essence as she left to return Home. Her father's gift was special as well and another instance of a parent seeing that his daughter was taken care of. A heavenly mechanic. You can't get much better than that!

****

That unforgettable laugh:

My brother, Rog, passed in 2000. He had been told in 1998 that he would probably not live through that year, but he was having no part of that! He told the doctors that he was going to live to see the year 2000. Not unlike him at all.

Rog had the most amazing laugh you ever heard. You'd laugh just from listening to him. It made no difference if you knew what he was laughing at or not, it was that infectious. I have yet to "see" Rog. I have had no dreams of him, but I hear that laugh at the most amazing times. There will be something on TV that I know he would have loved, and it won't be any time and I will hear his laugh. He was a master at one-liners and would never crack a smile telling them. He would patiently wait until you 'got it,' then would fall apart from laughter. He would 'get you' every single time. He enjoyed that more than anyone I knew. So I hear his laughter often and consider that my ADC from him.

Ellen Siddons

Bottom line: Memories are among the most cherished gifts our loved ones leave with us and the departed have no hesitation about using our senses to remind us that they're close by. It may be a smell, the scent of the cologne someone wore or the favorite pipe tobacco a loved one smoked, especially when you're alone and can think of no explanation or source for the aroma. In Ellen's case, it's her hearing, and clearly the sound of her brother's laughter is one she keeps close to her heart. The next time something of this nature happens to you, embrace it, cherish it and accept it as a sign that our loved ones are saying hello.

****

It doesn't matter if they're furry, feathered, scaly with two legs, four, or none at all, our pets are family. And when they die we grieve just as much and intensely as we would for a relative, because we loved them, and they loved us unconditionally. Therefore it should come as no surprise that they might want

us to know they're still around. And they do. Bless their hearts, they do.

Jerry, the Calico Kitty:

When my mother died in 1987, she left explicit instructions to have Jerry, her cat, euthanized. The cat was old and my mother feared that no one would care for Jerry. I looked at this beautiful kitty and just couldn't do it. I bought Jerry an airline ticket and she came home with me.

Jerry only lived for a few more years, but she was a pleasure to have in my household. Directly after she died, my daughter and I thought we were seeing her out of the corner of our eyes. We wrote it off as imagination and grief at losing her.

Then it happened. Watching TV one evening, we felt and saw the impression on the bed as our little ghost kitty decided to join us. I panicked, still not willing to believe my own eyes. We rationalized the whole thing and went to bed. I woke feeling Jerry curled up on my pillow, purring.

I got up and walked into my living room so as not to wake my daughter. I said, "Mom, you need to come get your kitty right now. She's still here and it's scaring us. It's time to take Jerry with you."

We had no kitty visits after that.

Vikki North

Bottom line: There's nothing quite as disconcerting as seeing a beloved pet from the corner of your eye and turning to find nothing there. It happens. I've experienced it firsthand after the loss of a particularly cherished pussycat named Rudy. Even after almost ten years he still prowls through occasionally. So I have no doubt that Jerry returned to visit Vikki for one last snuggle. Pets. God love 'em.

****

Pets understand more than we think they do:

My mother had been ill for years with a progressive respiratory illness. It was not a surprise when she asked to go to the hospital, because she was unable to breathe. She had asked that if there was no hope of recovery that we remove the respirator and make sure she was heavily sedated – "morphed out" was how she described it. This was done and during her last seven days in the hospital, she was unconscious while we kept a 24-hour vigil. She died on a Sunday evening with my younger brother at her side. Her death was devastating to all of us, for she was a determined, vibrant and spirited woman despite her many illnesses.

A day or so later I was lying in my bed, so very tearful, sad and inconsolable. I felt that each day that would pass would be taking my mother farther away. I could try to keep her with me by going over every detail of her final illness, but that could only last so long.

As I lay there I felt a warmth and a pressure on my left hand, which was lying on the pillow near my head. I thought it was my cat, Asia, known to come and comfort me in times of distress. I opened my eyes and there was no cat. Immediately I closed my eyes. The pressure became stronger and warmer. I was shocked at first, but quickly accepted it as my mother's final gift. I knew it was my mother who had come to comfort and reassure me. She had been a fierce and determined mother, always there for us. I fell asleep with her hand holding mine, comforted, and feeling that my mother was comforted as well with the knowledge that she had been able to reach me.

Seven years later in October 2004, my dad became ill while my husband and I were in NYC celebrating our anniversary. My brother had been staying with him while we were gone, so we made our way to the hospital where he was having a cardiac catheterization in preparation for surgery. However, his condition deteriorated and surgery was ruled out. We decided to discontinue active treatment and he died within ten minutes, a difficult death to watch.

A month later I had a pet communicator speak with his cat, Desi, whom I thought might be mourning Dad's absence. The pet communicator knew nothing of my parents' deaths. The pet communicator relayed that Desi 'knew' Dad was ready to go and so had no particular sadness. Desi also 'said' that he was very sad about his grandmother – my grandmother. She had been very sick, he said, and stayed in a place in a bed far away for a long time. He 'went' to her in his mind and got very upset because she did not respond to him when he wanted to say goodbye. He became very angry with her and shouted at her that she was dying, and afterwards felt very ashamed. He also said that after she died, my mother stayed here for a while, that she was confused and missed her family. Desi missed her very much.

After my dad died, Desi said that he tried not to think about Dad too much because he knew it would make me sad.

Desi was very accurate about my mom. She had a special relationship with him and after her death, he often sat on the footstool in front of her chair and looked around at us and cried. My mom was in a coma unrelated to the morphine for several weeks in the hospital; it was if she had withdrawn deep within herself purposefully to avoid being afraid. I believe Desi was right about her lingering here. Nothing made her happier than to be in our presence. And nothing, not even death, changed that.

Diane Manville

Followup from Diane: I shared these events with my family and several close friends. I think my brothers benefitted the most, leaving the skeptical one a little more open to such things. My other brother had no problem at all in understanding it and accepting it as reality. My mother had told him he was her favorite and he really needed to hear that from her. So as usual, Mom took care of us all.

****

Purrs from Prison:
My husband, Rusty, had a most amazing relationship with one of our cats. His name was Prison and he was eleven years old when he died in his sleep. Several years ago, my husband moved from Rhode Island to North Carolina. Prison became very depressed, so we thought of a solution to cheer him up. Rusty would talk to

Prison on the phone every day when he called me. After only two calls, Prison's mood was much happier.

Rusty came home for a couple of days to visit and to finalize my moving plans to North Carolina, and Prison would not leave Rusty's side. Prison had only one trick, which was jumping up on you without using his claws. He expected you to catch him.

My husband had two dreams/visits this week from Prison in which Prison had his favorite toys in his mouth (which we buried with him). He jumped up and Rusty caught him. We took it as a sign from Prison that he was helping us find one of the feral cats we were feeding that had been missing for several days. Sure enough, the cat showed up later on the second morning! We were able to catch this feral cat we named Baby Blue and bring him into our house. Our vet worked him into his surgery schedule to neuter him the day I called, so now Baby Blue is an indoor-only cat. We are positive we have Prison to thank for helping Baby Blue.

Peggy Smith

Bottom line: Just another example of how much our pets love us. They know when another cat or dog is needed to fill the hole in our hearts left by their departure. Prison did his part to help and now the Smith family is complete again.

****

Lest I leave the impression that I'm anti-dog (which I fervently deny), here's how Nan's beloved Quincy made her feelings known:

Our little dog, Quincy, had been with us for fourteen years and she was simply wearing out. The last few days she was slipping badly. It was time. So we took her in to the vet to stop her pain. She was a special member of the family (they all are, really, I know) and one of the smartest dogs I've ever known.

The vet did her job, then said, "She's gone," and left us to say our goodbyes just one more time. While we were standing there loving her and telling her what she'd meant to us, the lights flickered. They didn't flicker off. They flickered <u>brighter.</u> There was an actual quick flash of a bright light. We both looked up at the light fixture. Then I looked at hubby, he looked at me and we both had a smile on our faces, and the "Hmmm, I gotta keep this one in mind," look.

A few moments later I told Quincy again, "I love you," and dang if the lights didn't flicker a second time, almost on the heels of the words. And again, <u>brighter.</u>

It helped so much to have that from her. She knew we loved her and she's doing fine now. If there was doubt after the first flash of light, there was none after the second one. It was almost as if she was prancing around and poking the light with her nose, or whacking at it with her paw. "Oh, hey, my ride is here – it's been great. See ya later," kind of message.

I have no doubt that without that light flickering, I'd still be feeling the guilt that I didn't take her in soon enough. It gave me such a feeling of peace to know that her release was so instant and so complete. I don't know why, but it never occurred to me that a dog could or would "give a sign," and within <u>minutes</u> of her passing!!

I'm very grateful. It made everything alright. Everything had happened as it should and everything was as it should be. It made all the difference to me.

I don't really care if it sounds woo-woo. We <u>know.</u>

Nan Crowley

Bottom line: We'd be well advised not to sell our beloved animal companions short. They are every bit as capable as anyone else at sending signs after their transition. After all, they have souls, too!

****

It is not unusual for the death of someone close to us to cause the death of our religious beliefs. It makes us question them, put them through a wringer. That's where Jacki Butcher found herself after the death of her father, even as, she relates, "going through my Catholic motions of offering prayers and masses for my father and getting on with things, but actually I was treading water. I hadn't quite worked out what my father's death meant to me." A series of small miracles left her with all the answers she needed.

The following is the reason I began to investigate life after death. It had caused me a lot of angst, as it is contrary to my Catholic faith, but ultimately led me back to the Church with renewed vigour.

It was July 2000 and I worked as a mental health nurse in Accident & Emergency. My husband and I had been invited to a wedding. It was to be on a Sunday and I was due to work four to midnight. I tried for months to get one of the other nurses to take my shift for me, but no one would or could help. My husband went off to the wedding without me at my insistence. My parents stayed at my house to babysit.

At 9:15 I left our interview room to go into reception to wait for a social worker who was new to the area. As I walked through majors, my dad went by on a trolley and I said hello. I went into reception and saw my mum with her neighbor in the relatives' area. It was at that point I realized it was my dad I'd said hello to. I was concerned, as I couldn't see my daughter. (How strangely the brain works in these situations.) My mum explained that Dad hadn't been feeling well and had gone home. When he arrived home, my sister called an ambulance, as he looked very unwell. She then got the neighbour, who drove her to my house, then drove my mum to the hospital, leaving my sister to babysit.

I went and found my dad, who was busy telling the doctor to call him Fred and not to worry, as he had indigestion. My dad was insistent that the doctor go look after one of the sick people! A colleague was placing ECG lines on my dad, and as the readings hit the monitor, I knew what I was seeing. My dad, who never had a day's sickness, walked everywhere and never complained, was in the throws of a huge cardiac arrest, and looked as if he had been for a while.

He was moved to a cardiac care unit and started to recover. He still insisted that he had a touch of indigestion and swore never to eat my mother's cooking again. He agreed to stay overnight to 'keep us all quiet.'

That night, with my husband snoring like a steam train, I knew that my dad was going to die the next day. This was not medical knowledge; it was a gut feeling. I returned to the hospital with my mum and two sisters the next day. When we got there we were told we would have to wait for half an hour for doctors' rounds to finish. Again, I knew my daughter needed to be there. I called my husband, who removed my 8-year-old from school and brought her to the hospital.

The crash team ran past and I ran with them, taking my middle sister with me. We watched as the team tried in vain to resuscitate my dad. I heard someone praying the Our Father and Hail Mary and saw my husband behind me, eyes closed, rosary in hand, praying hard. He said later that he didn't want the last words my dad heard to be people counting chest compressions.

Next morning when I woke early and came downstairs, the house smelt of bacon and the kettle was warm. With everyone else in bed, I knew my dad was there. When my daughter awoke, she proceeded to tell me all about God's garden. She had drawn a lovely picture and proceeded to tell me that Granddad was fine, he was going to look after the garden and make sure it was lovely for when we all got there. Dad was letting me know he was okay just before I'd have reached the conclusion that God had deserted me.

Over the first year I felt my dad frequently, often talking to him in dreams where he would give me pertinent advice and once seeing him at the end of our garden sorting out my tomato plants. As for how I felt when I first saw him? I felt happy, then very, very scared – happy because my tomatoes were not doing well and I knew Dad could sort them out, then scared because this didn't happen to sane people, did it? I was sure I was hallucinating. I get now that he did this because he thought I could handle it. He was wrong! The first time freaked me out. I went to bed in the afternoon and hid under the duvet. I struggled with this due to my faith and was sure I was going mad. I spoke to my priest who stunned me by saying, "Why shouldn't he come back to give you advice? That's what he would do if he were here, isn't it?"

I knew for sure that it was my dad when, praying at the side of my bed, I felt someone kneel next to me. The dog sat staring at the space, and then I heard very clearly, "Teach me how to say it." My dad, who was not a church goer, asked me to teach him the rosary from behind the grave. We prayed the rosary together. My dad told me in full voice that my husband praying whilst he was leaving was beautiful. It had assured him swift passage to the garden. My dad went on to say that I was right, that the Church did hold the truth. He was annoyed when I married a Catholic and mortified when I converted later. He wanted me to make sure I never let go of my faith.

I again spoke to my priest, who suggested I look up John Edward. I have since developed my power so that I can talk to my dad – and my grandparents and anyone else who fancies a natter – whenever I wish. The pain of his loss seems trivial now. I hear him. I feel him and I regularly smell him – bacon, tea and buttered toast. I look forward to the day I can cuddle him again.

The first person I told was my husband, who was kind, but looking back, slightly incredulous. I told my mum almost a year later. She was really angry that my dad had not communicated with her, but I know he will when he's ready.

Something else happened recently. My daughter, at fourteen, was confirmed on June 6th. As is customary, the Mass was offered for the young people. However, during the prayers, the priest said, "We pray for those who are no longer here, in particular Charles Parker, known as Fred. He loved this place." The priest says a note was pushed through his door and I can find no one who admits to doing it. I suspect that now that my dad 'gets' this prayer thing, he wants all he can get.

My experience has made me see aspects of my father's character that I didn't see when he was here. It makes me feel sad that I took him for granted. I realize just how proud he was of me, something he never said here.

I see now that my experiences have made a huge impact on my understanding of faith, God, and all the other big things I thought I had a handle on prior to my father's death. It made me sit back and think, "Well, okay then. That's how this all works." Belated gifts, but better late....

Jacki Butcher, England

Bottom line: In the end, the transition of her father led to Jacki's embrace of her faith in a new way. It remains her rock, her foundation, along with the knowledge that her father prays along side her. She's been left with gifts of ineffable value.

****

The following is a two-fer, an ADC as well as an out-of-body experience. As the latter is not the focus of this book, I'll restrain from supplying the varying explanations for the phenomenon. Suffice it to say it does happen. Anyone interested should look into research into the nature of consciousness.

I was about 10-12 years old, living in a large two-story house. I'd gone to bed and something made me open my eyes and look at the far wall that had a wall-to-wall bookshelf full of books on it, up to the top of the ceiling and to the left. I saw what seemed like a foggyish vapor or thickness of some sort, but it was also transparent. I laid there for a few seconds in awe at what I was seeing, and all of a sudden I knew it was my great grandmother, Lizzie, who'd passed away a couple of years before, whose shape/likeness was beginning to form over there in the corner. I had been devastated by her death, since I'd known her fairly closely.

All of a sudden I was filled with anxiety and fear and I started screaming at the top of my lungs and crying, and pulled the covers over my head. My mom came running into the room and asked me what the matter was, and I told her. She sat there on my bed, comforting me and talking to me for a few minutes until I was calmed down. She asked me if I wanted her to stay in my room until I was asleep again. I said yes, so she sat in a chair next to my bed.

The next thing I'm aware of, my mom is standing up, looking over me to make sure I'm asleep. She pulled the covers up higher and walked out of the room.

I thought to myself, "HEY! She said she was gonna stay in here till I was asleep," pretty indignant at the thought that she hadn't kept her word. Then it dawned on me that I was seeing this from the ceiling viewpoint – and that my body was laying on the bed, face up, but I was floating, watching this all facing downwards and no gravity was pulling me in any way.

I thought this was amazing. I marveled at it, checking out the sense of it, how there was no gravity and how I was positioned. I wondered what I could do, so I must have thought about going downward, because I started slowly going down towards myself, slowly, slowly, thinking this was neat as could be. I got about a foot and a half to two feet above my body and I remember nothing else. But when I woke the next day I remembered every single bit of it, as I do to this day.

As a ten-year-old, I reacted with awe and amazement that it was my great grandmother in spirit until my mind took over and I got scared. This incident, however, became the foundation of the idea that we do live on after our physical death, even though I wasn't ready to deal with it at the time. But it left me assured that my Grandma Lizzie still loved me.

Other than my mother, I kept the experience to myself for many years, certain that most people wouldn't understand it or think me either unbalanced or lying. Fortunately, I now feel free to relate my first ADC as well as the first of my four out-of-body experiences.

Kim Hardie

Bottom line: Perhaps this type of out-of-body experience is a hint of things to come, since some who have had near-death experiences relate a similar phenomenon, i.e., seeing themselves from above their own body. Perhaps Lizzie appeared to help prepare her granddaughter, Kim, for her ability to travel beyond the confines of her physical body. Whatever her reason, it was

reassurance for Kim that we survive our transition, as does love.

****

Soul rescue strikes me as yet another category of after death communication. In poking around during my research, I discovered that soul rescues are frequently conducted during times of war or on occasions when the departed have, for whatever reason, failed to make the transition to the other side. The following is but one example:

My adventure began years ago in Denver, Colorado. In the mid-60's a friend attended the Spiritualist Church in Denver. I went with her one time and they were relaying messages from the other side. The minister, a very elderly person, seemed to be very accurate for many people, judging by their reactions. I had a question about my mother, but his answer was unsatisfactory. He said, "She is not here in this realm." It seemed strange since she had died seven years before.

During the following year I began to have occasional bouts with depression, unusual for me, but being a college student with three young children, and separated from my husband for two years, it seemed it might be normal. I didn't have time to figure it out.

After moving to Colorado Springs in late 1968, we bought our first house. We were in the house a few weeks when I lay down one quiet afternoon to rest in the warm sun coming through a south window, and had an unexpected experience. Just at the point between sleep and wakening, my father, who had died five years earlier, spoke to me. He said, "You are on the right track." Unmistakably his voice, not in my mind but in my ear. Unmistakably his words, the inflections, the small nuances and language usage, even the pauses. It was his voice and his words beyond question. I was shaken by the experience but with no doubts about it. He had believed that property was a great investment, and I had used some of my inheritance from his estate as a down payment on this home. So it seemed logical.

When we moved back to Denver in 1984, I abandoned my Colorado Springs business and had a lot of time to delve into new ideas. My daughter gave me the Course in Miracles books. I found an amazing study group there and began an adventure into a different reality. I also volunteered as a graduate research subject at the University of Denver and was accepted into a 16-week research project testing self hypnosis into past life discovery. Following that, at age 56, I decided to attend a Holistic Psychology Graduate School in Boulder. I tasted of many things of a metaphysical nature, but the outstanding events there were receiving an MA degree and a two-credit class I signed into. The class sounded like an easy credit in two long weekends. It was a class in "Spirit life." It actually started as a past life investigation, and ended in a "Spirit rescue," as the instructor termed it.

The instructor, a local Protestant minister, claimed to have performed many rescues of spirits who had not passed over. I was very skeptical about the idea. Late the final day of class he asked us about any event that we felt might be attached to spirit energy. Since I had not volunteered for any class demonstrations and, recalling strange episodes of depression I had experienced over the previous fifteen or so years, I raised my hand. I was the only person volunteering.

I described having a sense of sadness and depression come over me that felt like it belonged to someone else. The instructor questioned me carefully. We honed in on my deceased mother's energy as a potential source. She had suffered menopausal depression and weeping for several years before her death. I was still very skeptical, but agreed to assist in a spirit rescue – anticipating nothing from it. It turned out to be the most profound experience of my life.

The spirit rescue preparation seemed kind of unnecessary. Five classmates were instructed to hold my arms and ankles, and one sat at my head. His firm instruction was, "You can not go with this spirit, no matter what." *Okay, whatever*, was my thought. *This won't work anyway.* I was on an unexpected ride in seconds. There were prayers in the room, but I barely heard them because before me stood my mother. I noticed details I had all but forgotten about her.

With instruction, I engaged in silent conversation with her. I asked her why she was here, because she was dead. Her answer brought tears to my eyes. "I'm not dead," she declared. From here on I was asked to speak out loud and received instruction from the minister. I finally convinced her she was indeed dead to this physical life, and I asked her to go to the light. I had not seen any light but suddenly a huge round hole opened, filled with blinding light.

She wanted me to go with her and I told her several times I could not go, but she was afraid and literally hung onto me. I told her Daddy was waiting for her. Suddenly, a large light figure reached out for her hand. It seemed to me like my dad; he looked directly at her only. She took the hand and was whisked into the light. Then the hole closed. I thought to myself *I can recreate this any time I want to.* But so far, try as I may, I have never been able to do so.

Regardless, this experience left me feeling more complete in my relationship with my mother. Rescuing my mother's spirit was the most loving thing I had ever done for her, and the timing of it was pure serendipity, since it occurred during a weekend class at a location forty miles from home.

Following the Spirit Life class, my depressive episodes ended. I am still depressed at times, but it is different. I can relate any depression to situations in my life. I own them. I also gained a belief in continuing life and that our beliefs about that after may condition the way we experience it.

Norma Struthers

Followup: Norma reports that she has shared the rescue of her mother's spirit with various people over the years and can say that the event left her with a great love for those who have left us, especially those wandering as lost souls. That, she feels, must truly be purgatory.

****

A special reunion:

A few years ago my father went to the hospital to have a benign tumor from his prostrate. We had been told he would need to stay after surgery for at least a week. Yet to everyone's delight, he had such a speedy recovery that we were told he would only be kept for observation for three or four days. Other than antibiotics, he was taken off pain medication and all other drugs. I went to visit him and we sat and watched the World Series together. His spirits were good and we spent a great time teasing each other about rooting for opposite teams. That was about the third day after his surgery.

The following day once again, I went to visit. He was sitting up having breakfast. The first thing he said was, "Honey, I had quite a few visitors last night and we had some great conversations." I was a bit surprised, since I had left the night before because visiting hours were over. I asked him who had come so late and how had they gotten past the nurses' station.

He told me several names, as well as some of the content of their discussion. All of them were family and friends who had already crossed. My heart sank. I couldn't let it show. Instead I listened to him describe how they had come in one at a time, how they had looked, what they had said, how happy it had made him to see them again. My father was a very conservative man, a real skeptic. If you wanted to see him get upset, just mention something like astrology or tarot cards. I asked if there was any chance it had been a dream. The question annoyed him. He said he was sitting up awake and alert, watching TV when they came.

I excused myself for a few minutes, went to the bathroom and cried. I knew why they had visited. I spent the rest of the day with him. We talked and laughed. When I finally had to leave to catch the plane to fly home, I hugged him for a long time. I kissed him goodbye. I knew it would be the last time. I flew home and waited for the call.

It came two days later. "A sudden turn for the worse." "We don't know why." "He was pronounced dead at one p.m." I heard the words. I expected them. Yet....

My dad was a man of science and, as I mentioned, very conservative in his views. Somehow this made the experience I was able to share with him in his final days even more poignant.

Julie Bannister

Bottom line: Seeing "visitors" seems to be a common occurrence of those about to make their departure from this life. Most who witness it might assume that this is imagination, or that the person has become mentally impaired because of the severity of their condition. Others of us, like Julie, know that the time of the person's leaving is close and that the departed one's most beloved family and friends are there to welcome him or her Home. I would hope that those of us left behind will take comfort in that.

****

How can one find words that adequately relay the unique pain, bone-deep grief and anguish a parents feels at the loss of a child? Sweet Anthony, true to his nature has brought comfort to his mom:

Anthony was born on Christmas Eve, 1993, bringing with him the first snow of the year. He was the truest form of Christmas Spirit; his personality befitted his birth date.

He was the most caring, sensitive, loving person I had every known. He cared so deeply for people, even at the tender age of two. Every Christmas we donated for "Toys for Tots" and we could just get a toy for a boy, we would get one for a girl, too. Anthony would walk up to the Marine and happily hand him the toys! Wherever he went he made friends easily and always shared with others. He would come into the house to get a drink and walk out with three. I'd ask him why he was taking so many and he would say that his friends were thirsty, too! He'd give one to each of them, the same with cookies and snacks. He just cared about everyone. I was speechless, he was so admirable. He really enjoyed giving.

On July 7, 2000, my world as I knew it ended. I was at work and received a call from the hospital asking me if I had a son named Anthony. I was frozen and time seemed to have stopped at that moment. They told me that he had been in an auto crash. When I walked into the emergency room, the chaplain took my hand. Still numb and not knowing what had happened, I didn't give a thought to the seriousness of the situation. All I wanted to do was see my son.

I'm a smoker and I was outside the emergency room smoking when one of the police officers, a mother herself, put her arm around me and told me they were in a car accident. The woman who was watching Anthony was also watching another friend's boys, both of them Anthony's two best friends, along with her own son. Without my consent or those of the other mothers, she put the boys in the car to go get a video. Within 8/10 of a mile, she slammed head-on into a telephone pole. The police believed that she fell asleep and hit the gas, thinking it was the brake. There were four boys in that car. Anthony was in the middle of the back seat with his lap belt on. The others sustained injuries, but none were serious or life threatening, except for Anthony's. One of the other boys in the auto crash was also in the PICU unit for two days.

When I was allowed to see my son, he was on a respirator. It was simply beyond my comprehension that Anthony would not be okay. As soon as they stabilized him, I had him flown to a trauma hospital in the area. My family, all of his teachers, his friends and their moms, and my co-workers were there with me at the hospital every day.

That first night when I finally collapsed from exhaustion, I had a dream. My son, the other boy in PICU and I were outside the hospital. Anthony went into the middle of the street and I yelled, "Anthony, get out of the street, it's dangerous!" My son replied, "Watch, Ma, it's cool!" Then a car went right through him. The other boy then said, "Cool! I want to try it." My son turned to us and said, "I'm the only one that can do this."

I woke up and there were about eight doctors in front of me, including his pediatrician. I told them that I just had a dream about him and his pediatrician asked what the dream was. I told her not to worry about it. I was so afraid if I told them my dream, they would disconnect the life support machines.

Anthony was on life support for twenty days. Outside he was as beautiful as ever, not a scratch on him aside from the mark from the lap belt. Unfortunately, his most severe injury was a brain/spinal cord injury. I didn't want to let him go. After twenty days on life support and with his body starting to shut down, however, I didn't have much choice. I had to make the decision to let him go Home.

I also decided that he would be an organ donor, as am I. I heard him in my mind telling me, "Mom, I don't need them any more." So Anthony gave throughout his life and continued to give in his passing. He gave the gift of sight to an eight-year-old boy, and a heart valve to a seven-month-old baby boy. The baby's transplant was done on Valentine's Day. And the auto accident had been so highly publicized that it also helped to implement New Jersey's booster seat law. I will never know how many lives will be saved by this, or how many children can be prevented from being paralyzed by a head/neck injury. Even from heaven, Anthony continues to give.

After he passed I was driving from New Jersey to South Carolina. As I was driving through a tunnel in West Virginia, suddenly I felt elated. I was the only car in the tunnel at the time. I just wanted to go faster and faster. I remember seeing the lights on the sides and just had this anticipation and excitement, yet felt very peaceful about driving through it. As soon as I came out, there was a sign that said, "Welcome to Virginia." It was daylight again and there was greenery. Again, my first thought was that my son was allowing me to feel what it is like to go through the tunnel on the way Home.

Excerpted from www.geocities.com/anthonymg93/index.html with permission from

Veronica Georgiadis

Bottom line: One has to admire Veronica's desire to see something positive result from the death of her son. Together she and Anthony may well have saved the lives and health of many children. Anthony's legacy is a gift to us all.

****

Then there's Tyler. One can only pray that the possibilities reflected by his mother, Cyndi's experience will be taken to heart and engender hope:

My son, Tyler, died at thirteen years of age on August 6, 2004. Perhaps six or seven months before he died, I had a dream in which Tyler was driving his ATV with his cousin, Marley, riding on the back. They flipped over into a ditch and became submerged under water. Marley came up screaming for help, yelling that Tyler was going to die because he was trapped and neither of them could shift the ATV off of him. I awoke with tears streaming down my face. I told a friend that one of my kids was going to die.

When I told Tyler about the dream and tried to convince him to stay off the ATV, he said, "Oh, Mom, I can get that thing off me." I insisted that he wouldn't be able to, that I had heard a hundred times in the ER about ATVs flipping and rolling onto a driver who then couldn't move it. Telling him had no effect.

When I got the call that August night, I'd been in the bathroom crying uncontrollably and couldn't figure out why. I knew something was wrong even before the phone rang. I had tried to call Tyler all day and hadn't been able to reach him. I answered the phone, but no one was there. Caller ID announced that the caller was Out of Area. I realized later that the call had come at the time of Tyler's death.

Some time later, I went to the cemetery to visit his grave. There was a little girl in the cemetery standing next to the grave in which my Aunt Thelma is buried. Her face was round, her eyes blue, her smile so like my son's. When I jumped, startled at seeing her, she nodded at me. I could almost hear Tyler saying, "Mom, do not be afraid." I thought I was losing my mind. It was if I could hear what the child was thinking, yet it was my son's voice saying, "I am fine, Mom. Do not get out of the truck. Just believe. I know you believe in this stuff."

I drove on to my son's grave, got out and said a prayer. I looked back at the child and she kept turning to look back at me. I couldn't imagine why a child that young would be all alone at dusk in a graveyard. I wondered if I should go back, try to talk to her, especially as, for some reason, I sensed that she was there to deliver a message to me. But I didn't. When I stopped at my mother's house on the way home, she asked if I'd seen the little girl in the graveyard. She had seen her, too.

Her image stayed on my mind to such an extent that I wrote to Allison DuBois in search of answers. Somewhere I'd heard that victims of tragic accidents continue to roam the earth and I was so afraid that Tyler was among them. Allison assured me that he wasn't roaming. He was vibrant and happy and with me. She said the phone call that day had been from Tyler. He hadn't known how to come through yet and now understood why I had been so worried about him all the time.

She also said the little girl in the cemetery was a child someone in the family had lost earlier, that she had been there to let me know that Tyler was okay. My brother had lost a baby when she was three days old.

On a later occasion when I was visiting the cemetery, I kept hearing Tyler's voice saying, "Mom, go to the other side of the graveyard." That's where I found little Megan's grave. She would have been about the age of the little girl I'd seen.

It has been five years since my son crossed over. I am still grieving and will until I take my last breath, take his hand and hear him say, "Momma, what took you so long?" I know he is physically gone, but he is still present through the universe.

Our family shares everything. They have had things happen to them and they call to say, "We believe you." I think it helps them to see that we are living in a life of different planes. It helps to understand that when we die there is another plane we go to until we meet God.

Memories are what memories are and the ADC is a memory I will never forget. It was SO REAL. We connected for one last time in that graveyard and he got to tell his mother he was fine. But he never said, "Goodbye, Mom." I know he is still with me every day. He knows I believe and he can communicate with me whenever he needs to and I can understand. So I ask: do _you_ believe?

Cyndi Rucker

****

And Tyler's balloons:

On October 29, 2005, my son, Tyler, would have been fifteen. I had started a ritual the previous year in which I would take thirteen balloons to his grave, along with a yellow smiley face balloon to celebrate his birthday. So the year before I'd taken thirteen white ones and one yellow smiley face. In 2005 I decided on fourteen red balloons and one yellow smiley face.

I took my sister and mother with me. We got all the balloons placed into my truck safely. When we got to the graveyard, I said to my sister, "Do you have the balloons? Hang onto them and I will take the strings." Before opening the hatch all the way, I took the red balloons and the one yellow one, being careful not to pop them.

I started off to his grave and noticed that the yellow one was missing. I walked back to my truck and said to my sister, "Give me the yellow balloon."

She said, she'd given me all of them.

I said, "Geanine, look at me. I have only fourteen red balloons. Where is the yellow one?" My sister started looking frantically in the truck for the yellow smiley balloon.

By that time my mother is saying, "Girls, do not freak out. It is a sign from Tyler. We need to pray."

I thought, *Ooh, my gosh, she is going to make us say a whole rosary.* Laughing to myself and looking up to the heavens, I said, "Thanks, Tyler." We were all shook up and questioning how the one balloon could have slipped out of the truck.

My mother said, "Look at us. He gives us a sign and we still do not believe it happened." He knew he had to take the yellow one because we would not have missed one of the rest.

Cyndi Rucker

Bottom line: Clearly Tyler's personality remained the same after his transition. He reached out to comfort his mother in the cemetery, to assure her there was no reason to be afraid. And

he was wily enough to steal the one balloon he was certain his family would notice was gone. Still the Tyler Cyndi had loved. Still the rascal as well.

****

Someone's ringing:

On the evening I came home and found my tickets for the night's John Edward seminar in Washington, D.C., my husband, Phil, and I were talking about the anniversary of the death of our dear friend, Jim, and how we felt he had arranged the tickets. As we were talking, the doorbell rang. Phil got up and looked right away, even walked outside. Nothing. This is not something that happens in our neighborhood although there is always a first time for pranksters. So we said, "Hi, Jim. Glad you will be there with us."

Last night I was working on a list of names and dates to take to the seminar, just in case we got a reading. I had just worked on Jim's dates and the doorbell rang. Phil went to the door and there was no one visible anywhere around. Jim, when on this side, would always show up unexpectedly, and this is just such a perfect sign for him to give. We were sure Jim rang the bell. How coincidental could it be that each time we talked/wrote about Jim in relation to John Edward the doorbell rang? We were so excited that our dear friend could still come by unexpectedly, just as he had in life. It was yet another validation that life goes on and our loves ones continue to chime in from time to time.

We didn't need a reading from John. We knew Jim would be there. I had also been getting pennies and dimes all week that are significant to others. The other afternoon I was thinking about the seminar, and two butterflies (in April!) fluttered around my head right in front of me for a long time. The previous Saturday I had found the combination of coins my mom always sends. We definitely did not travel to Washington alone. So to all our loved ones who went with us, thanks for the signs and the support.

Sue Purdy

Bottom line: As someone who was also subjected to the doorbell sounding off with no one there to ring it not long after my husband's transition, I have no doubt that Jim took advantage of an old habit to remind Sue and her husband of their friendship. As easy manipulators of electricity, the departed clearly have no hesitation about ringing our bells to let us know that they are indeed still around.

****

A mother's caress:

My mother died in 2002. She lived in a senior citizen apartment building and we visited every Friday and Sunday. That last Sunday my husband came with me because I had a bad feeling and she wasn't answering the phone. We found that she had passed away in the night. Our son, who was twelve at the time, was also with us. It was upsetting, but at the same time not unexpected. She had just checked herself out of the hospital against medical advice for a heart problem. She was a stubborn soul.

Both my son and I woke up in the following weeks feeling as if something had been touching us in the night. My foot was sticking out of the covers and it felt as if something lightly touched my toe. I didn't think anything of it until my son said, "I think Me-Maw touched my arm last night."

Deb Tanner

Bottom line: Yet another experience I can share with Deb and her son. Apparently they accepted with far more grace than I did. Still, isn't it miraculous that we can find ourselves on the receiving end of such a gift? Gives "reach out and touch" a whole new meaning!

****

A sense of disquiet:

I was a child about 8 or 9. It was summer and I was at the public pool in our neighborhood. The pool hours were something

211

like 9:00 a.m. - 12:00 p.m., 1:00 - 5:00 p.m., and 6:00 - 8:00 p.m. I, along with my friends, were there when it opened, went home for lunch and then went right back until supper time. My great aunt, who lived in our house, was very ill and in the hospital with a heart condition.

This one day I was at the pool as usual and I just had this very strong feeling that I wanted to go home. I told my friends that I was going to leave. They asked if I was sick. I said no, I just wanted to go home. I grabbed my stuff and as I passed the lifeguard and asked what time it was. He said, "Three o'clock." I changed and walked the short distance home.

As I was rounding the corner near our house, I heard my mother's voice calling to another relative who lived across the street. "Marge died at three o'clock." Even at that age, I felt something significant had just happened.

Mary Ellen Gray

Bottom line: Had Mary Ellen's great aunt reached across the void with a message to go home so she'd be with her family when the news reached them? There's no way to answer that. But stranger things have happened, right? If nothing else it was a reminder to pay attention and honor one's intuition.

****

A comforting hand, a comforting light:
Shortly after my dad died, my mother said she was looking out the back door and thinking, "How am I going to do all this alone?" when she felt a hand on her shoulder. She told me it was so vivid that she spun around thinking that someone was actually there, but there wasn't. Maybe this was my dad's way of sending her comfort and reassurance when she needed it.

In 2002, my mom underwent major surgery. In the days immediately following, she was in the Critical Care Unit of the hospital. I sat there pretty much from early morning till night. She was asleep most of the time, but every once in a while, her eyes would pop open and she'd look at me, almost as if I had called her. I'd say, "Hi." She'd say, "Hi," then drift back off.

Finally one day she did it, then said to me, "Every once in a while I feel a hand on me."

I said, "Where?"

"Sometimes on my head, and sometimes on my shoulder."

I said, "They're here, Mom."

She said, "I know they are," and went back to sleep. "They" were her mom and dad and my dad. It's like they were comforting her.

Mom passed away on Wednesday, October 23, 2002. On the following Sunday, my brother was getting dressed for church when he sensed that someone had walked into the room behind him. He turned around expecting to see his significant other standing there. Two things happened. First, she wasn't there. No one was. And second, as he turned his head, he caught a glimpse of a very small point of light over near the other closet. When he looked directly at it, there was nothing there. He said he kept turning his head the same way again and again, trying to duplicate it, but he couldn't.

Mary Ellen Gray

Bottom line: Yet another instance of "reach out and touch," as well as support for the notion that we are all beings of light, perhaps a light that remains hidden until we've surrendered our dense physical shells. True or not, Mary Ellen's mother made her transition with her father and great-grandparents waiting to welcome her. Whether or not she was the source of the light Mary Ellen's brother saw is something we'll never know. But as the old saying goes, anything's possible.

****

Mom on the Lost and Found Desk:

My youngest son, Chris, had misplaced an expensive flashlight he had paid for. He cried for days about it. They were going camping and I told him I would look for it in the car one last time. I went out to the van and my husband had gotten it detailed. It was spotless, nothing anywhere in the van, not in the doors, pouches on the backs of the seats. It looked as if it came off the showroom floor.

Chris was still upset and I told him to go look in the van anyway. At this point I was just trying to give him something to do, since I was at work and needed to get him off the phone. He called me several hours later and told me that his grandma, my mom, had helped him find it. When he looked out in the van again, the flashlight was sitting in the pocket on the side door. I asked how Grandma had helped. He said because there were gift certificates for him to McDonald's with her name on them. They were not dated and she had been gone over two years. I have no explanation for it. They were just there.

Lori Messer

Bottom line: Lori's mother was still fulfilling her role as a caring and supportive grandparent. It seems perfectly logical that she'd use something from the golden arches to get the job done.

****

Reminders, regrets, reunions:

I found my fiance, Wade, on September 19, 2007. He had sedated himself and hung himself from my kids' bunk beds. Since then he has been with me and around me many times. Here are a few instances:

1. I had to move. It was our last day there and a highly emotional time. The day we moved the bunk beds out, he showed up in a picture taken of me outside the apartments. It looks like a double negative of his face, except it was taken with my mom's cell phone, so that was impossible. There is also an older man and an old woman over my shoulder as well. I don't know who these people are, except maybe some of his family that has passed. The woman seems to be wearing a black mantilla-type veil over her head. Wade was Italian and his grandmother came straight from Sicily. It is quite amazing.

2. I woke up in the middle of the night to find my living room lights on. I have come home several times to lights on that were definitely not on when I left.

3. I came into the old apartment while moving, and my mother and dad were with me. The alarm in my bedroom went off to the song, "I'm Coming Out." I walked in to turn it off and the entire side of the room was permeated with his cologne. I called Mom, didn't tell her why and she walked into the room and immediately said, "I smell it."

4. One night my mother and I were on a three-way phone call with my sister, who knew Wade and who lives in Florida. My mom and sister had been trying desperately to figure out what cologne it was that my mother had bought Wade. Later that evening the same cologne permeated a part of her house. All of a sudden, my father heard music coming from the upstairs. Mom went up and a CD she didn't even remember having was playing on a CD player she hadn't used in over a year. It was on track #3, a song called, "I'm There for You."

5. A day or so after Wade passed, I was at my ex-husband's home. His wife, Donna, has become my friend, and her neighbor came over with her three-year-old son, Noah. Noah had never met me or Wade. We were sitting outside when Noah came out and started talking about "the man sitting on the couch." Intrigued, we followed him. He went upstairs to the children's room and began talking about "the man sitting on Josie's (my daughter) bed crying." Noah said, the man said "He killed the bad guy." At this point I'm freaking but trying not to scare Noah. I begin asking what the man's name is. Finally Noah blurts out: "NAME WADE." Noah said the man kissed his forehead and pinched his nose.

6. The next day Donna had put in a DVD of Wade playing music – he played the drums in a band – and Noah and his mother once again came over. We weren't paying attention when all of a sudden, Noah yells out, "There! That guy!" and points at Wade playing the drums.

7. I also recall most recently waking up in the middle of the night and hearing Wade say, "I am going to be where I am for a long

time because of what I did to you." I had lifted my head from the pillow, but wasn't completely awake, then blasted up when I heard this. It was almost as if I was eavesdropping on a conversation I wasn't supposed to consciously hear. It was wonderful.

I have no doubt Wade is with me, can hear me and will always let me know he is near when he can.

Michelle Cooper, Burlington, KY

Bottom line: The impact of suicide leaves wounds for those left behind that may take a long time to heal, if they ever do. It is so sad that the victim of suicide can't envision the devastation loved ones suffer until they are viewing it from the Other Side. At least Wade appears to have made it his mission to comfort Michelle as best he can.

****

Gran pulls a fast one:

My 93-year-old grandma, my Mimi, passed on November 28th 2007. My mom called just as I was going to sleep to tell me, so I cried around a little bit, then settled down to pray and talk to Mimi and God, then laid back to go to sleep. Well, out of a completely meditative blank type state, I heard Stevie Nix singing the song "Landslide," except that I heard the words, "When you see my reflection in a rose-covered hill," instead of "snow-covered" as the song goes. I was thrilled because I knew this was a message from my Mimi, no doubt in my mind because I definitely associate her with the rose perfume she wore forever. But I thought how odd that she used Stevie Nix because I totally and completely dislike her voice. And this is who Mimi uses to connect with me. Funny. I was marveling about "Landslide," and thought it awesome that Mimi had come to say hi.

My grandmother was much like a mother to me. She often commented that I was more of her own child than a grandchild. That she came to visit me just after her passing means the world to me. I felt she was saying once again, "I love you, KimbyPoo." It gave me warm, loving comfort. This definitely changed the grieving process for me. It wasn't nearly so deep and raw. I was able to go to sleep with a feeling of peace about her passing. All was as it was supposed to be in the frame of life.

My two grown daughters and I flew to Texas for the funeral. In route, I'd spoken to my mom, and she told me that there was some tension and friction between two of the four daughters – her sisters – and that it might get ugly and for me to be prepared for it.

Well, my girls and I were in a rental car driving the 60 miles from the airport to my Mimi's house where we were planning on staying, and I filled my girls in on what my mom had said. So I said, "Let's make a White Circle of Light around us." They said, "Yeah," together. So I said, "We ask that a White Circle of love wrap itself around us, around this car and around this entire trip, and that none of this negative energy can permeate this shield around us. But also let us be able to share our energy of love with them all. We ask this in the name of Love, Peace and Mimi!!!"

We're high-fiving and "whoo-hooing" and the traffic gets pretty hairy since it was a Friday evening with folks leaving Dallas and going home and trying to get there fast. I was white-knuckling the steering wheel, and a song came on the radio that was completely offensive and just wrong, especially after the beauty of our little ceremony. I said, "NO! No, I'm not listening to THIS!" and I reached over, not being able to take my eyes off the road, just reached in the general direction of the radio and pushed anything I touched, and changed the station.

And we heard: "And when you see my reflection in a snow-covered hill...and the landslide brought me down...." Stevie Nix and "Landslide"

It bought every one of us up short and we all gasped in unison. Everyone in my family knows of my feelings about Stevie Nix, and I'd told my girls of the experience the night Mimi had passed on.

The most beautiful thing about it is there was absolutely, positively NO evidence of any kind of friction or tension between the sisters. All of us cousins expected World War 3 to happen, but it never did. Nor has it yet. Thank God and thank Mimi, I'm sure.

It's funny how a visitation can change the last thought or memories of someone. Mine had been of my grandmother suffering from dementia, scared and confused much of the time. Her contacts put love, hope and peace back in my heart and lifted that sadness and gave me back the true spirit of Mimi as I knew her – fun-loving and full of surprises.

My life after death belief system was already firmly in place, so contact with my grandmother confirmed that we don't vanish after death. Communication is still very open if we are open to it, and even sometimes when we aren't.

Kim Hardie

Bottom line: How clever of Kim's beloved Mimi to use a song guaranteed to get her granddaughter's attention. A lovely parting gift indeed.

****

As I said at the beginning of this chapter, it was difficult to fit some of these experiences into one particular category. Some overlapped others. Inexplicable. And minor miracles.

C.W.

CHAPTER TWELVE - WHEN THE MEDIUM BRINGS THE MESSAGE - PART VI

ROBERT BROWN

Robert Brown in an internationally known psychic medium from the United Kingdom. He travels extensively holding both private and group readings as well as weekend and week-long retreats during which he helps others develop their ability to become mediums. He spends part of each year in the US, and this hour-long private reading took place in Baltimore, Maryland. It was not typical of other readings I've had in that during our hour together, Mr. Brown stepped out of his role as medium, crammed on his psychic and spiritual adviser hat and read ME, offering sage counsel that was of great help. As most of that section is personal in a way that the mediumship reading was not, the transcript of the taped session has been edited to a degree. Occasionally, I've inserted comments in parenthesis for clarification and/or validation. Otherwise, for the most part what follows is as it transpired. Mr. Brown is both clairaudient and clairvoyant, able to see the departed.

****

RB: The 18th of May, 2005 and my name is Robert Brown. So the way that I start the sessions that we have, I always like to explain just a little bit about how I work. ... I say that my job is to link with people who have passed, to try and get the evidence of survival and then to see what they have to say about you. The theory is when working one- on-one, there's only me and you and spirit.

CW: Okay.

RB: Certainly what we try to do by sitting with one person is to limit maybe the people that are around them and connecting with them. I certainly feel that you have more influence than I have on the people that come through. ... But I do believe that you can think of, you can invite, you can ask for – maybe these things you've done. But from this point on, I tell people it seems to help if you can say "I've sent out my invitations, it's up to them." You know?

Now what I need from you as we go along is that you say yes, you understand or no, you don't. I don't mind you asking questions, that's not a problem.

Okay. Because I want to start here, it's a lady. She's a very interesting lady, right, on mothers' side here. (Indicating the area to my left.) There's about three people here, but the lady is on mothers' side here. I'm wondering if it's grandmother, rather than mother. Now, is your mother passed?

CW: Yes.

RB: And grandmother passed.

CW: Yes.

RB: Did either of them particularly like children?

CW: I think they both did.

RB: *(Indicating my left again.)* I've got a lady who was unwell before she passed. It wasn't a quick passing. It was almost as if she was drained of energy, then. (True.) But what I was really noticing, there was a lot of children around her, in the spirit world. Which I'll be happy to explain in a moment. But who had the long illness?

CW: My mother and my aunt.

RB: It's not your aunt. So it would be either mother or grandmother. Now …

CW: My aunt was old enough to be my grandmother.

RB: Okay. But I would know if it was an aunt. This lady would be standing over here (further left) but this one is right here. No, this is your mom. But was she not able to walk too well? Towards the end? Or was she not moving around so much? (True.) Because this lady is showing me herself being very active now, as if to say she had been slowed down by her health condition. But now she's moving around, and also the difference is one of them, not your mother, but one of the others, is quite religious.

CW: That's probably my mother in law.

RB: …No, I saw a bible and I saw somebody who might have even lived by the bible. (Indicating my right side this time.) And a gentleman who had a heart condition. You've got a little group around you here.

CW: I've got a whole mob over there.

RB: I know. … This is why I'm pointing here. This is mothers' side (on my left). This is your dads' side here. (On my right.) And was he fairly tall, your dad?

CW: No.

RB: 'Cuz I'm looking up to this man, unless you had him on pedestal in some way.

CW: No. (This is a case of my misunderstanding what he meant.)

RB: Right. So I've got this man with a heart condition that I'm kind of like, looking up to there. And it's chest and heart condition. Go to your husbands' family. And do you also know a younger person who passed?

CW: Yes.

RB: Wait there, for that. Because, again, it's like watching a line of people. This is your mom. Mother-in- law I feel is in here, too. The aunt could have been almost like a mother to you. She's there, the way she feels about you there. (She was. She had raised my mother and she helped to raise me.) Um. Father- in-law passed?

CW: Yes.

RB: You're sure he didn't have a chest problem?

CW: Yes.

RB: 'Cuz I felt that this man, if we say like a father, he doesn't have to be like a father to you, but how's he gonna fit in? … Um. Your father himself did never really show his emotions. As I'm seeing it. So I don't feel he's someone who dealt with emotion. That would make sense of the chest problem. But I'm not seeing him. But we'll wait. (Personal note: Mr. Brown seemed agitated that he couldn't "see" my father. The reason became clear later.) Your mother, were you with her when she passed?

CW: Yes.

RB: But I don't think for one moment you were nervous about coming here today. Maybe apprehensive or wondering--

CW: No.

RB: --what was gonna happen. But your mom said, "I'm here to hold your hand." Now the only thing that says to me unless you were holding her hand--

CW: She was in a coma when she passed.

RB: I feel that she was aware of it, you know? Because, I don't know if you realize this, but you kind of helped her.

CW: I hope so.

RB: You did. Because she was like, "I'm here to hold your hand like you were holding mine." I have to tell you something really interesting. I don't think she wanted to let go. I think she needed to let go. And she said, "You did me a great service." She taps you on the hand like this. "You did me a great service in letting me go." Now that's very interesting to me because we can't keep anyone here.

CW: Mm-hm.

RB: But I felt that she needed that encouragement. And that's why she said, "I'm here to hold your hand like you held mine." Certainly it is like hearing someone in the next room. Like we just heard the lady out there? (A cleaning lady in the hall.) That's how it is when you're in a coma. But you can tell if somebody's angry or if somebody's sending love. And I just kinda felt that your mom needed that love surrounding her. She said "I'm so pleased I was not on my own. I'm so pleased I was not on my own." At one point there was a small group around her, too. (Correct.) Cuz she was aware of other people around but she couldn't quite make out what they were saying. That might have been just prior or something. Now. Either of them have a large family? A large family is gonna be 7 or 11.

CW: My mothers' side was a large family. (Precisely seven.)

RB: This is where I've got all those children. Now they do not have to be children related to you.

CW: I see. (With every reading I've had, when my mother has come through to the medium, she has always come with a lot of children around her. I'm an only child, so I've never been certain where all the kids came from.)

RB: If someone ever brings me back and says "He's got children around," say: "That isn't Robert Brown." Because I don't have children around me. But your mum seems to be like a mother to more than one person, that she can have people around her. And in the spirit world, there are children around her.

CW: And you would be able to determine whether we're talking about my mother or my aunt?

RB: Yes. Because they're very much together. You see here's your mom, that was holding your hand. Here's your aunt. Your aunt seems to have a lot of patience, standing in the back there. And then (on my right) this is mother-in-law. That's the one with the bible. And I saw very clearly a gold cross on this bible, as if she was either somebody who lived by it or spoke it. That was her way, and that was it. Um, I didn't see her wavering from her own kind of beliefs there. (Absolutely correct.) Now, also, do you know somebody who had cancer that passed?

CW: Um, several.

RB: Any of these people that I mentioned?

CW: My mother, my aunt.

RB: Okay. Because what's happened here is that they're giving me this burning sensation, so I'm asking, "Who are you? What happened to you?" So that's with them, a confirmation of your mom and your aunt, and you have a group around you because you've been sending thoughts, not of being lonely but of standing somewhat on your own. So they're saying "Oh, no, you don't, you've got this whole group around you from the spirit world. " And that's why I was saying to them one at a time.

A family of four, where's a family of four? It has to be either like four kids or two kids, a mom and dad. Is that your family?

CW: That would be my husbands' family.

RB: Four kids. Okay. Do you have children?

CW: No.

RB: Did you lose a child?

CW: Yes.

RB: But, like, a miscarriage?

CW: Yes.

RB: There's a little white light up there. And that white light...You know that we don't get to say, "Oh, this is a boy or a girl." Maybe you didn't know. They are very highly evolved spirits who don't need to come to the earth plane. ... So that's why that little white light will attach to you as well. But I have another man coming through where I've got breathing problems. Your husband's still alive?

CW: No

RB: What happened with him?

CW: He died of sleep apnea.

RB: What's that?

CW: It's when you stop breathing in your sleep for a period of time.

RB: But you see, I'm going like, "I can't breathe," here. That's why I said I've got breathing problems. Now, he's with his parents, 'cuz that's right on that side and I'm going like, "Wait a minute. I can't go any further because I can't breathe." You see what happens, they will come through, and it's not that we've got to accept them, that's not the point. But they will not let me move on until I make sense of something. And I'm going, "Wait a minute, this is getting frustrating, I can't breathe here. I've got a man here with breathing problems." You see, they're not going to say to me, this is sleep whatever you called it, because in actuality, I wouldn't know what that is. They're going to tell me things or show me in a way that I'm going to understand it. This is your husband, there, he's right there. Do you think he was a man that I could be looking up to?

CW: He was about 6 feet.

RB: I'm only 5 foot 7. (I finally realized that when Mr. Brown said 'a man he could be looking up to,' he meant someone taller than himself. Occasionally the differences in the use of American idioms as opposed to those used in the United Kingdom caused momentary confusion – at least on my part.) And he seems a very strong person, though, so that would be very frustrating for him, to not be able to breathe. But did this go very quickly, his passing?

CW: I wasn't there.

RB: I have to tell you, I got this like, I can't breathe. But I didn't get pain. Cancer, I know is difficult. These different conditions, it's not that they complain, because they don't have those conditions now. But they showed me what it was like for them, and I know particularly for your mom, it was not an easy thing. But, thank goodness she wasn't physically aware of some of the things that were going on. But with your husband, it seemed to happen so quickly, that…

CW: It was a surprise.

RB: Yeah, that was more like shock than the pain. The best way I can describe what I was feeling; indigestion.

CW: Well he had a trach, but an infection is what really killed him.

RB: Did he pass late at night or early in the morning?

CW: Early.

RB: Because he said, "I didn't have the strength to see another day."

CW: They told me he, quote, "coded', at something like 5 in the morning

RB: Some things they were saying are like a code to me. … So, although, he, of course, was unwell, I think that his actual passing was a shock. Now, did you ask him to come here today because he said "I've done this before."

CW: Yes. *(He had come through at a previous reading with a medium.)*

RB: Because he's come with this army of people, like the world showed up. ... And they do hear us, and they do try to work with us. I'm gonna say to you that there is no doubt that your husband would have come through, anyway. Because of love, you know? He actually is claiming that he learned a lot from you. Now this is the interesting thing, that you get his mother coming through, who's quite a tough lady, I have to say, thanking you. Thanking you for what you did for her son. Although he's your husband, it's her son. I saw this strange thing then. I thought she was gonna hit you on the head with the bible. *(The same thing was said at a future reading.)* But she had this book and she says, "I want to thank you for what you did for my son." I said "Ok, I'll say that. That's not a problem." And I think that sometimes he was a challenge as well.

CW: Uh-huh.

RB: But you know what? He seems, to me quite a strong person. And this is the one I'm looking up to. So your husband is here because he wants to be. It is a confirmation that he hears you. So if you are thinking of him, we call that 'talking,' he does hears you. Now the trick for you is that you've got to listen.

CW: I'm trying.

RB: OK. Let me help you then. ... It's perfectly okay to get yourself to that point where you say, "I just need to know you're okay." He said that he has tried on several occasions to let you know. Several times you thought it was him, but you weren't sure. So I'm thinking maybe you've had some indications or some things that happened where you may have thought of him, but you might have dismissed it there. But certainly he's been trying to show you in a more physical way that he's around. So, can you think of anything?

CW: There is no doubt; he yelled my name several times.

RB: That takes a lot of energy.

CW: He was bellowing practically. He has jiggled with electrical things, telephone, doorbell, the bed. I had one lucid dream.

RB: And you know what I think the next thing is? If your husband can get through to you, it's not just, "Oh, nice, I can speak with my husband or he can get to me." But what we've got to do with you is create an environment, a period, where you can listen, because if you have that ability to listen to your husband, or that ability for him to communicate with you, you have that ability for other people, too. And I kind of feel that part of your life to date has almost been like a preparing ground, a training ground, because I'm seeing behind you. And all these different people that know you - mom, aunt, mother-in-law. That couple seem to go very well together -- the mother-in-law and the father-in-law. Were they always together?

CW: Yeah, for a long time.

RB: They've got to be together. But then your husband here. Behind, there are rocks, there are boulders. These are the things you've been over. And I don't think you chose the easiest of lives in this life. But then most of us have some issues and problems, but I feel that it's been like preparation, getting you to the point where you are now. And would you say that you're quite creative?

CW: I'm a writer.

RB: Yeah? ... I'm seeing yellow around you. And so—

CW: Why yellow?

RB: Yellow is the color of inspiration. Each color means something. Yellow is the color of inspiration, new ideas. It's a creative color. It is very close to you. Which means that um, it should be flowing, the inspiration. But it can be quite erratic. ... I'm gonna say something quite different to you than I've said to many people and it's something I can't prove but I know it's right. You're an old soul in a younger body, if that makes sense to you. Because I can see right behind you that there are different lives. I'm not going to go into the different lives because we can't prove them, but we only ever say it to somebody's who's got an inkling themselves that there was more to this. And I felt that that's those stumbling blocks that I saw, those were these different lives. ... It's not an area I'm going to go to because I've seen so many people spend this life concerning themselves with what they've been. Whatever we've been, it's a sum total of many things that we are now. ... But with you, I just think it's an old soul because they're saying, "We've brought her all through these different things, not just in this life, but in other lives, for her to make a difference in some of the information that comes through her." So you've got to see yourself like a, I choose my words very carefully so that they're not misconstrued, like a channel. But I don't mean a medium channel. ... And it will come out through the hands, if you'd like, written. So that you may consider them your works, but I also feel that they're inspired works. That's the yellow. Yellow is the color of inspiration, new ideas, it's a creative color, it's an intelligent color.

I feel that for some reason that your husband was a bit of a test in your life. Because he said that he taught you, he taught <u>you,</u> and yet his mother is thanking you. That's interesting. Alright. Are you working on something at the moment? Writing?

CW: Yes.

RB: What is it you're doing at the moment?

CW: It's a novel about a woman with psychic abilities who does not realize she has them.

RB: I think that's gonna be very topical. If you want the best example of that, look at you. ... I think through life this gut reaction, this intuition, what we call solar plexus, I think it's kind of guided you. Now without a doubt, you haven't always used it for your best intention. Sometimes you get involved with some people only to find out that they weren't what you first thought they were. Well, that's part of that developing. But I do feel that you absolutely have that psychic ability. Whether you go on to develop it, or whether you want to develop it to the full extent that it could be, that I believe is your personal choice and responsibility. ... It's certainly there. You would not have heard your husband the way you did without it. I think it's a case of finding the right developing thing. ... I feel that time spent with some good meditation, ... It's going to be your key to going forward, there. It's right there, and all this yellow is enveloping you, so I know it's right there, we've just got to open it in a way that it's gonna flood. Because it just needs a key to open it there, which would be really good.

It's extraordinary that your husband has shown an enormous amount of patience there. And I say extraordinary because he's, I don't know what he was like as a person, but he's showing to me, "I'm having to learn a lot about patience, 'cuz I got through to her." Although you've said, "Oh, yes, I know it was him," he needs that feedback to know he got through to you. You know?

CW: I'm pretty sure he knows it, because also, he also touched me, physically.

RB: He's a very strong person. You know why, though? Because how you touched him, the very soul of him, in his life. Now, I asked him, what was his life about? Now among many things, he held up love. So I believe that he was someone who came to this earth plane to know what it was like to be loved. And to be able to love. That makes sense, why his mother is saying thank you to you. And these bonds of love, you cannot fake it. You absolutely cannot. That's why the link is so strong.

CW: Oh, I don't doubt it.

RB: ... So I do feel that with some meditation... Spirit never ever told us that we had to be constant. They said we have to be consistent. It is better to do a meditation one day a week for 10, 20 minutes, and build up to it, you know, than to do it twice a day and feel that it's a chore.

And never lose sight of the key with this meditation is to change our perspective. A meditation should have an objective, right? ... I'm watching your husband there, he's actually kneeling down at the side of you, and I don't know why. Sitting on the edge, really.

And what I was watching was, sometimes I think you asked twenty or thirty questions and maybe they try to get you twenty or thirty answers. ... They've got to find ways of giving you those answers. See? So if you do it in a concentrated way, you'll get much further more quickly than trying to get a lot of things out there.

CW: I've never been aware of getting through, although when I asked for the sign and got it, I was purely shocked, because I've never had a sense that I've reached anyone. Or I reached a certain person.

RB: Is it because you're waiting to see? (As in actually see the departed.)

CW: Not really.

RB: Because I know many – not just American mediums, but many ... mediums will say, "Oh, I've got your grandmother here; she's like this." And I say, "Oh, you've seen her?" And they say, "Well, no." But it leads people to think, "Oh, we've got to see."

When I saw your mom come in, I saw her. I saw her hand go straight on yours. When your husband came in, it was really funny because he, uh ... was he close to his mom? Do you know?

CW: Yes.

RB: Because his mom seemed to be somebody who he does love, but she seems a little strong.

CW: It's another case of his mother actually being old enough to be his grandmother.

RB: Right.

CW: And his sister ...

RB: Was like the mother. (True.) But this was his mom. Because I just kind of felt as if she, she had this Bible, and she thanked you, and I thought "Well, she's from a different kind of school altogether."

CW: I believe that.

RB: But you know what? That was her way. Now that she's passed because she's seen what was a good way for the all around education of her son. And by all around education we mean spiritual education. She's thanking you for making a difference to him. Because it's helped him to find what he was looking for, and that was love. There seems to be a tremendous amount of trust as well. That word keeps coming up, trust. I do feel that with some more meditation, I'm sorry to bore you with that word –

CW: (laughing) That's okay.

RB: But with some more meditation, I think you'll make a breakthrough. ... It's almost as if you're almost really examining your whole self, and every aspect of your life there. Because I feel that if you recognize who that person is now, you can then follow the path from where she came.

Now, that came from Spirit. That did not come from me. They're saying to me, "See the person as she is now, and you'll be able to retrace her steps." What you're trying to do is something that you've been taught to: do things in the logical order. The first thing that we have to learn when dealing with spirit, suspend logic. That's hard

CW: Yes.

RB: That's why we have such trouble with the scientists, you know. ... The scientists think in the box. And I'm forever saying to them when I'm working at the Edgar Cayce Center (in Virginia Beach, Virginia) and with Gary Schwartz (during tests of a number of mediums at the University of Arizona) and all this, I say to them, "You know, the first thing you've got to learn as scientists is to think outside that box." Because, a spirit, if you see the process, a spirit, when we come to the Earth plane as children, we have to learn to communicate through the physical body. To walk, to talk, to communicate. Well, we have that ability, but when we pass, although we have an exact replica, which is what the mediums see and can describe, we don't have a physical body so we have to learn to communicate on vibrations. The strongest of those vibrations is clairaudience where we can hear because he's either gonna say his name is Bob or not, you know, or you're gonna know his voice. It's really unmistakable.

You tell another person that you heard your husband; the best you'll probably get is like, "Oh, that's nice." Or "She's a loony." Because you cannot convey how real that was to anyone else that they'll understand it. You see? So I always believe those experiences are extremely personal and I go here because it's like knowing. It's not "Oh, I think I heard him." "Oh, I've got an idea in my stomach that it might be…" I <u>know</u> that it was him. And you can't make anyone else know. That's what makes them so real.

Alright, now … But he certainly has decided, your husband, to work with you there. To work with you. Now, you know we all have guides.

CW: Yes.

RB: These higher beings who decide to work with us even before we're born, they agree on our path. But of course we have free will and we often venture off the path, you know? Let's be brutally honest. Who are we likely to believe in? Some 4000 year old Egyptian or Chinese man? Or our husband, who we knew? I'm gonna pretty much believe the husband, 'cuz we knew him, you know? So I believe that, he's not like your guide but he's agreed to work, as I say, as a go-between because he knows you, he can get on your wavelength. Now that doesn't stop you linking with your guides. But I certainly feel he's the one that will be able to help you. So you do need to speak with him more, in those meditations. Ask him, please. 'Cuz he's saying to me, "Tell her if she tells me what she wants, I'll find a way of getting it through to her." The one thing I know about your husband here, the way he's talking, if he says something you can believe it. He's one of those people that I just know, in his voice, a sincerity of his voice. That if you asked him something and he can do it, he'll do it. I know that.

Alright now, any questions? A very different reading than what we normally do, but what's intriguing is this potential that you've got and I just would like to get you to the right kind of development group for something like this. ...

So I think that that next step is doing some of that, sorry, I'm going to say it again, meditation, there. I think that for your own purpose, it's getting at the truth. And I have to tell you, that's kind of laughable, because it's like peeling an onion. Every time you do it, and you understand a bit more, then it has to be another one.

I always tell people, at 16, I was interested in this for all sorts of reasons, mainly because I wanted to prove it was a lot of nonsense. At 21, I thought I knew everything, mainly because everyone told me how wonderful I was, you know? And then 30 years later – mind you, at the same time, at 20, I thought 40 was old and when I get to 40, I thought 77 was a good middle age. But you know at 50, I feel that I can laugh at myself. Even though I feel I know or I'm better informed, I feel I've got a lot more to learn. Because it is like this continued period, so it's getting at the truth for yourself, but along the way, you can find some things that makes more sense of a lot of other stuff. It's your own improvement. Because that's what you're about. You're about your own self development, your spirit development there. Along the way some other people may learn from you. You know you're in good company. I don't want to boast you up there or anything like that. Maya Angelou is of that kind.

CW: Is she?

RB: Yeah. She's somebody that really, I met her once but she's somebody who really wanted to know, "What the hell is all this about?" So while she's looking for it along the way, some other people have benefitted. And that's what I see with you. You know?

They've learned through some of her investigations. That could be the same thing.

I know we have to come towards the end there. He's (Bob) tremendous support. He's tremendous support. If I say he feels he owes you something, don't take it the wrong way. But he says, "I feel that I want to do this. To give back a little what she gave me." And it's not an obligation, but he feels that he wants to do that. So I'm going to say, speak with him more. And I feel that you're gonna get through. Take their love, and your moms' and your aunts'. Ok?

Tape ends.

Chassie West

A reading with Robert Brown is not unlike sitting and chatting with an old friend. And my husband clearly likes the fact that he and Mr. Brown share the same first name. In an unanticipated reading almost a year later when Mr. Brown appeared before an audience of several hundred, Bob West came through again to chide me about getting my eyes checked, which I had been putting off for weeks. It seems that if I'm within hailing distance of a medium or psychic, whether it's a one-on-one situation or in a gathering of four hundred, Bob almost always puts in an appearance. As Abraham-Hicks says, "Nice to know."
****

Most mediums will advise you NOT to arrange a reading immediately after the death of a loved one. It is important that one gain a little distance and honor the grieving process. It also gives the departed time and space to adjust to being Home again. Once you're ready, ask someone you trust for a recommendation. If that's not possible or comfortable for you, information in Appendices A or B may help you. They are not comprehensive and all-inclusive lists by any stretch of the imagination, simply a place to start. Browse through the metaphysical section of your local bookstore; most of the better-known mediums have books

to their credit. You may have to stray beyond your comfort zone. Take the risk. You may find it to be well worth it.

C.W.

Afterword

The bottom line

That's it. We're done. And it occurs to us that some might assume that the ability to be on the receiving end of contact from the departed is unlikely unless one is psychic. To a certain extent, that's true. But an even harder sell is the fact that we are <u>all</u> born with psychic abilities, most of them dormant or squashed by the time we enter elementary school. Evidence of these abilities are routinely dismissed as childhood fantasies or overactive imagination, discounted and discouraged. Peer pressure contributes fear of rejection and a desire to fit in. We're left with the gift to which we refer on a regular basis and to which we are so accustomed to using that it never occurs to us that it is indeed a psychic ability: our intuition.

Think about it. How many times have you changed your route to work solely on a whim and found later that you had avoided the mother of all traffic jams? How many times have you ignored a strong negative feeling about someone or something, and suffered the consequences later? Protest all you like. It's all a part of your psychic makeup. And it is possible to reawaken and strengthen these latent abilities, ones you've never suspected you have. There are books, workshops and classes available nationwide, as well as on line (see Appendices A and B). All one needs to do is to suspend belief for a while and get into the spirit (no pun intended) of the occasion.

In spite of a lifelong fascination with the subject, I've always considered myself as psychic as your average rock, as John Edward describes the way most of us feel. I attended one of John Holland's workshops wearing an invisible **I'm a Skeptic, So Bite Me** button, but determined to get as much out of the weekend as I could. If nothing else, perhaps I could use it in my next mystery. So no one was more surprised than I was when I managed to identify several elements in a picture shown to only one half of the class. That half then projected the image telepathically to those of us in the other half of the class. One element I'd put down to sheer luck or percentages. But five?

I flunked psychometry - picking up energy from something being held – hands down. (So I find it ironic that years later I've become a Reconnective healer. Where is the focal point of the energy, light and information particular to this modality? My hands.) But there are no words to describe my reaction when, in a later workshop we took part in an exercise on mediumship, during which we chose a classmate as a partner and were to visualize and describe to that partner whatever or whoever popped into our minds. As a writer, visualization comes with the job, so I saw no reason to trust the figure who wandered on to my mental screen, nor the message we were told to ask for, and pass along. Big deal. I conjured up characters and dialogue every day. I felt badly for my partner, certain I would disappoint her.

And almost fell off my chair when she claimed that the description of the man I'd "imagined" fit her grandfather to a T, down to the pattern of his baldness, the khaki pants he'd worn and the way they had fit him. The message he'd given me consisted of two names. One turned out to be my partner's sister, the second that of her niece. The skeptic in me died an ignominious death. What John Holland's workshops did for me was to prove a point. We are all psychic to one degree or another, whether we care to admit it or not. If I, who had never been particularly intuitive or had exhibited anything remotely close to any sort of psychic ability, could do as well as I did in those workshops, so can you. Whether you wish to find out how to identify and strengthen your innate ability is up to you. And beside the point.

The only thing required to receive messages from the departed is an open mind and a willingness to entertain the possibility that consciousness survives physical death, that our bodies are simply temporary housing and once our bodies have worn out or have been irreparably damaged and shut down, our consciousness leaves and continues its existence on another plane.

A physicist friend explained it this way. We live in a vibrational universe. All matter, all energy vibrates. Energy can be transformed, but cannot be destroyed. Along with the purely biological mechanics that keep the brain alive and functioning, all of our mental busywork is electrical energy and as such is measurable – think EEGs. To use a more comfortable analogy, "We on this earth plane," my physicist friend, now among the departed himself, said, "vibrate at the speed of a merry-go-round. Freed of the confines of the physical body, the energy making up our consciousness can now vibrate at a rate beyond the ability of our senses to interpret. In comparison to our merry-go-round rate as physical beings, our liberated consciousness now vibrates faster than, say the blades of a helicopter."

He was fond of reminding me that the air around us is full of radio waves, television signals and the like. Do we see them? Our eyes interpret light and objects that fall within a narrowly defined vibrational range. Our ears detect sound within certain frequencies. Any above or below these ranges are invisible and inaudible to us without the aid of dedicated instruments. Think dog whistles. Ever heard one? Beyond our range to hear and interpret. Simplistic explanation perhaps, but true nonetheless.

So whether you're more comfortable approaching the subject of life after death from a scientific angle or from that of spirituality or metaphysics doesn't matter. The contributors to this effort don't feel it is our job to convince you to believe. Those of us whose experiences you've read <u>know</u> that existence beyond physical death is real. Acceptance leaves one changed, more aware of how much we <u>don't</u> know, how much is beyond our ken, how many of our beliefs and assumptions may be way off the track.

I repeat, our intent is not to make anyone a believer. We hope, however, that at the very least, you'll think about it. And keep an open mind while you're thinking. And, again, wonder.

Chassie West

Appendix A

Helpful Resources on Life after Death

After Life: Answers from the Other Side. John Edward (with Natasha Stoynoff). New York: Princess Books, 2003.

The Afterlife Connection - A Therapist Reveals How to Communicate with Departed Loved Ones. Dr. Jane Greer. New York: St. Martin's Press. 2003

Afterlife Encounters - Ordinary People, Extraordinary Experiences. Dianne Arcangel. Charlottesville, VA: Hampton Roads Publishing Co., Inc.

Believe Beyond...Seeing. Debra Martin. Bloomington, IN: AuthorHouse. 2006.

Beyond Knowing - Mysteries and Messages of Death and Life from a Forensic Pathologist. Janis Amatuzio, M.D. Novato, CA: New World Library. 2006.

The Biology of Belief - Unleashing the Power of Consciousness, Matter and Miracles. Bruce Lipton. Santa Rosa, CA: Mountain of Love/ Elite Books. 2005.

Born Knowing - A Medium's Journey. John Holland (with Cindy Pearlman). Carlsbad, CA: Hay House. 2003.

Conversations with the Other Side. Sylvia Browne. Carlsbad, CA: Hay House. 2002.

Crossing Over - The Stories Beyond the Stories. John Edward. San Diego, CA: Jodere Group, Inc. 2001.

The Dead Are Live - They Can and Do Communicate with You. Harold Sherman. New York: Fawcett Gold Medal. 1981.

The Divine Matrix - Bridging Time, Space, Miracles and Belief. Gregg Braden. Carlsbad, CA: Hay House. 2007

Don't Kiss Them Good-Bye. Allison DuBois. Phoenix, AZ:π Press. 2004.

Embraced by the Light. Bettie J Eadie (with Curtus Taylor). New York: Bantam Books. 1992.

George Anderson's Lessons from the Light - Extraordinary Messages of Comfort and Hope from the Other Side. George Anderson and Andrew Barone. New York: The Berkley Publishing Group. 1999.

Ghost Hunters - William James and the Search for Scientific Proof of Life after Death. Deborah Blum. New York: The Penguin Press. 2006.

Hello from Heaven. Bill Guggenheim and Judy Guggenheim. New York: Bantam Books. 1995

Is There an Afterlife? - A Comprehensive Overview of the Evidence. David Fontana. OBE, UK: O Books. 2005.

Just One More Question - Answers and Insights from a Psychic Medium. Yolana (with Mark Bego). New York: G. P. Putnam's Sons. 2006.

Letters from the Afterlife - A Guide to the Other Side. Else Barker. Hillsboro, OR: Beyond Words Publishing. 1995.

Life After Death - Living Proof. Tom Harrison. Saturday Night Press. 2004.

Love Never Dies - A Mother's Journey from Loss to Love. Sandra Goodman. San Diego, CA: Jodere Group. 2001.

A Medium's Cookbook: Recipes for the Soul. Suzane Northrop. New York: Northstar 2 LLC. 2005.

Never Say Goodbye - A Medium's Stories of Connecting with your Loved Ones. Patrick Mathews. St. Paul, MN: Lewellyn Publications. 2003.

The Next Place. Warren Hanson. Peabody, MA: Waldman House Press. 1997.

One Last Time - A Psychic Medium Speaks to Those We have Loved and Lost. John Edward. New York: Berkley Trade. 1999.

The Other Side and Back - A Psychic's Guide to Our World and Beyond. Sylvia Browne (with Lindsay Harrison). New York: Signet. 1999.

Psychic Navigator - Harnessing Your Inner Guidance. John Holland. Carlsbad, CA: Hay House. 2004.

Quit Kissing my Ashes - A Mother's Journey Through Grief. Judy Collier. Baton Rouge, LA: Forty-Two Publishing. 2002.

The Scole Experiment - Scientific Evidence of Life after Death. Grant and Jane Solomon. London: Judy Piatkus (Publishers) Ltd. 1999.

Second Change - Healing Messages from the Afterlife (formerly titled The Séance). San Diego, CA: Jodere Group. 2002.

Seven Steps to Heaven - How to Communicate with your Departed Loved Ones in Seven Easy Steps. Joyce Keller. New York: Simon & Schuster. 2003.

Spirit Messenger - The Remarkable Story of a Seventh Son of a Seventh Son. Gordon Smith. Carlsbad, CA: Hay House. 2004.

The Spirit Whisperer – Chronicles of a Medium. John Holland. Carlsbad, CA: Hay House. 2010.

Transition of the Soul - True Stories from Ordinary People. Nick Bunick. Charlottesville, VA:Hampton Roads Publishing Co., Inc. 2001.

Visits from the Afterlife. Sylvia Browne with Lindsay Harrison. New York: New American Library. 2004.

We Are Eternal. Robert Brown. UK: Hodder Mobius. 2004.

We are Not Forgotten - George Anderson's Messages of Hope from the Other Side. Joel Martin and Patricia Romanowski. New York: G.P. Putnam's Sons. 1991.

We Are Their Heaven - Why the Dead Never Leave Us. Allison DuBois. New York: Simon & Schuster. 2006.

We Don't Die - George Anderson's Conversations with the Other Side. Joel Martin and Patricia Romanowski. New York: The Berkley Publishing Group. 1988.

The Unbelievable Truth - A Medium's Guide to the Spirit World. Gordon Smith. Carlsbad, cA: Hay House. 2004.

Appendix B

Resources on the Internet
www.Abraham-Hicks.com

A.D.C. [After Death Communication] Judy Guggenheim and Bill Guggenheim, authors of *Hello from Heaven.* www.after-death. com

After Death Communication Research Foundation, http://www. adcrf.org

After Life – a site dedicated to the education of Afterlife Knowledge. www.afterlife101.com

Allison DuBois – http://www.allisondubois.com

BestPsychicMediums.com

Robert Brown, International Medium – http:robertbrown-medium. com

Connecting to Spirit – www.connectingtospirit.com

Duke Center for Spirituality, Theology and Health – http://www. dukespiritualityandhealth.org.

FriendsCommunities – www.FriendsCommunities.org

The Greater Reality – http://greaterreality.com

The Institute of Noetic Sciences – http://www.noetic.org.

Intuition Network – An organization that assist people to cultivate their inner, intuitive resources. Site lists articles and referrals for intuition development. www.intuition.org

John Edward, Psychic Medium – www.johnedward.net

John Holland, Psychic Medium – http://johnholland.com

Lily Dale Assembly – www.lilydaleassembly.com

Michele Livingston, Medium, Clairvoyant, Artist – http://www.nasc.org

The McCabe Institute - www.thepsychicandthedoc.com

The National Spiritualists Association of Churches – http://www.nsac.org

Nexus – http://www.nexusmagazine.com/articles/IADC.html

OfSpirit.com – http://www.ofspirit.com

Patti Sinclair – www.pattisinclair.com

SpiritDiscovery.com – http://spiritdiscovery.com

SurvivalAfterDeath.org – http://www.survivalafterdeath.org

Suzane Northrop – www.suzanenorthrop.com

Appendix C

Contributors and Featured Psychic Mediums
(on this side of the veil)

M

N

P

R

S

T

W

LaVergne, TN USA
17 February 2011
216951LV00001B/9/P